D0285617

The Art and Science of Transformational Leadership

Unleashing Creativity, Innovation, and
Leadership to Embrace Transformative Change

Raghurami Reddy Etukuru

THE ART AND SCIENCE OF
TRANSFORMATIONAL LEADERSHIP
UNLEASHING CREATIVITY, INNOVATION, AND LEADERSHIP
TO EMBRACE TRANSFORMATIVE CHANGE

Author Credits: Raghurami Reddy Etukuru

iUniverse books may be ordered through booksellers or by contacting:

iUniverse
1663 Liberty Drive
Bloomington, IN 47403
www.iuniverse.com
1-800-Authors (1-800-288-4677)

ISBN: 978-1-5320-6189-9 (sc)
ISBN: 978-1-5320-6190-5 (e)

Library of Congress Control Number: 2018913065

Print information available on the last page.

iUniverse rev. date: 11/06/2018

Contents

Preface

Transformation is a process of bringing radical change to an organization that sets a new direction and takes the organization to an entirely different level of effectiveness with little or no resemblance to the past. There is always a need for positive change and transforming the lives of the people, regardless of what has been achieved so far by the organization or society. There is always room for people to dream big, think big, make a difference, and make an impact to bring about transformative change. Transformation is required in virtually any field, whether it is business, technology, education, health care, banking, agriculture, politics, poverty reduction, entertainment, transportation, cities, or manufacturing. Transforming an organization or the lives of people in a society is purely a leadership-based mission that requires a creative and innovative mind-set. Aspects of the transformation process include purpose-driven vision, creativity, innovation, design thinking, agile transformation, cultural transformation, digital capabilities, human experience transformation, and business model transformation. Transformational leadership is about envisioning the future and making it brighter by way of bringing about transformative change. Transformational leaders must be courageous and empathetic. Several qualities that transformational leaders need to possess to embrace transformation include vision, creativity, inspiration, courage, collaboration, commitment, empathy, and emotional intelligence.

Every transformation mission must have a purpose that is driven by a vision. The vision must be shared with the people involved in the process. The success of the mission depends on the culture of the organization or the entity that is undertaking the transformation mission. The organization must change the mind-set of the people so as to renew the entrepreneurial spirit. The organization must ignite creativity among the people to come up with novel ideas addressing the complex problems in the organization or the society to thrive in an environment that is filled with volatility, uncertainty, complexity, and assumptions. The organization must foster innovation by way of experimentation. Business models must be transformed to provide the best human experience. Digital capabilities should be adapted to rebuild business models from the human experience point of view.

People care less about how an organization is doing than they do about why the organization is doing what it's doing and what it wants to achieve. A purpose-driven vision must be shared with the people within an organization. Transformational leaders must continuously inspire or motivate employees to make them courageous enough to take a risk and to foster a culture of collaboration. Transformational leaders and everyone else involved in the process must commit to the purpose-driven vision. It is imperative for a transformational leader to have emotional intelligence to deal with any situation. Transformational leaders must apply the right thought process based on the context. The aspects of transformational leadership, along with their appropriate components and subcomponents, are discussed in *The Art and Science of Transformational Leadership*.

Raghurami Reddy Etukuru
New Jersey, USA

1

Aspects of Transformation

1.1 Transformation

Transformation is a process of bringing about radical change to a context that sets a new direction and takes the organization to an entirely different level of effectiveness with little or no resemblance to the past. Transformation is the evolution or journey from the current level to a different level, producing an improved state of things. The journey of transformation is a long-runnning process requiring discipline and building blocks for future success.

The transformation process never stagnates. No matter how mature the industry is or how mature the organization is, there is always room for change. Change is the only constant. There is always room for people to dream big, think big, make a difference, and make an impact to bring about positive change to the lives of their families and friends, their organizations, and society as a whole.

Transformation requires courageous leaders with the ability to imagine and visualize far beyond the current comfort zone to discover unmet needs with a clear purpose and the ability to drive the mission to reach such a destination by taking bold action.

As human beings are continuously looking for improvements to their lives in a world of unprecedented disruption, organizations need to create new value, uncover unmet needs, uncover new opportunities, and drive growth to deliver new efficiencies. Transformation is a bold ambition that goes beyond incremental change to change the way we work and change the business models and operating models to deliver breakthrough value to the planet and beyond. Here the end beneficiaries do not necessarily include just the customers. The word *customer* is used in this book only for convenience purposes. In the case of business, there are customers or internal users. In the case of governments and nonprofit organizations, the spectrum is vast, including human beings and others such as animals and birds, nature, and the climate.

There is a need for transformation in virtually every sector— business, technology, education, health care, banking, agriculture, politics, poverty reduction, entertainment, transportation, cities, manufacturing, and more. Taking a hospital as an example, we find that improving value to patients is most critical. In the case of streets, creating safe conditions and improving the experience for pedestrians and bike riders is critical. Protecting the atmosphere from pollution, protecting wildlife, increasing the number of green reserves, saving the planet from climate change—these issues all require a radical transformation of the way we currently perform.

The bold ambition of the transformation process should include the democratization of products and services that are not easily available to the broader spectrum of people in all corners of the world. Specific blocks of transformation can fail at intermediate levels, but since transformation is evolutionary and occurs over a period of time, it should eventually lead to success.

The life span of companies has been decreasing decade after decade. While mergers and acquisitions are two reasons for this decreased life span, it is also true that many companies fail because they fail to change with the times. People are looking for improvements in their lives. Technological advancements are disrupting markets. Several companies have fallen victim to disruptive business models, from video rental companies to well-established photo companies. The "business as usual" concept is no longer a viable strategy if one wishes to survive against competitors. The new mantra for businesses to cherish is "change or perish." In a dynamic business world, the only constant is change; the only status quo is transformation.

While the ultimate goal of any transformation is to make a more meaningful contribution to society, the specific goals of transformation include broadening the company's reach, improving operational efficiency, transforming the company's culture, and transforming the leadership and the company's image. Digital technology is one of the core drivers that is making a massive contribution to overall transformation. Digital transformation is not the whole or sole purpose of the transformation mission; it is one of the essential things for overall transformation. Digital transformation is consistently putting traditional business practices to the test, requiring organizations to recognize technology's potential.

There are two types of transformation: linear transformation and exponential transformation. While the goal of linear transformation is to embrace the changes within a business to improve operations, the goal of exponential transformation is to transform the business itself by way of transforming its capabilities and business models.

Incremental innovation and breakthrough innovations are the critical drivers of linear transformation. They merely bring about technological advancements to help a company to do in a better way what it is already doing. Linear transformation improves a company's competitiveness without significantly changing the way the value is delivered to the customer. For example, a brick-and-mortar-style retail store can build an efficient online portal to enable customers to make purchases online. Offering a simple online shopping cart without increasing prices can add significant value to the customer and can increase sales for the retailer, thereby improving the marginal cost. However, even after such a change, the organization keeps its old business model intact, and the business's underlying economics remain the same.

On the other hand, exponential transformation is radically different from linear transformation. With innovation occurring much faster, accelerating month over month, the disruptive innovation that is part and parcel of exponential transformation fundamentally changes the business model and finds new ways of delivering value to customers. Disruptive innovations, whether they occur internally or externally, disrupt the organization's ways of operating, requiring changes to leadership, people, systems, products, services, processes, customer experience, pricing models, and more.

For example, Airbnb has brought about an exponential transformation to the hospitality industry by changing the way that customers access available rooms or houses for short-term rental and by creating a shared economy, allowing owners to offer available properties for short-term rental, thereby producing additional income. While incumbent hotels focus on providing access through their own or third-party websites and providing rate comparisons—linear value-added services—Airbnb has done things differently, bringing about exponential transformation to the hospitality industry. These transformations have created new business models and forced the incumbents businesses to change their practices and adopt new business models.

It is inevitable that transformation, whether it is linear or exponential, is required if a company is to survive in today's competitive world. However, linear transformation is no longer sufficient to stay competitive in the long term, as the pace of innovation is increasing at a speed demanding exponential transformation.

While it is easy for new entrants or start-ups to come up with a disruptive business model and create a new culture, bringing exponential transformation to the industry, it is a challenge for established organizations to do so because it requires new ways of thinking and disrupting well-established patterns. The organizations that are navigating an exponential transformation are required to disrupt themselves.

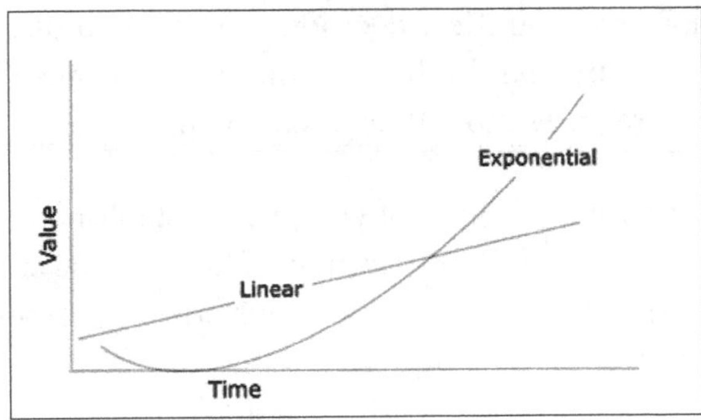

FIGURE 1.1. Linear vs. exponential transformation

While both linear and exponential transformation are good at capturing value, linear transformation does not create significant value. Exponential transformation goes through a period of value creation, creating value for both the business organization and its customers. As shown in figure 1, exponential transformation decreases in value as time progresses, but it captures value exponentially.

Exponential transformation has become the default phrase; there is no need to mention *exponential* explicitly. From here on out, it is referred to as just "transformation." However, the fundamental questions are these: Why we need exponential transformation? How do we do it? What do we achieve by transforming exponentially?

Transformation results include, but not are limited to, the following:

- Better human experience
- Economic benefit to the customers
- Improved work experience for employees
- Poverty reduction within society
- Better education across all sectors
- Value creation to the organization
- Survivability of the organization
- Economic benefit to the shareholders

How do we embrace transformation? Organizations have become hyperconnected, both internally and externally, with a mountain of information and countless decision makers who affect nearly all aspects of transformation. In this environment, a successful journey of transformation requires more than a road map.

From the organizational point of view, large established organizations are required to behave like start-ups in order to renew the entrepreneurial spirit. Overall transformation requires transformation in several areas of the organization.

- Transformation requires a comprehensive set of capabilities that include people, infrastructure, processes, operations, customer engagement, and tighter integration among these five aspects.
- It requires that the people have leadership capabilities and creative skills.
- It requires that the infrastructure include traditional technologies, digital technologies, and architectures.
- It requires that the operations include processes.
- For customer engagement, It requires that products and services be included.

A clear policy that facilitates integration within and across these capabilities is essential. Transformation initiatives require significant investment in resources to realize the transformation's ambition and to ensure that the return on the investment is directly proportional to the caliber and dedication of the talent aligned with the transformation.

The transformation program requires dedicated transformational leaders, not ones who share the responsibilities of existing programs. Sharing the responsibilities for other activities can dilute the effectiveness of the leader in all the shared programs.

"Transformation requires courageous leaders with the ability to imagine and visualize far beyond the current comfort zone to discover unmet needs with a clear purpose and the ability to drive the mission to reach such destination by taking bold action."

Various aspects that fuel and accelerate organizational transformation include the following:

- Leadership transformation
- Purpose-driven vision
- Creativity
- Innovation
- Design thinking
- Agile transformation
- Cultural transformation
- Digital capabilities
- Human experience transformation
- Business model transformation
- The absence of a narcissistic leadership approach

1.2 Leadership

For several millennia, leaders have shaped—as they are continuing to shape—the future. Their tireless efforts led to innovations at all times. We have reached the point where hyperconnectedness has become an integral part of people's lives. People's lives are transforming at a fast pace. Things in the hyperconnected world are changing faster than ever, and disruption is the norm rather than the exception. With exponential developments in technology, environment, and consciousness, the amount of human knowledge is now doubling every few months. However, the benefits are not reaching all corners of the world. Corporate organizations have a more significant role to play in improving people's experience. Because of hyperconnectedness, the movement of the changes is becoming more unpredictable. With these changes, we are entering a new situation with full of volatility, uncertainty, complexity, and ambiguity, known as VUCA. Though we have more data than ever, we are more uncertain about the future than in the past as rapid and radical transformations across industries are making things that used to be stable more volatile. That is why the acronym VUCA has become the norm in this context.

- Volatility is a result of fast-changing needs of people on a large scale.
- Uncertainty is caused by lack of clarity about the desired outcome.
- Complexity arises from multiple factors such as connections.
- Ambiguity comes from lack of clarity on the impact these changes can have on the society.

Organizations need to prepare to translate these problems and challenges into a clear vision and pointed actions so as to innovate in order to keep up with the disruptive changes. Transformation is critical to ongoing sustainability and growth. Indeed, the demand for leadership capabilities is higher in the VUCA environment than in any other environment.

More start-ups are emerging to challenge incumbent firms and are even disrupting the industry; new technology breakthroughs are being made, new customer trends are developing, and customers are expecting a better experience. Entrepreneurs are challenging the status quo in the industrial world. The only process for which an organization should maintain the status quo is the transformation process. This means that the process of transformation must continue as a journey. Several transformations are under way in many organizations: digital transformation, marketing transformation, business model transformation, and so forth.

Transforming people's experience requires first that organizations be transformed. Organizational transformation requires an individual focused on achieving an outcome. Such a characteristic is mandatory if one is to have the capacity to be the right leader. Leading innovation and transformation involves adopting principles that fall outside the realm of traditional leadership principles. Disruptive change requires leaders with postconventional thinking, and in particular, they need to be operating at the level of strategist. Leaders need to be more agile and transformative to adapt to the occurring problem(s). There is a considerable gap between traditional leadership and the leadership that is needed to lead transformation. Therefore, an integrated focus on strategic leadership development is needed to identify and develop both the current and the future state of leadership.

This leadership strategy must move away from the traditional people-management style and toward functional brain management. The brain, the most complex object in the world, has more than one hundred billion nerves and one hundred trillion connections. The new trend is to encourage neuroscientists to examine the activities and mechanisms of brain cells that affect human behavior and leadership abilities. Neuroscience helps us to study the nervous system and identify the patterns of human thought and action.

Transformational leaders are required to navigate disruption. They need to uncover people's deeper motivations and drive meaningful opportunities for society. They need to prepare to travel into the unknown with uncertainty and be prepared to fail at the intermediate stage. Failure is not always a failure but rather a stepping-stone to learning and progress. Leading innovation and transformation requires disrupting the most fundamental mind-sets and behaviors that have led us to our current success. The fundamental mind-sets and behaviors of people in an organization are not necessarily wrong, but workers need to be agile to embrace further innovation and transformation. Transformational leaders should lead their people by example and instill in them a passion for what the leader is doing with a clear vision. Transformational leaders should have the ability to inspire and motivate their followers by injecting them with energy, passion, and enthusiasm and uplifting them.

Transformational leaders should implement new ideas by following through with the process of challenging, motivating, and engaging people from start to finish and beyond. Leaders who want to successfully guide their organizations through transformation must have the courage of their convictions. In a situation where volatility and uncertainty exist, the leader may not know the exact route to move forward, but courage and determination will lead him or her to the desired destination. Courage comes from a wealth of knowledge. There will be situations where the leaders do not have all the answers, but there may be more information out there. In such cases, leaders should act confidently and decisively.

Transformational leaders should know that there are going to be failures in the interim, but by maintaining persistence and consistency, they can achieve the end goals. Therefore, the leadership must be adaptable and flexible during the journey of transformation but should have the commitment and persistence to reach goals and fulfill needs. Transformational leaders should create trust and integrity among their followers. They should celebrate others and share the credit with others, and they should be the first to shoulder the burden in case of failure. These actions will strengthen the leaders because they are giving credit as well as taking the responsibility. Leaders should have the ability to influence their followers to follow the right path and encourage them to make a change in the environment around them. Transformational leaders must have confidence, but this does not mean that they will do the right thing all the time. They should always listen to their followers. Transformational leaders should provide intellectual simulations to their people to enhance their creativity and innovation, which will show them a new way of looking at old problems. A leader's innovative thinking will motivate the entire organization and inspire followers to excel.

Unlike traditional leadership, transformational leadership should mobilize people and make them self-sufficient. A transformational leader's strong sense of purpose is able to mobilize people in a way that pursuing profits alone never will.

An organization's culture has a significant impact on the success of any transformational change initiatives. The new strategies, structures, systems, processes, and technologies are likely to be different from the current state of affairs and will require that people adopt new ways of being and working. Transformational leaders should create a culture wherein the transformation process runs smoothly.

Transformational leaders should reflect on and learn from their experiences and see them as multifaceted. They should lead with inquiry rather than advocacy, with encouragement rather than command, and with a sincerely held humility. They should facilitate opportunities for others to thrive.

Any transformation will have a profound impact on the relationships of every person involved in it. It is vital for leaders to be present to see and feel the impact that organizational changes have on the people. This requires that transformational leaders have empathy toward the people involved in the process. Empathy helps leaders to earn the confidence and respect of their people. They show empathy by being emotionally and physically present during the organization's transformation.

There is the difference between leading a start-up and leading an incumbent organization. In the case of a start-up, the culture starts at zero. The implicit entrepreneurial spirit will help to attune the leadership style to the most current level. Therefore, start-up leaders are aligned to deal with volatility and uncertainty. Their desire to grow fast and continuously will diminish the uncertainty and allow them to find ways to achieve value. However, once the start-up becomes successful and mature, a different game starts. The rate of change slows down. Just like with any other larger organization, start-up leaders soon will have to deal with more components, stakeholders, and dependencies. They will need to deal with complexity and ambiguity. However, they will still have an advantage over the incumbent if the founder's mentality still exists and if they have not entirely abandoned it. By showing strong transformational leadership, start-ups have the potential to transform the industry itself.

Start-ups and large organizations will have to deal with all four dynamics: volatility, uncertainty, complexity, and ambiguity. The core pillars of purpose, vision, and mission will support transformational leaders in the context of VUCA.

The transformational leader must create a collaborative culture to energize teams, to promote creativity, to make the environment more productive and joyful, and to connect siloed thinking and link those who practice it within the context of the bigger picture.

Even during the transformation process, transformational leaders must reinforce past commitments that are still benefiting the customers. Also, they should learn how to identify the past commitments that are becoming roadblocks to the needed changes and replace them with new and rejuvenating commitments.

Transformation takes time. If change is easy, it is not sustainable. The transformational leader must maintain a positive attitude and a strong sense of opportunity during periods of turbulence. When faced with ambiguity, the leader finds ways to move forward and avoids getting stuck. Therefore, transformational leaders must be highly emotionally intelligent. Emotional intelligence is the ability to identify and manage one's own emotions and the emotions of others. Emotional intelligence will give the leader the ability to manage his or her own emotions, regulate the emotions of others, and solve problems.

Transformational leaders encounter problems quite often during transformation. Problem-solving skills are essential for leaders because they all have to make decisions. The transformational leader must know the right thought process to apply depending on the nature of the problem.

The success rate of transformational leaders is not measured by their reaching a particular position or achieving a precise net worth. Their success is measured by the positive difference they bring to the lives of their colleagues, their organizations, their families, and society as a whole. Transformational leaders are willing to change, and they encourage others to change to ensure that the organization will change.

Considering everything that we have discussed thus far, there are several areas where transformational leaders need to excel in order to embrace transformation within the organization, the industry, or elsewhere. The areas are as follows:

- Purpose
- Vision
- Creativity
- Innovation
- Inspiration
- Courage
- Collaboration

- Commitment
- Emotional intelligence
- Thought processes

1.3 Purpose-Driven Vision

Transformation starts with envisioning a zone that is far away from the comfort zone. Such a destination should have a clear sense of purpose. The purpose is most important not only for the organization but also for the members of the organization and, for that matter, even for our personal lives. When we live our lives with a clear sense of purpose, we begin living positively and start seeking out new opportunities. The experience makes us feel that we can make a difference. Knowing life's purpose helps us to find our real passion, which is a significant driver to achieve something extraordinary. Knowing the purpose helps us to focus on what matters the most in our life. Purpose gives us clarity about what we want and therefore spares us from spending our time on irrelevant things. A purpose comes with values, which are an integral part of life. Knowing the purpose of life helps us to live life with integrity. All these things deepen our trust and faith in other people.

Having a purpose causes a person dig deep to identify his or her true passion. This purpose should give real meaning to the things that we do in our lives. For example, Steve Jobs's purpose was not merely to make computers. His purpose was to build the tools to help people unleash their potential. The characteristics of the tool may change from time to time along the path. In the beginning of his career at Apple, Jobs built the computer, and later he transformed the company to unveil the iPod, iPhone, iPad, and more. Purpose fuels the work, vision directs the person or team to the ultimate destination, and the mission drives the person or team. The vision sets the direction in which an organization needs to move during the transformation process. The vision is the destination of the transformation journey. Without a vision, the transformation effort will dissolve into a list of discrete and incompatible efforts that can lead the organization in the wrong direction. Transformational leaders must have a clear vision to cut through the clouds.

1.4 Creativity

Creativity is a way of turning dreams into actions. Creativity is a brain function that unleashes the potential of the mind to conceive new ideas to change the lives of the people of the world. Creativity is the driving force behind innovation and transformation. Many of the current world problems can be solved using creativity, and indeed, many problems of the past were solved using creativity. The human being's ability to create novel solutions to problems has allowed us to thrive on the path to the current state from the point of origin. However, many organizations have ignored creativity in their rush toward short-term benefits. Transformational leaders should ignite creativity among the people in the organization to unleash their potential to root out the problems and discover the solutions to those problems.

1.5 Innovation

Innovation is the process of implementing new ideas to create a new product, service, system, or process, or to enhance existing ones to bring about positive change. Whereas, by definition, creativity is about original, unexpected, fresh ideas, innovation does not necessarily arise from those original ideas. Transformational leaders must foster a culture of innovation throughout the organization. Innovation is not something that can be deployed overnight or within a short time frame. It is a process of continual learning and bringing about change. It is an iterative process through which we learn more about customers, markets, and existing internal capabilities and then offer new things. Adopting design thinking and agile innovation within the organization can make the innovation process successful and may mitigate the risk associated with innovation.

1.6 Human Experience

How people perceive their interactions with a product, service, process, or organization is what builds a company's reputation. Perception is guided by emotional and psychological responses when people interact with the product, service, process, customer, or environment. Human experience is one of the mechanisms through which transforming organizations create value. The human experience also brings a durable competitive advantage to the organization. The term *customer experience* is widely used in the field of commerce. However, the experience matters for any entity, such as a nonprofit organization, a government, a patient in a hospital, or a public place such as a park or street. Therefore, the terms *customer experience* and *human experience* are interchangeably used throughout *The Art and Science of Transformational Leadership.*

Digital capabilities have emerged as a primary driver in reshaping the human experience in almost every sector. The growing user expectation for superior service is pitting incumbent organizations' profitability against their ability to deliver services in new ways. Every entity, even traditional players in sectors such as chemicals and steel, should make a bold move to build dynamic shared digital ecosystems around human needs and transform the user experience.

1.7 Design Thinking

Design thinking is a methodology used to solve complex problems that draws upon empathy, imagination, intuition, ideation, and systemic reasoning to explore possibilities of a desired design and outcomes that benefit users. It is one of the human-centered design methodologies.

Innovation and transformation are associated with risks because of the uncertainty and unknown factors that are accumulated because of rapid changes in consumer behavior, disruptive technologies, hyperconnectedness among the systems, shifting economic winds, and increased social connectedness. The transformation process is a nonlinear process. To drive a transformation program effectively, one should look for a systematic process that minimizes risks and produces consistent results. Design thinking is best for nonlinear problem-solving. Business models that use linear problem-solving attempt to define everything up front and then implement the solution in a systematic way. While design thinking is also very systematic, it is more like nonlinear thinking, where one can uncover the problems and then find the solutions to those problems. Linear thinking is good if one's aim is value capture, whereas nonlinear design thinking is good if one's aim is value creation.

Design thinking is not problem focused; it is solution focused. However, one who implements design thinking may not expect the solution to be achieved in one shot. The process is more experimental and iterative. Design thinking solves problems by way of design. Design thinking can be applied in order to design tangible things such as products and intangible things such as services, processes, and business models. It can be used to solve problems in several fields such as business, society, politics, education, and engineering.

1.8 Agile Approach

The process of transformation is not a revolutionary event that can be achieved within a short time frame. It is an evolutionary journey. The agile approach can help manage the complexity and unpredictability through development processes that are iterative and incremental. Since the landscape in which businesses operate is also continuously evolving, there is no doubt that a big-bang delivery approach will lead to delays and even failure. Fostering agility into every transformation initiative will help one to determine the right path to the destination. The agile approach can help deliver quick wins and iterative progress aligning with the desired transformation value. The agile approach can provide early benefits through incremental value creation, which can help fund the subsequent steps in the process of transformation execution. Therefore, the organization that is going through or planning to go through a transformation should transform itself into an agile development culture.

1.9 Organizational Culture

Organizational culture plays a crucial role in the success of any transformational change initiatives. An organization's culture is its collective mind-set. Organizational culture evolves from the patterns brought about by widely shared assumptions, beliefs, and values. The organizational structure, whether it has hard barriers or soft barriers, will impact how the people interact, how people are influenced, how people get inspired or motivated, and how projects are managed. Those behaviors will be directly reflected by the organizational culture.

In the journey of transformation, the target-state strategies, structures, technologies, systems, and processes are likely very different from the current state of affairs. Creativity and innovations are the fundamental drivers of transformation. The organizational culture should encourage employees at all levels to think creatively and innovatively at every point of the transformation journey. The changes that arise from transformation require people to adopt new ways of being and working. An organization's culture shapes everything that takes place in that environment. It can either support the new state that is being implemented or block it. For the organization's change initiatives to be successful, the organization needs an evident shift in cultural norms and expectations. Without cultural transformation, the organization's change initiatives are likely to fail as the employees will show resistance to the changes and may soon revert to their old ways of working. Organizations should design a new culture so that the employees are able to see how the new corporate culture will fit into the big picture.

Certain pieces of the transformation can lead to an unknown state or even to failure. In the hyperconnected world of business, as there are multiple factors increasing uncertainty and creating fear of failure in the workplace, fear keeps millions of individuals from reaching their potential. Transformational leaders must create a courageous culture where people can think creatively, present innovative ideas, and challenge the status quo, even at the cost of failure.

1.10 Digital Capabilities

Digital transformation is one of the components of organizational transformation that unleashes the full potential of digital technologies.

Digital transformation serves as a tool for the organization to embrace overall transformation. The emerging digital economy and shared economy, and fast-changing consumer behavior and expectations, is forcing incumbent organizations to adapt to digital technologies. Digital transformation is an evolutionary journey with multiple intermediary goals. Digital transformation is linked to all other transformations described herein. It focuses on continuous optimization across the processes in a hyperconnected ecosystem. Digital transformation will innovatively bring new capabilities and opportunities. Digital technologies will eventually transform the human experience and will lead to new business models.

The portfolio of digital technologies is highly dynamic in that modernized technologies are being added to the portfolio rapidly, making some of the old technologies obsolete. The list includes, but is not limited to, advanced analytics, artificial intelligence, machine learning, cognitive computing, quantum computing, in-memory computing, the Internet of Things (IoT), blockchain, cloud computing, robotics, drones, social media, mobile capabilities, visualization, 3-D printing, driverless vehicles, open APIs, microservices, augmented reality (AR), and virtual reality (VR). Combining these digital technologies effectively will create synergy for an organization.

1.11 Business Model

Linear transformation is not new to the business world. The emergence of the internet and related technologies brought about the concept of e-commerce. However, this merely transferred the physical store to the online environment. These new technologies have never transformed an industry on their own. Exponential transformation has the potential to transform the business model linking digital technologies to an emerging market need. Indeed, business model transformation and digital transformation are connected in two ways. To unleash the full potential of digital technology, it is necessary to transform the existing business model and discover a new business model that will use digital technologies to their full potential.

A business model is defined as a way of creating and capturing value by business organizations. It is a system where various features interact, often in complex ways, to determine the business's success. The features that define a business model include customer value proposition, pricing structure, the partners with whom value is produced and delivered, and how customers interact with the business. For example, Airbnb, having realized that technology had great potential, designed an entirely new business model challenging the traditional economics of the hotel industry. Airbnb's business model included a platform for producing value for both guests and property owners and also producing value for itself, eventually creating the shared economy.

Some of the fundamentals that contribute to an excellent business model are the following.

- Products or services that are better tailored to customers' individual and immediate needs.
- A model that allows the sharing of precious assets. Uber and Airbnb are the best examples.
- A fee structure based on the use of the product or service, rather than requiring customers to buy outright.
- An ecosystem that allows seamless collaboration among the partners.

1.12 Avoiding the Narcissistic Leadership Approach

Transformational leaders should avoid certain behaviors at all times. A leader's reputation is tarnished as he starts exhibiting narcissistic leadership and toxic behavior. Behaviors such as manipulating others, devaluing others' work, overemphasizing one's own work, and putting one's own interests first at the expense of the other people in the organization are common in narcissistic leaders. Though such leaders have the charisma and required abilities to move the organization forward in the short term, their narcissistic behavior can create havoc and lead to organizational failure in the long run. Narcissistic leaders always try to win at any cost. They have a strong sense of entitlement, and if they do not receive the special treatment, they become very impatient or get quite angry. Narcissistic leaders fail to show empathy and do not identify with the feelings and needs of others. Narcissistic leaders take reckless risks. While it is necessary to have courage to take risks for transformation to happen, such reckless risk-taking for the purpose of self-interest and personal incentives will cause the narcissistic leader to bring trouble upon the organization in the long run.

Narcissists leaders are highly distrustful. They always put their interests first, at the expense of the team. While it is true that narcissistic leaders have clear vision and the ability to see the big picture, their overall characteristics make them unsuitable for the purpose of transformation as they don't maintain good relations, they don't accept criticism, they don't digest failure, they are not good listeners, and they lack the empathy.

Overall, narcissistic leadership goes against the principles of transformational leadership and is harmful to the organizations that seek to transform themselves.

2

Purpose-Driven Vision

Why, What, and How

When we travel, we begin at the origin, take a specific path, and eventually reach the destination. There should be a reason to travel. Alternatively, at least, we ask ourselves *why* we are traveling. What do we expect to find or do when we reach our destination? Then we plan *how* we will get there. In this scenario, there are three factors: why, what, and how.

The why factor is the spirit of everything we do. It is the origin of the things we do, whether in professional or personal life. When we ask a student why she is going to college, if her answer is to get the degree or certificate, then there is no spirit there. She goes to college to acquire knowledge so that she can do better things for herself, her family, and society. Acquiring knowledge is the "why" factor. Why a person acquires knowledge is so that she can do good things for herself, her family, and society. That is the "what" factor. How she acquires knowledge is determined by the college curriculum, her study plans, and more. That is the "how" factor.

These factors are applicable everywhere, whether in corporate organizations, nonprofit organizations, education, politics, or personal life.

Translating why, how, and what factors in different words, they become purpose, mission, and vision, respectively.

- We begin with a purpose.
- The vision is the destination.
- Our mission follows the right path.

In other words:

- Why = Purpose
- What = Vision
- How = Mission

Vision is the ability to imagine the future by looking far away from the current comfort zone and realizing the possibilities and opportunities for solving problems. Vision is an intellectual aspect and is biased toward a clear aspiration for how the world should be.

Purpose, vision, and mission are the three pillars of any transformation that a transformational leader undertakes. What do these pillars do?

- Purpose guides us.
- Vision is where we aspire to be.
- Mission drives us.

2.1 Purpose

Passion is everything. Transformation does not happen without passion. Knowing the purpose will make a person dig deep to identify his or her true passion. Steve Jobs's purpose was not merely to make computers. His purpose was to build the tools to help people unleash their potential. The characteristics of a tool may change from time to time along the path. In the beginning of his career at Apple, Steve Jobs built the computer, and later he transformed the company to unveil the iPod, iPhone, iPad, and more.

Purpose fuels the work, vision directs the person or team to the ultimate destination, and the mission drives the person or the team. At the time when personal computer ownership was limited to select people, Steve Jobs and Apple cofounder Steve Wozniak had the vision to democratize the personal computer and put it into the hands of many individuals. A bold vision inspires the leader and sets the forces in motion. Jobs believed that the role of a leader is to hire the best people and keep them aligned with the vision.

"Knowing the purpose will make a person dig deep to identify his or her true passion."

The purpose is most important not only for the organization but also for the members of the organization and, for that matter, even for our personal life. Having a clear sense of purpose in life helps us to live positively and start seeking out new opportunities. The experience will cause us to feel that we can make a difference. Knowing our life's purpose helps us find our real passion and drives us to achieve something extraordinary. Knowing our purpose helps us to focus on what matters most in our lives. The purpose will give us clarity about what we want and therefore spares us from wasting time on irrelevant things. Purpose comes with values, which are an integral part of life. Knowing the purpose of life helps us live life with integrity. All these things deepen our trust and faith in other people.

"Knowing our life's purpose helps us find our real passion and drives us to achieve something extraordinary."

Purpose is something that an organization is committed to exploring in creative and innovative ways, no matter what the current environment is or the future environment will be. The purpose statement is short and precise, and it is the mantra that inspires everyone in the organization. The people in the organization care less about the how of things until they know why they are doing what they are being asked to do. Many dreamer entrepreneurs fail to achieve success because they fail to communicate with the people in their organization and their investors why they are developing the product. People get inspired if they know that the initiative, product, or idea can improve their own lives and the rest of society.

A clear sense of purpose and meaning for one's work will enlarge the context and help people to see why they are doing what they are doing through a bigger lens. The purpose will help the people to align their roles with the mission and vision. A clear purpose will allow leaders to get approval to change the business model to completely align with the intended transformation. The purpose serves as the basis for the courage to act, to step out of the comfort zone, and inspires the passion to persevere in the face of volatility in a world of uncertainty.

Traditional leadership focuses on managing people, whereas transformational leadership should mobilize people and make them self-sufficient to perform their tasks. An organization without a purpose merely manages people with a traditional leadership approach, whereas an organization with purpose mobilizes people. Purpose fosters a healthy, sustainable, scalable organizational culture. The purpose is intangible and so is not visible. It is the spirit within. Even some organizations that claim to have a purpose do not do anything to integrate that purpose into the day-to-day activities of their employees and customers. Such an approach to purpose fails to unleash the full potential of the organization's resources and will lead the company to miss out on a fundamental element of purpose: a positive impact on society.

"The purpose serves as the basis for the courage to act, to step out of the comfort zone, and inspires the passion to persevere in the face of volatility in a world of uncertainty."

A strong correlation exists between purpose and performance. The more meaningful the purpose, the higher the performance. When an organization defines its purpose and shares it with the employees, the organization lives the purpose, and the business results follow. If the organization's purpose is integral to its corporate social responsibility, instead of being only a philanthropic effort, the community will see the profound impact and the organization will see business performance. Unlike market-driven organizations, purpose-driven organizations are driven by values, culture, and ethos. Instead of being an obligation, social responsibility is seen as an opportunity. A purpose-driven organization can assert that if it were to disappear tomorrow, the world would lose something meaningful.

Organizations with meaningful purpose attract the best talent as leaders are raising their aspirations and shifting their priorities. People are giving preference to the organizations that value social responsibility and strive to make the world a better place instead of just focusing on moneymaking.

There are two ways that people get motivated, and both these ways are essential. Extrinsic motivators focus on individuals' desire to be rewarded through incentives, and intrinsic motivators include meaning, connection, and joy in the work, as well as the desire to contribute, develop, and achieve. Purpose is one of the most potent intrinsic motivators. Digitization reduces interpersonal interaction, but without in-person interaction, the emotional bonding among people will become insubstantial. In such an environment, the purpose enables digital interactions to be more meaningful by bonding them with a sense of the shared values that create communities. Unlike the traditional initiatives that can be launched and driven from the top by a program management office, specific transformations such as digital transformation tend to be a bottom-up phenomena involving many people across the chain. The purpose of transformation is to create positive energy, which provides an emotional connection that inspires more significant commitment. In a hyperconnected transformation process, the purpose serves as hidden energy to illuminate the path to the destination by linking and steering various transformation efforts in a way that is logical and accessible to everyone.

Though vision statements and mission statements are typical in the corporate world, few organizations have purpose statements as well. An organization may have a purpose statement either at the organizational level or at different levels within the organization. Business organizations should make a profit, but they exist to make a difference by serving a cause. The purpose statement should articulate why the organization or the business unit within the organization is doing what it does and why the cause is meaningful. There is no standard agreement on what the purpose statement should be like and no stanard definition of a purpose statement. Few organizations use mission and vision for their purpose statements. People connect with the mission if there is clear communication about why and how the organization is going about its work (the what). The purpose statement should communicate the values of the organization and reveal the character that guides its culture. Customers will connect more deeply to the purpose and character than to the mission statement.

Following are some guidelines for a successful purpose statement:

- It must state the cause that defines the contribution the organization makes to society through its work.
- It should mention how the organization makes a difference and is part of a meaningful legacy.
- It should be inspirational and motivational.
- It should use powerful words.
- It must be easy to remember.
- It should be broad in scope to allow for future opportunities and change.

2.2 Vision

From everyday life, we learn a lot about the most successful leaders and draw so much inspiration from them. The story of every successful leader is unique. Successful leaders serve as social innovators and change agents. They want to disrupt markets with a definite purpose. However, to fulfill a purpose, a leader must have a clear sense of direction. This is called vision. The foundation for purposeful disruptive change is the vision that leaders establish. They develop a vision based on a positive picture of the future with a clear sense of direction. Their thinking is different and often called big-picture thinking, which is the way a person looks at problems and comes up with solutions. Successful leaders bring about disruptive changes and substantial opportunities to create new business by generating new ideas through creativity and putting those ideas into practice by way of innovation. The transformational leader can be an entrepreneur who wants to bring about a new dawn or an intrapreneur who wants to bring disruptive change to the existing organization. In either case, they work with imagination, intuition, and courage. They observe the truth behind most of the polarized issues in society. They search for solutions in unconventional ways to address the systemic causes of problems and create real breakthroughs.

While having vision at the individual level is highly desired, the vision will not be successful if it is not shared with others. People feel honored when they are allowed to contribute in a meaningful way. Sharing the vision at all levels of the organization creates a strong force field that brings about positive energy and gives it form. Clear vision helps the leader to anticipate change and be proactive, rather than react to events. Vision cuts through the clouds and helps leaders to see where the organization will be in the future and to frame the actions to get the organization there. Creating and sustaining a vision for an organization calls for discipline and creativity. The leader turns a vision into reality by creating a vivid image of the target he or she needs to attain and creating a specific strategic plan for the coming year. Through the vision, leaders embrace positive change by turning dreams into reality by way of strong leadership skills, creativity, innovation, and transformation. Through the vision, the leader explains what goals the organization must accomplish and the specific responsibilities of each key team member. Along the way, the leader keeps the team informed of their progress.

"Sharing the vision at all levels of the organization creates a strong force field that brings about positive energy and gives it form."

Transformational leaders must focus on situating the vision within the bigger context of transformation and sharing it with all the members of the organization. Building such a vision will enable the members and bring about a radical shift in the way they think about innovation, creativity, and transformation. Vision building must be based on in-depth sources of intuition and imagination. The vision reflects the personal culture of the thinker.

"Through the vision, leaders embrace positive change by turning dreams into reality by way of strong leadership skills, creativity, innovation, and transformation."

Transformation does not mean that we should change everything. The vision tells us about what to preserve and what to change. The vision consists of a core ideology and an envisioned future. The core ideology sets the core values of the organization, and these are the glue that holds the organization together as it changes. The envisioned future will identify the goals and elicit vivid descriptions of what it will mean to achieve them.

The transformation process requires leaders to lead people into the future by connecting them deeply to the present. A vision is created by looking into the minds of the people, by listening to them very carefully, by appreciating their hopes, and by attending to their needs. In simple words, a vision is created by observing the human condition. An organization that does not have a clear vision for the future may succeed in the short term and may continue to operate quite nicely, but it will fail to thrive in the long run. It will shrink its chance of growing, expanding, and improving in a bigger context because it identifies no clear direction for the expansion to take. Whatever the idea, it will not be implemeted without a clear vision of where the institution is heading.

Communicating the vision to the public audience in straightforward and inspiring words and making it visible in the talent recruitment process will tell the public where the organization is heading and will attract the best and most passionate talent. Doing this will help to ensure that all new staff are aware of the institution's stated vision and how they can play their part in achieving it. That is where the vision statement plays a vital role. While the vision statement communicates the message of the overall organization, the vision must exist at all the levels of the organization and for each product and service.

Let's take a look at the vision statements of some organizations:

Alzheimer's Association
"Our vision is a world without Alzheimer's disease."

Norfolk Southern
"Be the safest, most customer-focused, and most successful transportation company in the world."

Sweetgreen
"To inspire healthier communities by connecting people to real food."

Reston Association
"Leading the model community where all can live, work, and play."

Disney
"To make people happy."

Honest Tea
"To create and promote great-tasting, healthy, organic beverages."

Avon
"To be the company that best understands and satisfies the product, service, and self-fulfillment needs of women—globally."

Cradles to Crayons
"Provides children from birth through age twelve, living in homeless or low-income situations, with the essential items they need to thrive—at home, at school, and at play."

JetBlue
"To inspire humanity—both in the air and on the ground."

Ikea
"To create a better everyday life for the many people."

Some organizations try to combine their purpose, vision, and mission in one statement. While all three of these have some attributes—such as aspiration, inspiration, and motivation—in common, they indeed must be distinguished.

What should the vision statement look like?

- The vision statement is what the organization aspires to be.
- The vision statement should help drive decisions and goals.
- The vision statement indicates a commitment.
- The vision statement should inspire the people who are involved in the process.
- The vision statement does not necessarily reflect the current state of the organization.
- The vision statement should reflect the optimal desired future state.
- The vision statement can be imaginative but should be realistic.
- The vision statement must be creative.
- The vision statement must be descriptive.
- The vision statement must be clear.
- The vision statement must be consistent.
- The vision statement should be able to create synergies.

Mission

The mission maps the "how" factor of the why–what–how framework. An organization typically has a purpose statement describing why it exists, and usually it has a vision statement expressing where it wants to be in the future. The next thing is how the organization will get to the future in order to fulfill the purpose. That is the mission. When people connect with the purpose, they believe in the mission. When all these things align, the organization will make a more significant impact on the cause. The purpose is the foundation of the mission and the vision. The mission drives us to the desired destination (vision) to serve the purpose.

"The mission drives us to the desired destination (vision) to serve the purpose."

When the purpose, vision, and mission are aligned, the transformational leader thrives and brings disruptive changes to the world. When the purpose, vision, and mission are aligned, the organization thrives and disrupts the market.

"When the purpose, vision, and mission are aligned, the transformational leader thrives and brings disruptive changes to the world."

Similar to the purpose statement and vision statement, a mission statement is a must-have for an organization. The mission statement should not be combined with the purpose and vision statements. It should be unique and distinct.

- The mission statement defines the company's business.
- The mission statement outlines the approach to reach the desired goals.
- The mission statement gives a clear picture of the corporate culture, values, and strategy.
- The mission statement states the commitment the organization has to its key stakeholders, including customers and employees.
- The mission statement develops the buy-in and support throughout the organization.
- The mission statement guides the leadership's thinking on strategic issues, especially during times of significant change.
- The mission statement helps to define performance standards.

3

Igniting Creativity

3.1 Creativity

Creativity is a brain function that unleashes the potential of the mind to conceive new ideas. Ideas have the potential to change the lives of people around the world. Creativity is the driving force behind innovation and transformation. While creativity is about conceiving something original, innovation is about creating something new from either creative ideas or existing ideas. The real innovation comes from recognizing an unmet need and designing a creative way to fill it.

"Creativity is the driving force behind innovation."

Creativity lays the foundation to turn the vision into action. Embracing a change to any product or process has two stages. The first stage, which is creativity, involves idea generation and is the free flow of experimentation and the creation of a new concept. The second stage involves rehearsing, editing, and assessing the final product or process as it evolves into its final form, all of which is called innovation.

"Creativity lays the foundation to turn vision into action."

Many of the current world problems can be solved by using creativity. Indeed, many problems were solved using creativity for millennia. Human creativity has driven almost every significant advance achieved by society, such as the advancements in the arts, science, technology, residential planning, transportation, entertainment, and economic prosperity.

Even in the modern business world, certain organizations are thriving based on their creativity. However, not all businesses are fostering creativity and adopting it into their culture. Is this because these businesses lack creative skills, or is it because they do not recognize the significance of creativity? What makes some business leaders lack creativity? Either they think that they were not born with a creative brain or else they believe that creativity has something to do with painting pictures or crafting art. In some cases, business leaders think that creativity does not yield instant revenues and therefore does not fit into their current revenue model. Even in cases where creativity is recognized as important, it is not made a strategic part of the business model. There is a misconception in some business organizations that creativity is unmanageable, too elusive, and too intangible to apply to business cases. There is another perception that focusing on creativity produces a less immediate payoff compared to improving existing products or processes.

The truth is that everyone has the potential to be creative. Creating something novel on a continal basis is essential to growing a business.

According to the CEO Study published by IBM in 2010, creativity is the single most important competitive edge for a business to have if it wishes to succeed. The enterprises that ignite creative thinking are thriving in today's dynamic environment, while their less creative competitors are struggling to sustain themselves. Many business, education, community, and government leaders identify creative thinking as an essential skill for the twenty-first century to solve problems. Creativity is the most important leadership quality for transformational leaders to have. Transformational leaders invite disruptive changes and inspire others to drop outdated approaches.

Everyone has the potential to unleash their creative mind. Everyone possesses the divine spark of genius within. Anyone anywhere, and in any profession, can conjure a creative insight that has the power to transform the lives of people in society or even create a new history.

Every child is very creative. Kids come up with lots of new ideas and play creatively. If we put them on a beach, they make sandcastles that elders cannot even imagine. If we give them paper, they make toys that we have never seen before. Even if those things are not new to the world but are new for the children who created them, we can call them creative thinkers.

Over time, people lose creativity as they move toward analytical thinking and boxed thinking. With practice and by following a methodological approach, however, one can establish a creative mind-set. With practice, one can cultivate the traits of curiosity, observation, intuition, and imagination. It requires pushing beyond one's self-limiting beliefs about how creative one is to unleash the creative genius within. By way of creative thinking, one will become a more innovative problem solver.

The secret behind creativity is to bombard the mind with new experiences and ideas entirely outside one's field, filtering out the noise, and connecting the dots among the remaining ideas.

Unleashing creative potential within an individual will require training by applying methodological approaches. Some of the methods that will help to train the brain to unleash its creative potential are as follows:

- Empathy
- Curiosity
- Observation
- Listening

- Questioning
- Experimentation
- Metaphoric thinking
- Divergent thinking
- Courage
- Intuition
- Analytics

Unleashing the creativity within an organization will require implementing the foregoing techniques on an individual level and also integrating the following methods on an organizational level:

- Cultural change
- Collaboration
- Leadership

Many types of research conclude that the functions related to creativity are performed on the right side of the brain. Therefore, it is said that right-brained people are more creative, are risk takers, and are future-oriented. This does not mean that the creative process is performed by the right brain alone. The highest form of creativity depends on engaging the whole brain by alternating the thinking process between the right hemisphere and left hemisphere of the brain. The creative process is said to be a whole-mind process.

"The secret behind creativity is to bombard the mind with new experiences and ideas entirely outside one's field, filtering out the noise, and connecting the dots among the remaining ideas."

3.2 Thinking Outside the Comfort Zone

Creativity is ignited by the intellectual courage to think big and dream big. Opportunities lie in the extreme end of the zone that is far away from the comfort zone. Unlocking the mind to think about extremes, to find the problems, and to find the solutions requires an extraordinary amount of energy, relentless dedication, commitment, and cognitive skill. As a result, one will be able to see the unmet opportunities with the potential to disrupt the markets to improve the lives of everyone in society.

Creativity comes from the power of finding the problems. While it is critical to find a right solution to any problem, it is even more important to find the right problems. In other words, find a problem and then find a solution. That is where creativity plays a critical role.

> "Unlocking the mind to think about extremes, to find the problems, and to find the solutions require an extraordinary amount of energy, relentless dedication, commitment, and cognitive skill."

Human beings enjoy the outcomes of innovation as these make them feel comfortable. At the same time, it is true that one will encounter resistance from some people when one attempts to change the current process to bring about positive change. Moreover, these people will resist the change even when it is in their best interests. It is quite the paradox that people enjoy the outcome of the innovation process but feel pain when being involved the innovation process. The latter is because the change process gives one a sense of physiological discomfort because of the unknowns. Thinking outside the comfort zone is crucial to embracing creativity.

> "While it is critical to find a right solution to any problem, it is even more important to find the right problems and the solutions to those problems."

When we think about something new, the new information and ideas are first compared with the information that already exists in the brain's working memory. The same thing happens when we try to buy some unknown brand instead of our regular brand. The working memory rationally compares its benefits to the product we currently use. At this time, the working memory activates the prefrontal cortex, an energy-intensive part of the brain. When we try to purchase the regularly used brand, the basal ganglion, one of the parts of the brain, is invoked. The basal ganglion requires much less energy to function compared to the energy required by the working memory. This is because the basal ganglion links to the brain modules that have already been trained by experience.

"Thinking outside the comfort zone is crucial to embracing creativity."

The working memory can hold only a limited amount of information at any given time. When an activity is conducted repeatedly, the information will get pushed down into the basal ganglion so as to free up the processing resources of the prefrontal cortex. Thinking outside the comfort zone requires much effort in the form of focus and dedication. Dedication makes a person pay attention to what he is doing. This activity creates chemical changes in the brain. Neurons communicate with each other through a type of electrochemical signaling. These ions travel through channels within the brain that are, at their narrowest point, only a little more than a single ion wide. Paying attention to the thoughts and insights makes the brain state rise in association with that experience. Over time, paying enough attention to any specific brain connection keeps the appropriate circuitry open and dynamically alive. These circuits then eventually become not just chemical links but also stable, physical changes in the brain's structure. Attention continually reshapes the patterns of the brain.

When we think of a solution to a problem, we usually impose specific constraints. This is called thinking inside the box. If we do not reach the solution in time, we sometimes give up on the problem. The self-imposed constraints or the restrictions governed by the leader limit people to thinking inside the box. However, when we relax the constraints, the brain moves into divergent thinking. It crosses the borders searching for fresh ideas. This is called thinking outside the box. The goal of divergent thinking is to generate many different ideas about a topic in a short period. Divergent thinking breaks down the topic into smaller parts to gain insight into the various aspects of the topic. Divergent thinking typically occurs in a spontaneous, free-flowing manner, such that ideas are generated in a random, unorganized fashion. Following the period of divergent thinking, the ideas and information will be organized using convergent thinking, which will put those various ideas back together in some structured way. While divergent thinking distracts a person to allow for the creation of several ideas, convergent thinking requires dedicated focus. Convergent thinking is mostly analytical. It excludes some of the ideas gathered by divergent thinking. This means that while finding a solution to a problem, the brain functions steadily, alternating between divergent thinking and convergent thinking.

Putting the brain in autopilot mode and performing the repeated day-to-day activities does not cause the brain to think creatively.

A guilty feeling of failure creates fear within people. However, a winning idea does not come about all of a sudden. Failures and obstacles are common in creativity. Fear stops a person from thinking beyond his or her comfort zone. Fear stops a person from thinking about extremes. Courage makes a person transcend fear. Courage is resistance to fear, mastery of fear. Courage to think outside the box and to move farther away from the comfort zone helps to ignite the creativity within.

3.3 Neuroscience of Creativity

Neuroplasticity is a quality of the human brain. It helps the brain to rewire and regain the creative thinking that everyone has when young. It is believed that the adult brain was pretty much hardwired after critical developmental periods in childhood. While it is true that the human brain is much more plastic during the early years and that capacity declines with age, brain plasticity remains all throughout one's life. Neuroplasticity is the ability of the brain to reorganize itself. The environment we live in, the behaviors around us, our thinking, and our emotions cause the brain to reorganize itself, both physically and functionally, throughout one's life. Neuroplasticity makes the brain remarkably resilient over time. It is the process by which all permanent learning takes place in the brain. Thanks to the advancements in neuroscience research and functional magnetic resonance imaging (fMRI), we now have the ability to see into the brain visually. This capability has confirmed the incredible morphing ability of the brain.

"The environment we live in, the behaviors around us, our thinking, and our emotions cause the brain to reorganize itself, both physically and functionally, throughout one's life."

Let us see what exactly happens during creative thinking and where creative thinking occurs in the brain. The brain is symmetrical with a left hemisphere and a right hemisphere. While the left hemisphere of the brain is more analytical, the right hemisphere is visual. The right brain is capable of seeing more deeply and subtly than the left, immersing itself in what's there, in all its richness. Researchers have discovered that there are four predictable stages in creative thinking. They have also found that the stages take place alternating between the right and left hemispheres of the brain. The stages are as follows:

Insights

When the problem for which we are hoping to find a solution is presented to the brain, the left hemisphere starts observing what information is already there in the brain pertaining to the problem, starts collecting new information, and tries to come up with a creative breakthrough.

Incubation

This stage comes into the picture when the brain fails to find a solution during stage one. It knows that the left hemisphere cannot seem to solve the problem. Incubation involves mulling over information, often unconsciously. The thinking process shifts to the right hemisphere to access new ideas and solutions.

Illumination

Aha moments are spontaneous, intuitive, and unbidden. The aha moment is the third stage of creativity. When we give the left hemisphere a rest and do something else, whether it is walking or relaxing, the idea is suddenly illuminated in the right side of the brain.

Verification

This is the final stage of creativity. During this stage, the left hemisphere reenters the playing field to challenge and test the creative breakthrough we have just had. The same is done externally as part of the experimentation process to confirm the viability and feasibility of the idea.

To further understand what happens in each step of these stages, it is essential to examine the structure of the brain. In addition to neuroplasticity, several other neuroscience phenomena help humans to regain the ability to think creatively. Before getting deeper into these phenomena, it is helpful to understand the structure of the brain and the cognitive components of creativity. The demand for creativity and cognitive computing made it imperative to explore the structure of the brain and cognition processes. The most complicated biological object in the universe is undoubtedly the human brain. When the brain engages in creative thinking, the activity within it changes. Observing how creative people produce their creativity and understanding how the brain functions during creative thinking helps other people practice being creative.

There are three critical aspects of the brain to learn about from a creativity point of view:

- Biological structure of the brain
- Functional structure of the brain
- Neurotransmitters

3.3.1 Biological Structure of the Brain

The brain is symmetrical, having the right and left hemispheres. These two hemispheres are joined by neurotransmitters that deliver messages from one side to the other. While the left hemisphere controls speech, comprehension, arithmetic, and writing, the right hemisphere controls creativity, spatial ability, artistic skills, and musical skills. Figure 3.1 shows the left and right hemispheres of the brain.

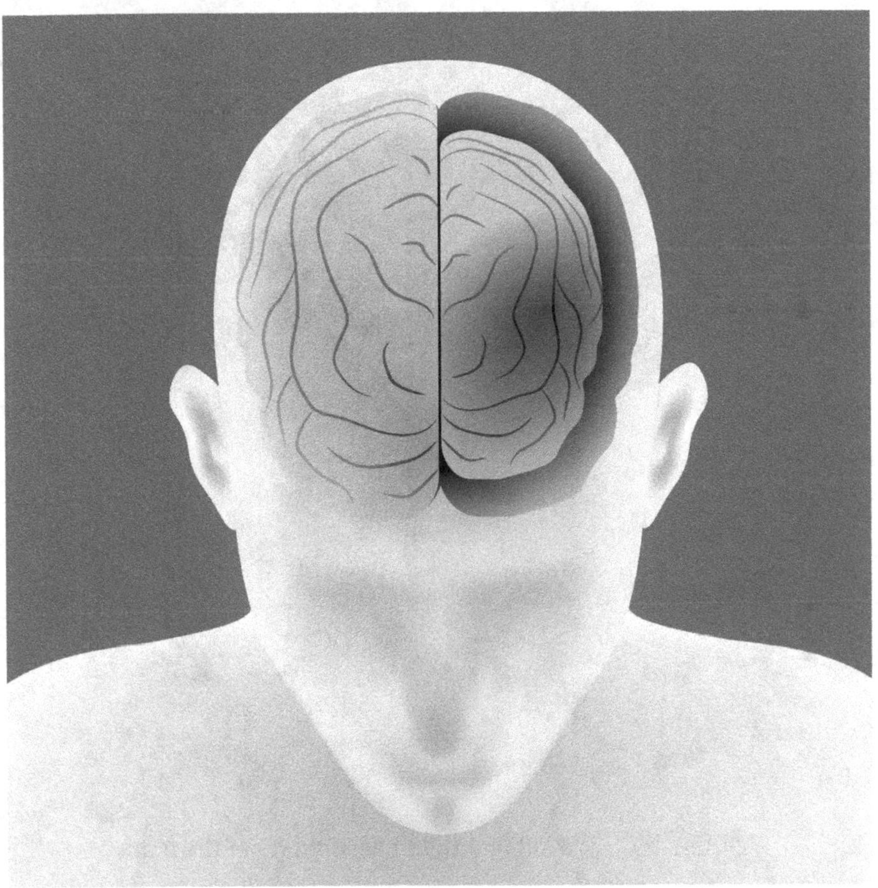

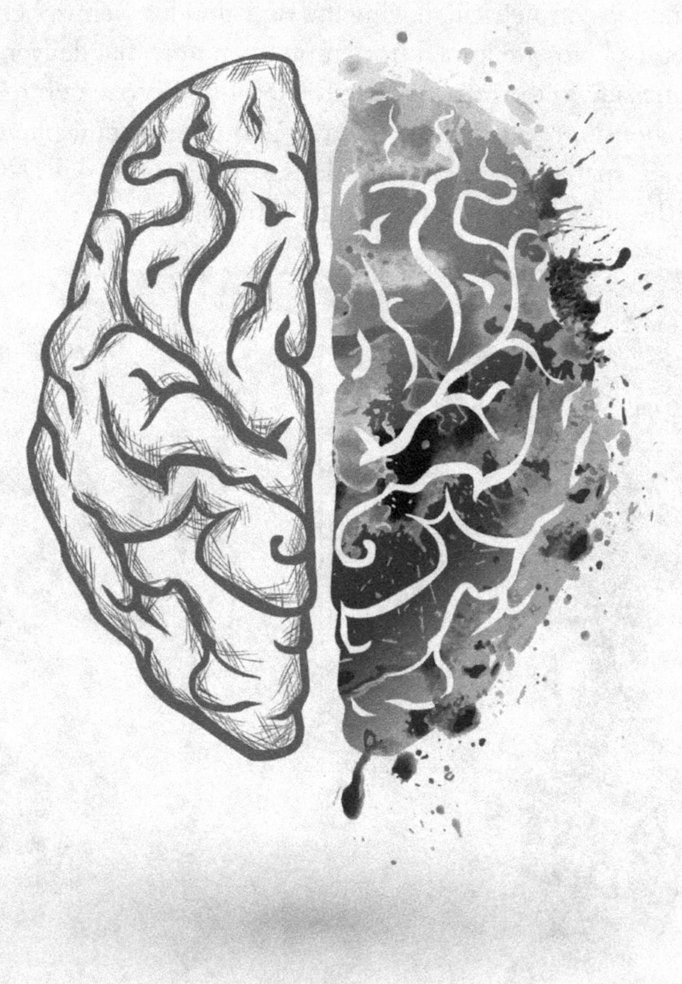

FIGURE 3.1. The left and right hemispheres of the brain

Each hemisphere of the brain is composed of three parts, as follows:

- Cerebrum
- Cerebellum
- Brain stem

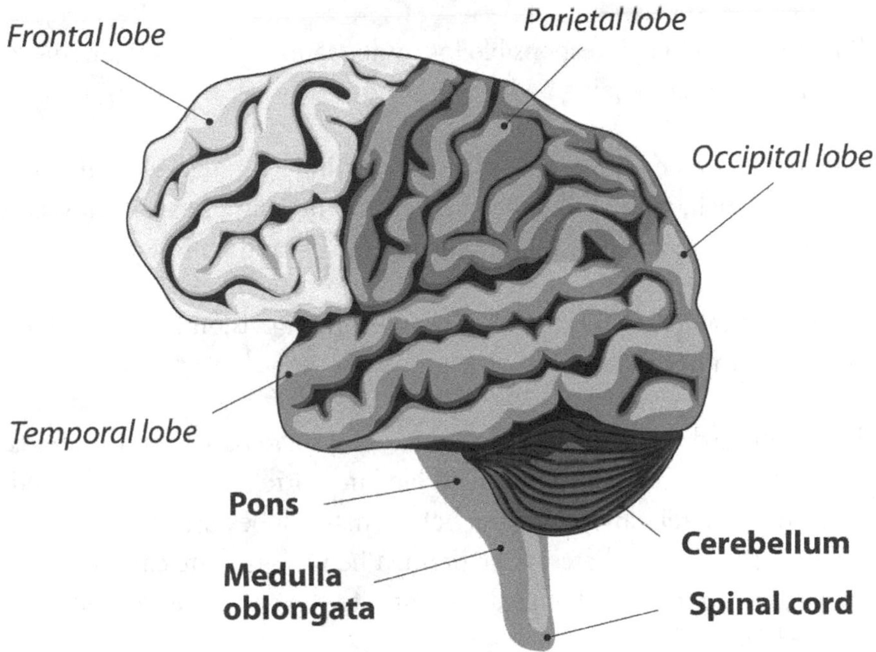

FIGURE 3.2. Lobes of the brain

Cerebrum

The cerebrum, also called the cortex, is the most substantial part of the brain. Its wrinkled nature makes it most useful as the wrinkles cover a great deal of the surface area of the brain and a significant number of the neurons within it. The cerebrum contains about 70 percent of the brain's one hundred billion nerve cells. It is divided into two halves, the right and left hemispheres. The cerebrum is responsible for interpreting touch, vision, hearing, speech, reasoning, learning, and emotions. It has four distinct lobes, as shown in figure 3.2:

- Frontal
- Temporal
- Parietal
- Occipital

The frontal lobe is responsible for behavior, emotions, judgment, planning, problem-solving, speech, body movement, intelligence, concentration, and self-awareness.

The temporal lobe is responsible for understanding language, memory, hearing, and sequencing and organization.

The parietal lobe is responsible for interpreting language; word use; the sense of touch, pain, and temperature; interpreting signals from vision and hearing; motor skills; sensory experiences; and memory.

The occipital lobe is responsible for interpreting vision to detect color, light, and movement.

Each lobe is divided into multiple areas that serve particular functions. The lobes do not function alone. They are all related and connected, and complex relationships exist between the lobes and between the right and left hemispheres of the brain. The messages are carried across these lobes, across the hemispheres, and to the structures buried deep in the brain.

There is another crucial system buried within the cerebrum called the limbic system, which is also called the emotional brain. The limbic system contains the thalamus, hypothalamus, amygdala, and hippocampus.

THE HUMAN BRAIN

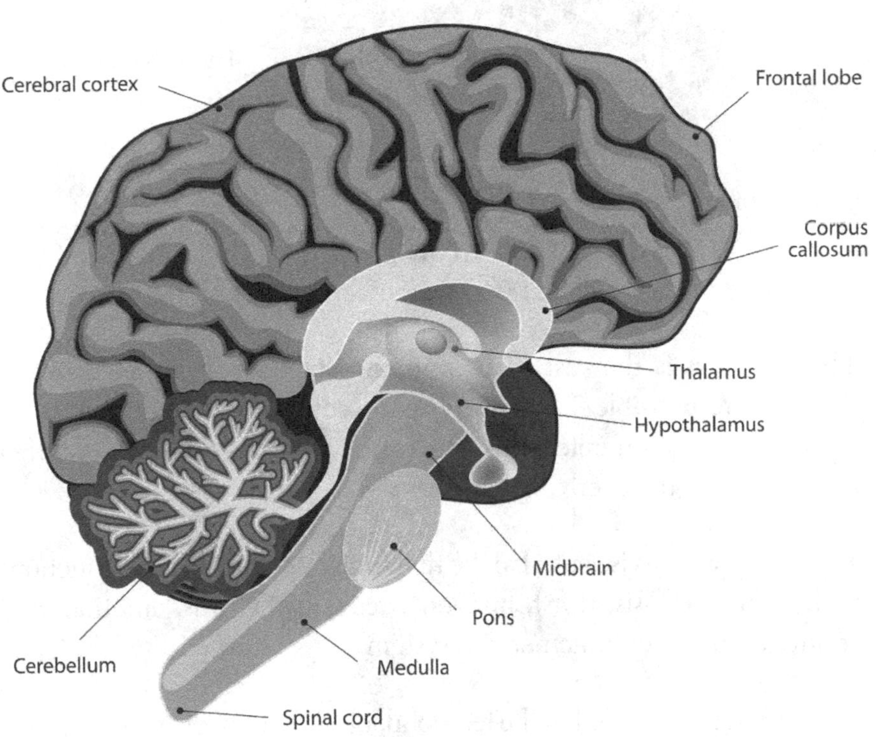

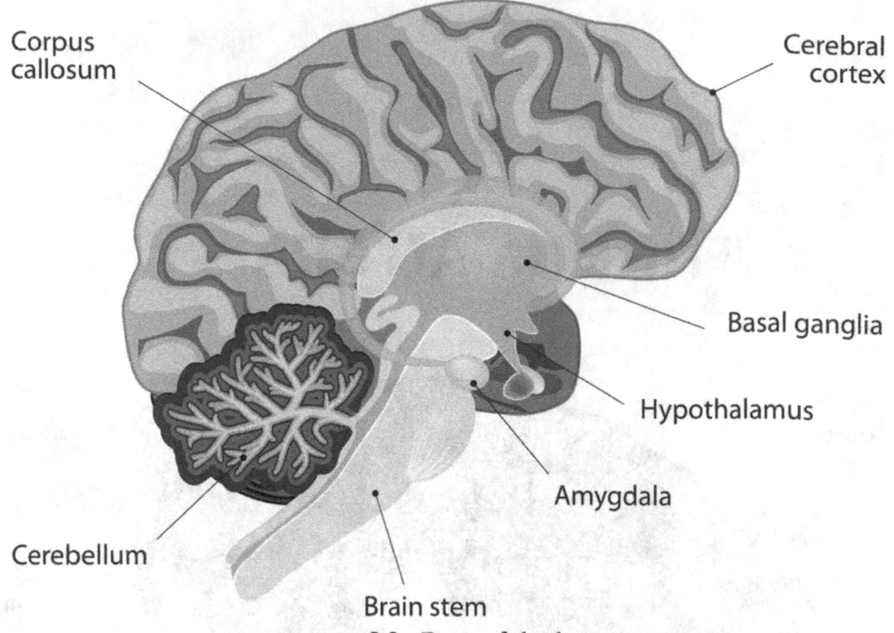

FIGURE 3.3. Parts of the brain

The thalamus is the vast mass of gray matter deeply situated in the forebrain responsible for sensory and motor functions. Almost all sensory information enters this structure, where the neurons send that information to the overlying cortex.

The hypothalamus is ventral to the thalamus and is involved in functions such as homeostasis, thirst, hunger, circadian rhythms, emotion, and control of the autonomic nervous system.

The amygdala is located in the temporal lobe and is involved in memory, emotion, and fear.

The hippocampus is essential for learning and memory, for converting short-term memory to permanent memory, and for recalling spatial relationships in the world.

Cerebellum

The cerebellum is located under the cerebrum and behind the top part of the brain stem. Like the cerebrum, the cerebellum is also made up of two hemispheres. It is a relatively small portion of the brain with about 10 percent of the total weight. However, it contains roughly half the brain's neurons that transmit information via electrical signals. The cerebellum receives information from the sensory systems, the spinal cord, and other parts of the brain and then regulates motor movements. The cerebellum coordinates voluntary movements such as posture, balance, and speech, resulting in smooth and balanced muscular activity.

Brain Stem

The brain stem includes the midbrain, pons, and medulla. It acts as a relay center, connecting the cerebrum and cerebellum to the spinal cord. It performs many automatic functions such as breathing, heart rate, body temperature, wake and sleep cycles, digestion, sneezing, coughing, vomiting, and swallowing. Ten of the twelve cranial nerves originate in the brain stem.

The midbrain is the rostral part of the brain stem. It includes the tectum and tegmentum. It is involved in functions such as vision, hearing, eye movement, and body movement. The anterior part has the cerebral peduncle, which is a massive bundle of axons traveling from the cerebral cortex through the brain stem. These fibers are essential for voluntary motor function.

The pons is part of the metencephalon in the hindbrain. It is involved in motor control and sensory analysis. It has parts that are important for levels of consciousness and sleep.

The medulla oblongata is part of the brain stem, between the pons and spinal cord. It is responsible for maintaining vital body functions such as breathing and heart rate.

According to the theory of human brain evolution, the brain stem is the oldest and indeed the original form of the human brain that evolved hundreds of millions of years ago. This part resembles the present-day brain structure of the whole brain of reptiles. That is why it is often called the reptilian brain. It controls life functions such as breathing, heart rate, alertness, survival, and the fight-or-flight mechanism.

Over millions of years of evolution, an additional two layers capable of more sophisticated reasoning have been added to this foundation. These additional layers provide the emotions and the intellectual and rational thoughts that have helped human society to evolve to its current state. When we are under threat, the reptilian brain overrides any rational brain components.

3.3.2 Functional Structure of the Brain

The foregoing structures of the brain are responsible for various functions in a human being's daily life.

The three core functions are as follows:

- Survival
- Emotions
- Thinking

The order is reflected in the brain structure from the bottom to the top. The bottom part of the brain stem is connected to the spinal cord. Let us discuss these functions of the brain.

Of the above three functions, the reptilian brain is responsible for survival, the limbic system is responsible for both positive and negative emotions, and the neocortex is responsible for cognitive thinking.

Survival Function

The reptilian brain is made up of the brain stem and the cerebellum. The behaviors of the reptilian brain are mostly unconscious and resistant to change. The reptilian brain keeps us away from danger. It has helped human beings survive for millions of years. For this reason, it sometimes prevents us from advancing. The primitive reptile survival instincts are either to fight to protect ourselves or else escape. That is why it is often referred as "fight or flight." Also, the basic emotions such as anger and aggression are still generated at the reptilian brain level. It is a way for the reptilian brain to try to protect people from others.

The reptilian brain does not feel any pain and looks for pleasant sensations automatically. This is what keeps people in a comfortable zone of thinking. The reptilian brain reacts quickly by triggering a punishment, which is a behavior that can lead to the spreading of a conflict without even trying to solve the problem. By serving as gatekeeper, this part of the brain sends information to the basal ganglion and also receives information from the higher levels of the brain, such as the cerebral cortex and limbic system. This means that unless it is controlled by the higher levels of the brain structure and function, the reptilian brain will give resistance to change and restrict thinking to the comfort level, preventing unconventional thinking, preventing risk-taking, and even initiating conflicts in the hopes of self-protection. Such resistance and conflict can always be managed by other parts of the brain cognitively, as described below.

Emotional Function

The limbic system, which is buried deep under the cerebrum, is concerned with both positive and negative emotions. By linking emotions with behavior, the limbic system serves as a layer of control to the fight-or-flight responses of the reptilian brain. The limbic system consists of the thalamus, hypothalamus, amygdala, and hippocampus. The amygdala performs a crucial role in the formation and storage of memories associated with emotional events. As it is connected to the prefrontal area, it makes it possible for the amygdala to play an essential role in the mediation and control of essential behaviors such as love, affection, fear, and aggression. When triggered, it generates fear and anxiety, which puts the person into a state of alertness, getting ready to fight or flee. The amygdala receives input from the medial prefrontal cortex. The prefrontal cortex is involved in the planning phase of the response, after the initial reflexive reactions, if one has to choose the best course of action to get out of a dangerous situation.

Cognitive Function

The neocortex is the place where all cognitive thought happens. The third and newest part of the human brain in light of evolution, the neocortex is associated with the function of making judgments and with the knowledge of good and evil. It is also the site from which our creativity emerges and is home to our sense of self. It is an area where matter is transformed into consciousness. It makes up more than two-thirds of our brain mass.

In the realm of intuition and critical analysis, the neocortex is the area where we have our ideas and inspirations, where we read and write, where we do mathematics, and where we think about the arts. Human civilization is the product of the cerebral cortex. The neocortex is the largest portion of the cerebral cortex that covers the outer portion of the brain. The convoluted or wrinkled shape increases its surface area and therefore the number of neurons that connect to the rest of the body. The neocortex enables executive decision-making and purposeful behavior and allows us to see ahead and plan for the future. It has specialized areas that make sense of and process information received from our senses, for example, touch, sight, air temperature, facial expressions, and tone of voice, and is responsible for voluntary movement.

Unlike the other two parts of the brain, the neocortex operates on a mostly conscious level. Participation of the cortex and interaction of the cortex with the reptilian brain causes us to behave and think in a more flexible manner. In short, to make decisions, our neocortex interprets the information that comes from the reptilian brain and the limbic brain. Thus, it tries to inhibit impulses that are not adaptive and to deploy behaviors more appropriate for the situation.

3.3.3 Neurotransmitters

The brain has two most potent neurotransmitters called dopamine and oxytocin, and they both are directly connected to the exploration and connection required in the pursuit of one's passions. Oxytocin also functions as a hormone. Oxytocin is produced in the hypothalamus and is associated with empathy, trust, and relationship-building. It impacts emotional, cognitive, and social behaviors when it is released into certain parts of the brain. It also causes a reduction in stress responses and anxiety. As covered in an earlier section, the thalamus, hypothalamus, amygdala, and hippocampus are part of the limbic system, which is mainly associated with the emotions. Being released in the hypothalamus, oxytocin targets the amygdala and hippocampus, and it interacts with the hypothalamic–pituitary–adrenal axis, reducing the stress and positively impacting the dopaminergic reward-processing circuitries. In this way, the oxytocinergic circuitry becomes pivotal in creativity by increasing global processing, reducing attention to detail, and enhancing cognitive flexibility, original ideation, and creative insight.

The brain releases oxytocin when we connect with like-minded people through all sorts of social interactions. Higher levels of oxytocin allow for more trust, empathy, and generosity. Dopamine, the other neurotransmitter, gives us pleasure and increases our motivation to pursue an anticipated reward. Dopamine drives our passion for exploring. When we start exploring our challenges, the brain releases dopamine. Neurons fire together and wire together. With more practice, the brain evolves its patterns. When these two transmitters are released in greater quantities into the brain, the brain becomes more adapted to pursuing challenges and coming up with creative solutions.

3.4 Empathy for Creativity

Having empathy means being able to understand the needs of other people by better understanding their feelings and their thinking. If we understand that creativity helps to improve the lives of people within society, we will quickly understand that the core factor that plays a role in this context is empathy. Though empathy and sympathy are somewhat related, they are different from one another. To have sympathy means to express sorrow for someone else's misfortune. Empathy is a much deeper feeling. Through empathy, we can understand and share another person's feelings and emotions. Empathy creates a secure bond between a person and society. Empathy is the ability to look outside ourselves, walk in someone else's shoes, see with someone else's eyes, and think with someone else's mind to feel what someone else is feeling. Empathy is the broader topic, and therefore it is also covered under the chapters on innovation and leadership.

"Most successful entrepreneurs, both past and present, are highly empathetic."

Why does empathy matter for creativity? Creative thinking needs real perspectives and insights in a real-world context. There are so many places in the world where people face challenges in their day-to-day lives. However, as discussed earlier, they feel comfortable with what they are facing. If we ask them what kind of solutions they need, they mostly say that they are okay with what they have. However, there may be exceptions, such as a need for water and food, which they want to solve immediately. If we want to change the way people live, we need to fully understand how they live now and what challenges they are facing. For businesses, finding a solution means creating something that people want to use. The problems a business leader is trying to solve are rarely her own but are the customers'. To give people the best solution to their problems, one must gain empathy for the people for whom one is seeking solutions. With empathy, we will understand the unique pain points and experiences of the people around us and will come up with creative solutions to address their problems. An empathic perspective will drive a person to step outside her own biases, think outside the box, and think divergently. Most successful entrepreneurs, past and present, are highly empathetic.

According to the research carried out in the field of neuroscience, empathy activates different networks in the brain. When we see other people's distress, we feel emotional distress. This is accompanied by activations in the brain in the anterior insula and anterior medial cingulate cortex—a core neural network that is involved in both firsthand experiences of pain and vicarious pain. Though we do not have the physical pain ourselves, we still activate this shared network. Such empathetic distress compels us to help the other person. Empathy is essential for creativity as it puts us into other people's shoes.

Empathy may refer to an emotional response, a cognitive response, or both.

There are three components of emotional empathy. They are as follows:

- feeling the same emotion that another person feels;
- feeling distress in response to perceiving another's plight; and
- feeling compassion for another person.

Cognitive empathy gives one the ability to gain an understanding of someone else's thoughts and feelings without actually feeling what that person is feeling. Cognitive empathy requires us to have complete and accurate knowledge of the contents of another person's mind, including how that person feels.

The best way to gain empathy is through immersion. Going out to other places and experiencing life, understanding the full contexts, observing the environment and activities of other people, and so forth will help to immerse one in empathy.

3.5 Idea Generation

The first step in the creative-solution-finding process is to generate as many ideas as possible. While a deep understanding of the problem and context will help us to find the solution, insights are most important for creativity. Insights are gathered through various methods with the direct involvement of humans:

- ➢ Curiosity
- ➢ Observation

- Listening
- Questioning

The two methods described earlier, thinking outside the comfort zone and cultivating empathy, augment the methods listed above to help one gain more relevant insights related to the problem for which a creative solution is needed.

3.5.1 Curiosity

Curiosity is the display of probing behaviors to gain more knowledge about something and to go deeper into ideas. Curiosity fuels high levels of creativity.

Albert Einstein once said that he had no special talent but rather was passionately curious. Curiosity ignites creativity by enabling us to lean into uncertainty with a positive attitude, searching for clues.

In business, people work hard to find solutions to problems. However, there is another angle to consider. Business should be able to find the right problems as well. Finding the problems and finding the solutions are both essential to the transformational business. One needs to be curious enough to identify the problems worth solving, and then one should come up with creative solutions. The curious mind takes an interest in exploring a wide range of subjects and finding the connections among them to help solve problems.

> "Curiosity ignites creativity by enabling us to lean into uncertainty with a positive attitude, searching for clues."

Curiosity will provide more building blocks to allow one to develop creative solutions. To spark new levels of creativity in the workplace, one should step outside one's comfort zone. Curiosity makes a person walk outside the comfort zone. Curiosity will look for the questions that inspire answers one cannot possibly predict. Divergent thinking brings several pieces of information into play. Making connections among these pieces of information, which appear meaningless at first glance, is the most crucial creative thinking skill we can ever master. Such a skill is made possible by curiosity. Curiosity makes connections between existing ideas that seem impossible to conventional thinking. Having past experiences and knowledge, combined with the curiosity to learn and discover more, will lead to original thinking and breakthrough creativity.

For several centuries, curiosity has been the force behind several scientific and technological discoveries and advancements. Curiosity sustains our interest and motivates us to inquire or explore. By having a curious mind, we gain new information which otherwise we would usually ignore.

There are two types of curiosity: specific curiosity and general curiosity. General curiosity is associated with the breadth of the subject rather than the depth of the subject. It leads us to learn about unfamiliar topics and gives us broader prospects in finding solutions. Specific curiosity is associated with depth of the subject. It causes us to seek the information to fill the gaps in already collected information.

General curiosity directly leads to higher creativity. Exploring industries other than one's own, even if they are entirely unrelated, can lead to the breakthrough ideas we have been waiting for, for a long time.

3.5.2 Observations

Observation is an untapped skill a creative person must possess. Practicing active observation will help one to tap into new ideas for a business. Making observations in the right way will connect a person to the environment in a new way. It will make a person open-minded to allow for new possibilities and to build a repository of experiences that can spark original ideas.

Observing the problem closer to the context will suppress the biased thinking that is formed by engaging in repetitive life experiences. The best way to capture people's best moments while observing them is by immersing oneself in empathy. Our brains are wired to automatically filter out some information without our knowledge. We need to observe things with a fresh set of eyes. By observing people, one can gain an understanding of the environment and receive clues about what people think and feel and what values they hold. With these observations, one can capture the physical manifestations of people's experiences, which will help one uncover insights. The best creative solutions come from the best insights into human behavior. One should observe the problem as it occurs naturally without affecting the behavior of the people involved. Also, the same problem must be observed under different circumstances.

"Observing the problem closer to the context will suppress the biased thinking that is formed by engaging in repetitive life experiences."

The why–what–how method covered in earlier chapter is useful in practicing observation as well, but in a different sequence: what, how, why. By doing this, we divide the observations into those three groups: what, how, and why. We should start with what the person is doing and what is happening in the background. Then we observe how the person is doing what he or she is doing. Based on the "what" and "how" observations, we should be able to draw conclusions about the emotional drivers to guess why the person is doing what he or she is going.

The motivation for thinking of creative ideas comes from an emotional connection with people and the environment. There is a smaller possibility of drawing emotion from mainstream or average users. Going to the extreme users and observing them will inspire and motivate us to find the problems and the solutions to those challenges. When we observe extreme users, we need to stretch our thinking. This does not necessarily mean that we are going to find the solution just for the extreme user. However, we will have more of an opportunity to learn from extreme users and understand extreme emotions. Then we should start thinking about the solution that will be acceptable to both extreme users and mainstream users. A solution that suits the extreme user will undoubtedly suit mainstream users.

The outliers will shine a new light and will offer richer insights because they are the ones for whom the experience matters. For example, as of today many banks still use the checkout mechanism online and at their physical locations, as it is suitable for the highest number of users and for most sectors. That "highest number" is average or mainstream consumers. And while this method works for most, some consumers and sectors struggle with the payment mechanism. Observing retailers in various sectors struggling to accommodate the many ways that consumers want to pay will help banks design a more flexible payment method. Later such a mechanism will naturally be accepted by mainstream users.

3.5.3 Listening

Listening is the most underrated skill that can bring enormous value to the creative process. Hearing and listening seem to be the same, but they have significant differences. While these two activities involve the use of ears, there is more mind process involved in listening. In other words, the sounds are perceived by the ears, and the brain understands it by paying full attention to the meanings behind those sounds. Listening is the process of diligently hearing sounds and interpreting the meanings of those sounds.

Successful business leaders are excellent listeners. They actively listen to everyone who is involved in problem-solving. What makes a person be not such a good listener? Our brains are wired to collect information rapidly, combine it with past experiences, interpret it, and generate predictions rapidly. The brain continuously employs memory of past experiences to interpret sensory information and predict the immediately important future. Such interpretation by the brain influences the speed of the present environment given the nature of multitasking work, information overload, and distractions. When we listen to people to understand the problem, our goal is to achieve comprehension. We should not feel that we are listening to criticism or praise. We should avoid engaging in judgment, prejudice, and assumptions.

> "The purpose of listening is to have comprehension, and therefore we should avoid engaging in judgment, prejudice, and assumptions at the time of listening."

So, we need to challenge our brain's habit of listening and override it with active listening. With the advancements in the field of neuroscience and with the help of fMRI, researchers have found differences in brain activity when in active listening mode versus nonactive listening mode. The right anterior insula, a region of the cerebral cortex, is more active in listening mode. The right anterior insula is also involved in evaluating positive emotions.

Based on the above findings and based on what we know about empathy, it is understood that empathetic listening will override the brain's predictive habit and make the brain open to more input. Empathetic listening allows us to let go of old habits and embrace new ones.

Active listening can make people more cooperative, make them feel good, and strengthen emotional bonding. Active listening techniques can also improve a client's outlook on past events. If another person is revealing an experience that is negatively impacting their life, the use of active listening can enhance their ability to reframe past events in a more positive way, which can be an essential step in the healing process.

The challenge to many creative people is to put aside their advocacy habits and acknowledge an existing problem. We cannot solve a problem if we cannot see it.

Active listening helps to make sure that we have all the facts from the relevant sources and outside experts to solve the problem. Practicing active listening and staying away from quick judgments will override the brain's habit of making quick predictions and jumping to conclusions.

One should combine curiosity and observation skills with listening skills. Active listening can make one discover a breakthrough solution.

3.5.4 Questioning

Just as curiosity, observation, and listening can help us to gain the most relevant insights so as to discover a creative solution, questioning or interviewing is another useful tool to help us gain a deep understanding of the problem. Questioning will bring a creative person close to the people involved in the problem and help him or her to understand the people from their own context, emotions, and behaviors. To make the most out of an interview, one should sufficiently prepare the questions. The objective is to learn something new and also to get inspired to solve the problem.

The core principles behind interviewing are a contextual inquiry, making people feel comfortable in a pleasant environment, using appropriate gestures, and understanding the interviewee's gestures. Contextual inquiry is the most important aspect to understanding people, their needs, and the context in which they will use the product or service. Contextual inquiry helps one to understand what people are already using and their unique environment to uncover their unmet needs.

During the interview process, we should not influence the outcome for those we are interviewing. We should engage them without the influence of our judgments. We should actively listen as outlined in the previous section. Their facial expressions and body language are crucial to grasp, as these things reveal why exactly the interviewees feel frustrated with the current solution. We should question things even if we already understand them so as to understand how those we are interviewing perceive the problem. We should look for exciting patterns and take note of the surroundings.

"During the interview process, we should not influence the outcome for those we are interviewing."

3.6 Idea Incubation

The techniques discussed in the previous section will help the new information flow into the brain. It will take some time to sink into the brain. All memories are fragile in the brain at the beginning. Over time they become concrete. It can take a few minutes, a few hours, a few days, or a few years for the memory to concretize and flow down to the unconscious part of the brain.

When we start thinking about a solution, we first set the challenges and goals of the information-gathering phase before we start collecting the information. The details about the problem must have already been transferred to the unconscious mind. This means that the unconscious mind already knows the goals and that it needs more information than the conscious mind does.

After setting the challenges and goals, we go on to explore the information to achieve the best solutions. When we stop gathering information and give the conscious mind a rest, the information starts moving down to the unconscious. At this stage, the information is reorganized and the neural connections are strengthened. This stage is called incubation.

Creative thinking relies on both new concepts that have just been accumulated and the information that has been stored in the brain over time. The brain makes the connections between past information and new information and will try to find the solutions we are interested in. If it finds any gaps in the information needed to find the solution, it will attempt to work the problem using the information it has. If it faces any difficulty in finding the solution, it will provoke us to get more information, at which time we will resume the insight phase.

Any relaxation that does not involve thinking can improve the incubation process. Sleeping well, practicing mindfulness meditation, walking a few minutes in a day, doing some deep breathing, and staying away from distractions will all help to strengthen the incubation.

Sleep is the best source for idea incubation. Sleep has several stages to it, each stage having its own pattern and momentum. One of those stages will remove the weak information that is blocking the idea. This means that the brain will forget the unuseful information. By doing so, it has a clean set of information for generating creative insights.

The other practice that helps the incubation process, but not when during sleep, is mindfulness meditation, which we do while awake. There is a link between mindfulness and creativity. Certain mindfulness traits will cause an increased level of creativity. Practicing meditation after the information absorption phase will help to ignite creative ideas.

Mindfulness meditation reduces the reactivity of the reptilian brain, increases resilience, improves emotional intelligence, and stimulates the neocortex. As a result, ideas flow directly to the neocortex, where creativity happens.

Incubation requires frequent pauses of conscious thinking. If we are trying to solve a problem and have failed to solve it, the brain stores the unsolved problem in a specialized area of memory. If we take a break from conscious thinking, then the problem-solving process is taken over by the unconscious mind. Mindfulness helps people to work on a creative task by focusing the attention entirely on the problem and giving the mind a break to focus entirely on something unrelated. Switches in thinking modes help ideas to incubate and generate creative insights. These frequent switches also result in scattered attention. Such scattered attention helps the brain to mix the patterns existing in the brain with expected ways of seeing the problem to provide possible novel ways of solving the problem.

"Mindfulness meditation reduces the reactiveness of brain, increases resilience, and improves emotional intelligence, which results in a flow of ideas and ignited creativity."

3.7 Idea Illumination

The illumination part is different from the incubation phase. The moment that gives the insight into what needs to be created is referred to as illumination. It is also called the aha moment or eureka moment. The earlier two stages, idea preparation and idea incubation, help the brain to illuminate the insight. Various studies have found that the best ideas come when a person is walking, working out, or swimming, but not while actively thinking about the solution. This means the eureka moment or aha moment that sparks unexpected solutions pops up when the mind is quiet and the consciousness is at rest. Quieting the mind helps to solve the complex problems that are too big for the conscious mind. The fact is that these flashes of insight are not as random as they seem and can be fostered by specific activities, for example, taking breaks between meetings and taking the time to take a walk outside.

Mind wandering is another crucial mechanism that often goes hand in hand with internal focus. Thomas Edison used to routinely let his mind wander, hoping to capture short bits of innovative thought, and then writing down those thoughts, believing that they were often creative. Scientists have since found mind wandering to be crucial for triggering insights. To stimulate optimal daydreaming conditions, one should not overschedule one's day. Allowing some downtime on a regular basis can have a significant impact.

After considering a problem to find the solution and spending some time on it, if we move on to thinking about other tasks, the part of the brain that was activated when we first considered the problem remains active, but in an unconscious state. That means we keep working on things unconsciously. Unconscious thinking is a hidden but powerful cognitive process that occurs outside our conscious awareness. Taking a break from thinking about the problem can allow us to access this untapped resource to process the deluge of information that is required if we are to make an insight-driven decision.

Anxiety is an enemy of creativity, but unfortunately, the process of finding a solution for a problem can induce anxiety. Anxiety creates much noise in the brain, disturbing one's ability to gain insight. On the other hand, pleasant times with happy feelings will spark the eureka moments leading to insightful problem-solving and decision-making. People with positive emotions and good moods experience more aha moments and solve more problems compared to those with negative emotions and toxic moods such as anger, frustration, and anxiety. A pleasant mood alters brain activity and promotes an insight-friendly neural environment. When dealing with a complicated decision, doing something to lift the spirits, such as reading a book or listening to music, can bring a much-needed breakthrough.

By leaving space for quiet time, being internally focused, and taking a positive approach, one is more prone to have insights every day. More insights mean solving complex problems faster, whether it is solving a client's problem or changing the world.

"People with positive emotions and good moods are more creative in solving problems compared to those with negative emotions and toxic moods such as anger, frustration, and anxiety."

3.8 Idea Verification

Creativity is not about coming up with a new idea. It is about coming up with a new idea that is useful. Once the brain is flooded with information and goes through the incubation and illumination stages, it enters the final stage of creativity called idea verification. During this stage, the left hemisphere comes back into play, challenging and testing the creative breakthrough that has just been had to ensure that it is useful for the context. The same is done externally as part of experimenting and confirming the viability and feasibility of the idea.

3.9 Whole-Brain Creativity

It is a common belief that the right side of the brain is responsible for creativity and the left side of the brain is responsible for logical thinking. Such a belief may be right for certain types of creativity. Just as the increased level of hyperconnected and complexity in the world brings about more volatility and uncertainty to the creative process, the number of unknown factors is increasing. Courage will drive a person to overcome the unknown factors. The importance of analytics cannot be ruled out entirely in the creative process. Whether it is within the human brain or the organization, analytics undoubtedly augments the creative process.

Let us take the two paradoxical thinking processes, divergent thinking and convergent thinking. Divergent thinking, which is creative, devises various ideas and solutions to the problem. Divergent thinking is the ability to come up with many ideas for problems that do not have a solution. It refers to associative and intuitive thought and thinking that requires flexibility. It is the ability to develop many possible solutions to a problem, some of which may be novel and differ in their quality. Because of the number of unknown factors of the problem, it is imperative to apply divergent thinking.

Following divergent thinking, convergent thinking, which is mostly analytical, puts these ideas back together in some organized fashion. Convergent thinking is mostly analytical as it uses cognitive activities that filter out the many to result in a few. Convergent thinking refers to intelligence and measures analytical problem-solving abilities. As such convergent thinking is analytical, logical, and controlled. It insists that there is one right solution for a given problem.

While the right hemisphere is heavily involved in divergent thinking, the left hemisphere of the brain is heavily involved in analytical thinking. This means that the functions steadily alternate between divergent thinking and convergent thinking to find a creative solution to the problem. The same is true in cases of the best analytical thinking. The right hemisphere of the brain augments analytical thinking to come up with the most exact reasoning. Higher levels of creative and analytical thinking require significantly more nerve connections between the right and left hemispheres.

Whole-brain thinking helps people to break out of traditional mind-sets and reframe their views and their perceptions of the challenges to come up with a strategic road map for creativity, innovation, and transformation. The techniques and methodologies used in science, the arts, engineering, and business can be combined to get a holistic view of the problem being solved and to design a creative solution for it.

3.10 Collaboration for Idea Generation

In the previous section, we covered the techniques to ignite ideas in the human brain from the individual point of view. While individuals have undoubted potential to tap into insights for idea generation, synergy plays a highly significant role in idea generation. According to Dictonary.com, synergy is "the interaction of elements that when combined produce a total effect that is greater than the sum of the individual elements and contributions." Such synergies are possible through meaningful collaboration. Collaboration is a defined process where various shareholders work together constructively, share the responsibilities, and facilitate collaborative problem-solving and decision-making. Utilizing the mechanism discussed in the previous section in a group has the potential to produce tremendous results.

Several creative historical scientific and artistic ideas emerged from collective thinking, passionate conversations, and emotional connections. In a world where change is happening very rapidly, it is not entirely possible for one individual to keep up with everything. It is not required for one leader to have answers to all the questions. The most valuable resources in any organization when it comes to generating ideas are the organization's members. When we bring various people onto the team, it is quite common for these different people to think in different ways. Not everyone thinks in the same manner, and not everyone *has* to think in the same manner. Diversity helps the leader to consider perspectives and possibilities that would otherwise be ignored. The thinking and ideas of each member may be correct in their contexts. This is called siloed thinking. Here the silo can be a person or a unit of the organization. Siloed thinking may not meet the expectations of the organization if it is taken as stand-alone, but it will help if the ideas from several silos are taken together and their meaningfulness harnessed. Embracing collaboration among the individual team members will create synergy. The transformational leader must know how to connect siloed thinking and link it to the context, the bigger picture. The leader must create a collaborative culture to energize the teams, to promote creativity, and to make the environment more productive and joyful.

"Diversity helps the leader to consider perspectives and possibilities that would otherwise be ignored."

The collaborative process is more than working together. There must be the glue that binds people together and gives them the ability to think together and to act on complex projects. The traditional or legacy processes are not modeled in such a way that they welcome organizational transformation. In a legacy process, individuals come together naturally but reluctantly based on a forced need. Collaboration is essential in a business where the problems are so complex that no one person or unit has either the information or the power to make decisions. The collaborative process helps to foster creativity in an organization. Collaboration helps people to listen, explore, learn, adjust, align, link, and leverage the information that is not otherwise available to an individual.

Collaboration improves the creative process in ways including, but not limited to, the following:

- Facilitating a better understanding of the problems
- Bringing previous experiences to bear
- Leveraging broader areas of expertise
- Suppressing biases

An understanding of the problem can fall short of the information when compared to the full context. In other words, there will be a potential gap between how we understand the problem and how it is related to the context. The gap can be even larger if we are dealing with a more complicated problem. In a collaborative team, each member contributes to the shared understanding and brings his or her unique perspectives. The collective knowledge of the team will help to explore the problem, which in turn will help to bridge the gaps in understanding.

The brain creates patterns and stores them based on past experiences. Such patterns will help people to analyze information quickly and make decisions. It is a fact that having done something right in the past will make us do the right thing in the present. At the same time, the current success level depends on the new context and environment, as there is a potential for previous experiences to create false assumptions. Working as a team will pool the knowledge and previous experiences and also facilitate the challenging of assumptions. Challenging the assumptions will help team members to adjust their knowledge and align it with the context.

The people on a collaborative team will have different areas of expertise. For example, if we are trying to find a creative solution for the problem that a patient is facing, solving the problem together with the patient, doctors, product experts, and other staff will help us to make better and more-informed decisions.

Most people find it is easy to spot other people's biases, but these same people overlook their own biases. This is not necessarily intentional; over time, we fall in love with the things we do and develop an emotional attachment to our creations. Working as a team helps to suppress the biases we have formed because, on a mutual respect basis, all team members give and receive critiques, which helps build trust.

In summary, when collaborating, people discuss, share knowledge, share experiences, come to understand the problem, review the solutions, and come up with the best creative idea that will suit the customers. Transformational leaders should cultivate a collaborative environment within the organization, where teams are empowered to work across departments and create cross-functional teams with the autonomy to make better decisions. The higher the proportion of experts on a team, the more creative the outcome.

To fully gain the benefit of collaboration, we should follow a structured ideation process called brainstorming, which is covered in the next section.

3.11 Brainstorming for Creativity

As covered in the previous section, collaboration creates synergies and strengthens the creative process. While there are several ways to foster collaboration and have it turn into creativity, the process must be structured, systematic, and disciplined to produce the best results. Two of the collaborative processes are codesign and cocreation. The one that best suits the idea generation phase is brainstorming. A brainstorming session should involve people from diverse fields to get more ideas so as to improve the chances of finding the right ones. The session should pull in key people, either on-site or virtually.

Brainstorming is not a single event that occurs once in a blue moon; instead, it is an iterative process with the following stages:

- Generation of new ideas
- Discussion of the generated ideas
- Short-listing of the potential ideas
- Storytelling
- Reflecting on what was learned

Brainstorming sessions should not get into the stages of experimenting and testing the ideas. These stages are covered under the chapter "Innovation."

Generating Ideas

The idea generation part of the structured brainstorming process should follow certain inspirational, motivational, and positive-thinking norms. The norms include, but are not limited to, the following:

- The individuals should first offer their ideas to the group.
- Other members' ideas should be endowed.
- Members should avoid blocking any ideas.
- People should be encouraged to come up with ideas even if they seem a bit crazy. Crazy ideas sometimes spark more new ideas.
- Avoid criticizing or rewarding ideas during brainstorming sessions.
- Avoid judgment during the brainstorming session, as it hinders idea generation and limits creativity. Judgment creates a fear of rejection in the members and unnecessarily filters out the good ideas, preventing them from surfacing.
- Defer the evaluation part to the end of the session.
- Provide an open environment that encourages everyone to participate.
- When one member gets stuck with an idea, the other members' experience should take the idea to the next stage.
- Everyone should feel that they have contributed to the solution.
- Create an environment where the brain can be creative. Providing plenty of writing space and utensils, selecting a conference room with a great view, and so forth will create a joyful environment.

The above norms are meant to separate the idea generation phase from the discussion stage. The core idea behind the brainstorming session is to share the topic with the team and get plenty of ideas. The leader should not act as an anchor and should make everyone an equal contributor to the process of idea generation.

Discussing and Short-Listing the Ideas

The purpose of phase one of the brainstorming session is to collect a diverse set of ideas from various people. Creativity thrives when there is a place for different ideas and different perceptions, where information can be judged. At the same time, conflict can occur among the people who come up with ideas. It can hinder the creative process when people do not understand one another. Some organizations dislike conflict, so they try to ensure that a team contains like-minded people. However, such a practice leads to the comfortable clone syndrome. In such a scenario, there will be no conflicting of ideas, but the session will result in the same type of ideas with the same type of assumptions. On the other hand, some organizations hire employees with a variety of thinking styles. While this is good for the organization, the leadership may fail to assess the possible conflict of ideas that occurs when people don't understand or respect one another. For example, an analytical thinker will dismiss future-oriented ideas, whereas the creative thinker will dismiss analysis-based ideas.

Fostering a healthy creative process requires bringing all the people together and getting a comprehensive set of ideas, whether they are analytical, intuitive, conceptual, experiential, social, or values-driven. A brainstorming group should encourage cognitively diverse people to respect each other's thinking styles.

During the discussion phase, the leader should encourage cognitive differences and individuals' preferences. Likewise, team members should not be rigid in their ideas and should not operate within narrow cognitive boundaries.

As discussed in the section on whole-brain creativity, the team as a unit should serve as the single whole brain. Both left-brain thinking, influenced by the analytical, logical, and sequential approach to problem-solving, and right-brain thinking, influenced by intuition, values, and nonlinearity, are crucial to finding the creative solution. That is where diversity adds value to idea generation and idea short-listing. Indeed, just like convergent thinking excludes specific ideas that are not relevant to the context, the short-listing session should exclude nonrelevant ideas and be based on healthy discussion.

The short-listing phase should be based on evaluation through a structured, logical process. It should also be based on the values and emotions of the people involved in the process. The whole idea behind the brainstorming session is to come up with valuable ideas, not to move into the experimentation phase. The goal is to learn something new and get fresh ideas rather than directly implement solutions.

Though the diverse cognitive preferences can cause tensions in group discussions, the innovation process requires the cross-fertilization of ideas. As the product is a system containing multiple pieces rather than one stand-alone piece, the transformation process cannot proceed without the cooperation of people who provide different ideas. Taking the sting out of intellectual disagreements is the most valuable contribution that different thinking and communication styles bring to the process of innovation. Personalizing the conflicts or avoiding conflicts does not yield the best results. Understanding that people do have the cognitive preferences and realizing that another person's approach is not wrongheaded but is merely a different approach can diffuse the anger and foster a friendly environment. Empathetic listening enables individual perceptions to dovetail into collective understanding.

"Fostering a healthy creative process requires bringing all the people together and getting a comprehensive set of ideas, whether they are analytical, intuitive, conceptual, experiential, social, or values-driven."

Storytelling

We can have great ideas, but if we cannot convince others to buy those ideas, they will not turn into innovative new products and services. Storytelling is a crucial skill that people must have. Mastering storytelling requires refinement over many years and hours and hours of practice. The story should involve a deep understanding of human emotions and motivations and help people to connect with the product or service.

Reflection on Learnings

Reflection is the concept of mentally wandering through where we have been in the learning process and trying to make some sense out of it all. The lessons will become meaningful and long-lasting if reflection is made an integrated part of the learning process. Without reflection, learning becomes only an activity. Reflective learning helps people in the collaborative process to look back rather than move forward by taking a break from what they have been doing. Basically, we ask ourselves what we have learned from doing the activity. Then we apply what we have learned to contexts beyond the original situation about which we learned something and link the past experience and current lessons with the future. Especially if we are learning from direct experience, reflection is more useful as it attempts to synthesize and articulate the key lessons taught by experience.

3.12 Creativity with Cocreation

Cocreation, as opposed to reflection, involves customers in the building of products and services. The most common definition of *cocreation* is "an active, creative and social process, based on collaboration between producers and users."

Cocreation is a way of developing new product and service ideas together with the customers. It is a way of turning customer engagement and direct insights into a creative process. During the course of this action, the organization provides public or private platforms granting the freedom to customers to participate in the production of things they intend to use and exchange valuable insights.

The evolution of digital capabilities and social networking is bringing about a fundamental shift in business thinking in the form of cocreation to achieve value creation. The convergence of business and technology, the rapidly emerging shared economy, the digital economy, increased connectivity, and well-equipped customers has changed many aspects of the business world. Adapting collaboration is the fundamental driver that allows a company to best utilize the cocreation approach. Cocreation gains more importance as consumers actively create their own value.

In many organizations, value is jointly created by customers, who express their requirements, bring their own insights, and even actively participate in the production process. Collaboration requires organizations to relinquish some of their control on the resources that the customer consumes. By placing what is tagged proprietary information in the consumers' hands, and by allowing customers to engage in active dialogue, businesses create individualized value propositions. This new class of privileged customer builds transparency into the products, services, and processes, and introduces new ways in which the organizations and consumers can achieve mutual benefit. Cocreation gives consumers the opportunity to utilize organizations' expensive and time-consuming processes, from R&D to maintenance. The prevailing customer base will bring synergies to the organization; in other words, the sum of customers' creative energy is larger than what the company can achieve alone.

4

Fostering Innovation

4.1 From Creativity to Innovation

We hear about innovation everywhere as it is one of the most used words in global business today. In the previous chapter, we discussed the idea that creativity is the driving force behind innovation. *Innovation* is defined as "the process of implementing new or existing ideas to create a new service, system, or enhancing existing ones to bring the positive change."

While creativity is about original, unexpected, and fresh ideas, innovation does not always necessarily spring from original ideas. For example, let us assume that a vendor company creates an entirely new system using creativity and that this system is ready for its clients to use. Though it may not be the original idea of the client, the adaptation of such a system will bring positive change to the organization and therefore still be classified as innovation.

Whether it is an original in-house idea or an adaptation of a third-party idea, as long as it brings positive change to the organization, it is called innovation. Innovation challenges the traditional ways of how things have been done and brings ideas from in-house, or from one industry to another, or from one region to another. By way of positive change, innovation fulfills the unmet needs of people, improves their lives, makes their jobs easier, makes them happier and more productive, creates new leaders, creates new businesses, and creates new industries.

"By way of positive change, innovation fulfills the unmet needs of people, improves their lives, makes their jobs easier, and makes them happier and more productive."

We can bring positive change to one market by taking something that has been long utilized in another market and applying it to the initial market. For example, lightweight material that is used in aircraft manufacturing can be used to make lightweight equipment for disabled people.

In our rapidly changing world, people have become busy with multiple engagements. As a result, people are looking for new, better, faster, more convenient products and becoming habitual much more quickly. The rapid change in customer habits is changing the mind-sets of people and organizations virtually in every sector, even those sectors that were subject to prolonged changes in the past.

As the consumers focus on how the products add value to them, the traditional business model focuses on how the current product can be improved to become more competitive in the market. However, that competitive edge vanishes quickly when new parties come out with a much better competitive product. The success of an organization in offering innovative products comes from building business models that offer new ways to create and deliver the products that add value to people. In other words, for an organization, innovation is a double-edged concept in that innovative products must come from a business model of innovation. Innovation must be a business discipline with a portfolio of innovation strategies designed for specific tasks. Each innovation strategy is different because innovation is about bringing about positive change by solving a problem—and each problem is different. Plus there are many ways to solve a problem.

Innovation is not something that can be deployed overnight or within a short time frame. The process of innovation requires continuous learning to bring about change. We must continuously learn more about customers, markets, internal members, existing internal capabilities, and competitors, and we must offer new things. It is a never-ending, iterative process.

Innovation does not have to come from inside the organization all the time. Actively collaborating and using open innovation can foster innovation within an organization. Open innovation creates an environment where individuals and organizations can collaboratively develop products. These individuals include suppliers, partners, and the broader business community. Knowing about who knows what things is a way of achieving goals when an organization does not have all the capabilities internally. The use of "knowledge of knowledge" will help to accelerate innovation. Instead of entirely relying on their own research, organizations should acquire inventions or intellectual property from other companies to advance their own business model. A competitive advantage comes from discovering and leasing others' innovations. Open innovation is an inclusive social way of solving complex problems and bringing about innovative solutions.

"The use of 'knowledge of knowledge' will help to accelerate innovation."

While open innovation brings about collaboration between different organizations and the sharing of intellectual property, it does not actively involve the customers. The digital economy has made customers a new asset class to an organization. The value is measured by way of how much insight the customers bring to an organization.

Innovation is a process of turning a vision into reality. However, innovation is not a risk-free process. There are risks associated with innovation. There is the potential for failure at certain stages of the innovation process. However, reluctance to innovate poses an even more significant risk to the organization. Change is the only constant. Failure is not a hurdle to the innovation process. We learn from failures and are able to strengthen the innovation process. As discussed in an earlier paragraph, innovation is a continuous-learning-based iterative process.

"Failure is not a hurdle to the innovation process. Failures provide an opportunity to learn new things and strengthen the innovation process."

The risks associated with innovation come from many sources. Some of these sources include customer behavior, which is not predictable; competitors, who sometimes move faster than we do; internal leadership not tuned to the entrepreneurial spirit; and senior management that is slow to grant approval.

In most cases, the innovation process starts with several unknown factors. That said, the more complex the system that we are trying to innovate, the more likely we will encounter uncertainties. Many of the risks associated with a complicated innovation process come from internal leadership capabilities, culture, and the existing infrastructure.

Initiating the innovation process is the key to the success of any business. The magnitude of innovation varies based on what kind of change the organization is anticipating.

At its core, innovation is of four types:

- Incremental innovation
- Breakthrough innovation
- Disruptive innovation
- Nonlinear innovation

Before discussing these four types of innovation in detail, let us look into some of the companies that failed due to lack of innovation and also some of the companies that are successful based on their innovation.

4.2 Companies That Failed to Innovate

Blockbuster

Blockbuster was thriving as the top video rental company with thousands of retail locations and millions of customers. It was serving as a facilitator for weekend entertainment through video rental for most US families. What made Blockbuster fail abruptly? First, it had high operational costs in the form of physical locations and a workforce that was too large. Second, it had no respect for its patrons. The company's profits were highly dependent on penalizing its patrons by charging late fees. Third, it failed to recognize the strength of the booming internet.

Blockbuster's lack of empathy for its customers and inefficient operating model opened the path to the rise of Netflix. Blockbuster's competition did not directly come from the current business model of Netflix. Indeed, the business model of Netflix was different in its early stage. Netflix was offering DVDs on a rental basis by shipping them to customers' homes. However, Netflix did not penalize customers for late returns. Since Netflix did not have physical locations, it was able to lower the cost of renting DVDs. Moreover, it offered its customers subscriptions, which allowed customers to keep the DVDs as long as they wanted or return them to get different ones.

While Netflix's model had some compelling aspects, it also had some glaring disadvantages. Netflix faced some hurdles in the beginning because without retail locations, people weren't aware of the service, and given that customers were receiving their videos by mail, the mail service was somewhat slow and cumbersome. People could not just pick up a movie for the night on their way home. Still, customers loved the service and told their friends about it. The concept of charging no late fees made the customers who subscribed early happy. Still, some people were reluctant to switch to Netflix, as they liked the ability to browse the movies at the Blockbuster stores and pick them up instantly. However, over time people fell in love with Netflix and convinced their friends to give it a shot.

Customers exhibit several levels of resistance. While new ideas are usually met with resistance by the majority of people, they are still acceptable to some early adopters. Once these early adopter are on board and begin to feel comfortable, people with the next level of resistance start giving the product or service a try. As each threshold is passed, the next group becomes more likely to adopt the new idea. That is how disruption happens.

However, the actual disruption at Netflix came from another business model. Netflix might have quickly failed had the company neglected to recognize the strength of the internet and streaming. It was courageous to compete with its own business model, renting DVDs through the mail and also offering streaming to customers.

The two principles that helped Netflix succeed were the company's empathy for its customers (by removing late fees and making movie watching more pleasant) and its courage to compete with its own business model and innovate (by offering streaming).

Lessons Learned:

- Do not penalize the customers by taking advantage of their emotions.
- Do not ignore the changing conditions in the industry, even if they are not immediate threats.
- Have the courage to disrupt yourself by having the courage to compete with yourself.

"Have the courage to disrupt yourself by having the courage to compete with yourself."

Kodak

Refusing to innovate was the biggest risk that Kodak took, which eventually led the company to go bankrupt in 2012. The most prominent opportunity that Kodak missed was digital photography. The evolution of digital photography in the market destroyed Kodak's film-based business model.

The company actually created the first digital camera in 1976. However, they were afraid that the new camera would hinder film sales. Eventually, Kodak shelved the project. By the time Kodak decided to enter the digital photography market in the mid-2000s, the new entrants had already taken hold of the market, and the prices of digital cameras had fallen. At the same time, sales of traditional cameras started declining.

Kodak perceived digital photography as the enemy to its successful business model and thought that it would kill the chemical-based film and paper business that had fueled Kodak's sales and profits for decades. Indeed, Kodak conducted extensive research on digital photography. The research produced mixed results. It indeed found that digital photography had the potential to replace Kodak's established film-based business. At the same time, it found that it would take some time for that to occur. It also found that the cost of digital photography equipment was high and that the quality of images and prints was low. Kodak thought that the low-quality prints of digital photographs would impact its reputation.

Therefore, Kodak concluded that the adoption of digital photography by consumers would be minimal and it would not be a threat for a while. History proved the study's conclusions to be remarkably accurate, both in the short and long term. Kodak failed to prepare for the next disruption and failed to transform the organization to digital. Instead, it went for incremental innovation by using digital technology to improve the quality of film.

In fact, Kodak's founder, George Eastman, had adopted disruptive photographic technology twice in the 1980s and 1990s. It was not digital, though. Nevertheless, this tendency shows that the founder was indeed open to innovation. However, the management successor was unwilling to consider digital as a replacement for film. Kodak's unwillingness to change to digital technology made it miss the opportunity that could have given it a leading position in digital image processing.

Lessons Learned:

- Have the courage to disrupt yourself by having the courage to compete with yourself.
- Do not ignore the founder's mentality even if he or she is no longer with the organization.

"Do not ignore the founder's mentality even if he or she is no longer with the organization."

MySpace

MySpace, which was founded in 2003, quickly became the top social network within three years of its inception. At the time, Facebook was in its early stage and was not even open to all potential users. With the entry of Facebook, MySpace started losing its position. The main reason was not that Facebook used superior technology but that MySpace failed to innovate.

MySpace was started as a site to help users make friends, write blogs, and share their passion for pop and rock bands. MySpace was indeed founded with an innovative mind-set. A group of people had found that Friendster, another social networking site, was less innovative and was not able to address the growing potential of social networking. These people started building a working prototype and created a site. It was later acquired by Rupert Murdoch's Fox News, which took it to the global space by extending the site into other language markets like China. With the use of the accessibility capabilities at Fox News' disposal, MySpace became popular quickly. MySpace was able to exceed the traffic levels of its competitor Facebook consistently. However, the pace of its innovations soon started stagnating. MySpace believed that it would be able to create its own products and therefore was rejecting other material from other developers. In an attempt to become more dominant, MySpace started morphing from a social networking site to become a self-proclaimed social entertainment site. With this approach, MySpace lagged behind in providing the elements that users were demanding. MySpace's core purpose of serving advertisers made it fall behind in facilitating the social part of social networking.

On the other hand, Facebook started to let third-party developers create apps on the site to provide a much better platform. This helped Facebook to catch up and surpass MySpace. That means Facebook was able to recognize the power of continuous improvement to the user experience. Facebook's innovative user experience made more and more people migrate from MySpace to Facebook.

News Corp's old-school thinking was the main reason for MySpace's fall. The acquisitions of Instagram and WhatsApp by Facebook shows News Corp's mistakes in not sticking to its promises. The fall of MySpace proved that customer expectations are changing quickly enabled by technology; that continuous innovation is required if a company is to remain cutting edge and unbeaten; and that users will abandon products and services if they are not innovative and moving forward.

Lessons Learned:

- Do not plan the strategy around small goals; plan it by having big-picture thinking.
- Meet customer expectations by making the platform open to further innovations.

"Do not plan the strategy around small goals;
plan it by having big-picture thinking."

BlackBerry

Founded in 1984, Research in Motion (RIM) created several wireless products, including radio modems, wireless point-of-sale devices, and the first two-way messaging pager. It later developed a wireless handheld with a built-in keyboard to handle email, contacts, and calendaring. Subsequently, it unveiled the BlackBerry Enterprise Server (BES) to provide a conduit between the wireless handheld and the corporate exchange mailbox, with contacts and calendar, putting business email in the hands of mobile users. This success led BlackBerry to boast over five million worldwide subscribers by 2006, which tripled to fifteen million by 2008. How did the growing company come to an end? Though it had numerous ideas, it failed to make the correct adaptations.

BlackBerry devices were enjoying success as they provided small QWERTY keyboards that made it easier to compose emails and instant messages. BlackBerry targeted mostly two types of consumers, company executives and teenagers, for the BlackBerry Messenger platform.

On the other hand, the market was seeing the entry of touch-screen handheld devices and continuous improvements around them. The concept of "bring your own device" (BYOD) started catching on in companies. Smartphone companies made continuous improvements to meet the need of consumers to use the device for business purposes. The app economy that evolved around iOS and Android caused even those users who were using BlackBerry to switch to smartphones with the BYOD concept.

BlackBerry failed to notice the gaining importance of the touch screen and failed to adapt it. Similar to the case of Kodak, BlackBerry missed an opportunity. BlackBerry failed to anticipate that a broader consumer base, not business customers, would drive the smartphone revolution. Also, it failed to recognize the emergence of the app economy. BlackBerry responded to this threat by introducing new phones, but it was too late.

Lessons Learned:

- Develop a product that is useful to a broader spectrum of people.
- Do not fall in love with a creative invention forever. Creative things can quickly become outdated in a rapidly changing world.

"Do not fall in love with a creative invention forever. Creative things can quickly become outdated in a rapidly changing world."

Yahoo

Yahoo was started as a passionate project by Jerry Yang and David Filo, who were PhD students in electrical engineering at Stanford. Their dissertation involved designing automation software. They had a passion for browsing many websites and exploring the World Wide Web. However, new sites were coming online every day. They started cataloging the sites at http://akebono.stanford.edu, calling it Jerry's Guide to the World Wide Web, which allowed other students to find them. Word of mouth spread the news to the public, and people started emailing Yang and Filo suggesting that new sites be added to the list. As the list was growing, the two students had to continuously reorganize it by breaking it into a hierarchical directory based on a site's relevancy. They even developed software to search for newer sites.

By September 1994, they compiled a directory of more than two thousand sites. The little project they had started as a hobby became their full-time project. They gave the project a name: Yahoo. Stanford had a long history of supporting student-run projects, some of which later evolved into start-ups. So, Stanford was generous to host Yahoo's traffic and content free of charge. When Netscape launched its beta browser in 1994, it made Yahoo the default link for the Directory button. By January 1995, Yahoo got its domain, Yahoo.com, and it was getting more than one hundred thousand unique visitors a day. Soon, venture capitalists recognized the growing popularity of Yahoo and started investing in it. Yahoo became the most popular portal. As of 2005, Yahoo owned 21 percent of the online advertising market.

What went wrong to slow the growth of Yahoo? Though Yahoo was providing search capabilities, it failed to see the growing importance of the search engine. Instead, it was focusing on an online portal to become a media giant. Yahoo did not recognize itself as a technology powerhouse. It prioritized content such as news, sports statistics, and financial data, with the idea that it could display ads along with the content it published. However, Yahoo is not a traditional media company.

The company failed to adapt to the significant trends of consumer interests: social networking and mobile devices. The traditional display ads did not translate well on smart devices as consumers spent more time on apps than they did surfing the mobile Web. Yahoo later recognized that it had failed to capture the audience for its content on smart devices. It started developing a large number of apps to bridge the gap. However, the company's efforts were unfocused.

In the past, Yahoo missed a few opportunities. There was reportedly a deal for Yahoo to buy Google for five billion dollars in 2002. The management refused it. Buying DoubleClick would've helped Yahoo strengthen its ads market to compete with Google, but Google got the opportunity to acquire DoubleClick. Yahoo had a deal to buy Facebook for $1 billion in 2006. Facebook backed out as the offer was lowered. Yahoo turned down an acquisition deal from Microsoft in 2008.

To continue thriving in a fast-paced market, organizations should either continuously improve their offerings and capabilities or acquire such capabilities using strategic mergers.

Lessons Learned:

- Develop a product strategy that meets the changing behaviors of the customers.
- Let the community contribute to the platform if it is open to the community.

"Develop a product strategy that meets the changing behaviors of the customers."

4.3 Innovative Companies

Just like some companies fail because of a lack of innovation, some companies continue to thrive and even disrupt their industries by way of creativity and innovation. Some of those companies are discussed here.

Apple

Steve Jobs is considered to be a role model for creativity. In his early life, Steve Jobs took a calligraphy course in college, which had no application to his life. However, that course helped him to design the first Macintosh computer, which offered beautiful typefaces, fonts, and calligraphy. Jobs proved that one could bring innovative ideas from one field and apply them to the products in a completely different field. By thinking creatively, we can perform miracles in any field.

Apple was close to bankruptcy before Steve Jobs returned to the company after a twelve-year absence. Upon his return to Apple, he wanted to build a digital hub around which all of the company's innovation efforts would revolve. As part of the exercise, he eliminated a significant portion of Apple's hardware and software products and positioned the Mac computer as Apple's core product. The goal was not to cut costs but to innovate the company's way out of its traditional operations. Jobs promised the community that he would unveil simplified tools that would easily and efficiently manage every aspect of digital life.

Apple made acquisitions, entered into partnerships, and hired the talent to execute its digital hub strategy. To fulfill Jobs's business promise, Apple brought a broad range of digital capabilities such as iPod, iTunes, iMovie, iPhoto, and GarageBand. While other smartphone makers were making phones more complicated by adding features and buttons, Apple launched the iPhone in 2007, which was simpler, cleaner, and user-friendly. The iPhone demonstrated the potential of the smartphone and made those who owned one feel like they had a mobile computer. Apple Store, which was started as a complementary innovation to support Apple's strategy, has become very successful and has made the customer purchase experience better. Instead of looking at its competitors, Apple focused on the consumer experience at retail stores. The products and services that Steve Jobs launched around the Mac are still driving the company's success.

Apple believed that selling the products that the company makes should not be the goal. Instead, selling the products that help people to achieve their dreams should be the goal. As a founder of Apple in 1970, Steve Jobs's purpose was not meant to build computers but to build the tools to help people unleash the computer's potential, knowing that the characteristics of these tools should change from time to time along the journey. Jobs built the computer in the beginning and later transformed the company to unveil the iPod, iPhone, iPad, and more. Purpose fuels the work, vision directs the person or team to the ultimate destination, and the mission drives the person or team. At the time when personal computer ownership was limited to select people, Steve Jobs and cofounder Steve Wozniak had the vision to democratize the personal computer so that it could find its way into the hands of many individuals. A bold vision inspires leaders and sets forces in motion. Jobs believed that the role of a leader is to hire the best people and keep them aligned with the vision.

Innovation requires the courage to dream big and pitch completely different ideas. Steve Jobs followed his heart and did not let the noise of others' opinions drown out his inner voice. He believed that one should have the courage to follow his or her heart and intuition.

Lessons Learned:

- Build products based on purpose and not based on available talent.
- Make the customer experience simple and straightforward.

- Make complementary innovations, as they sometimes become core products.
- Ignite creativity by finding the passion in people.
- Transformation should be centered on the core ideology or product.

"Innovation requires the courage to dream big and pitch completely different ideas."

Adobe

Innovation is associated with risks, and small failures at various stages of the innovation process are common in any industry. While founders and key stakeholders generally have a tolerance for failure, most employees are unable to digest failure. Employees want a perfect track record and don't feel the pleasure of experimentation. That is why organizational leadership should take necessary steps to ensure that their teams feel empowered.

One of the best examples of empowering teams is Adobe Systems. It wanted to drive innovation from within and appointed Mark Randall for the innovation program. He took the challenge of creating an experimentation-friendly culture and launched a program called the Adobe Kickbox. The Kickbox is a small, red cardboard box containing what is needed to generate, create a prototype of, and test a new idea. The goal is to improve innovator effectiveness, accelerate innovation, and improve outcomes.

The instructions in the box are framed as a six-level curriculum. Each level contains exercises guiding employees from the ideation stages to the testing stage. It encourages employees to take each level as a challenge, to beat each level. The sixth level is to sell the idea to management. The Kickbox challenges the conventional process where ideas first need to be sold to senior management to proceed to prototype and test them. Kickbox gives employees an opportunity to prototype, test, and then look for buy-in. It is designed to unleash the potential of employees' creative minds and allow them to come up with many ideas and experiment with them. This model would not have been survived a more bureaucratic vetting process.

The Adobe subscription model was one of the successful changes that the company implemented. Though it has witnessed initial pushback from the community, eventually the subscription model became the primary driver for Adobe's growth. Internal engineers are pleased with this model as it has smoothened their work as well. Earlier, they had to come up with new features every two years or so and then go to market to convince consumers to buy the new version based on those features. There was no guarantee that every customer would upgrade their version to avail themselves of the new features, so Adobe had to support multiple versions. The subscription model encourages all users to stay current with the newest versions of the software. Users are also happy as they get any new features right away.

Lessons Learned:

- Engage employees at all levels to contribute to innovation.
- Foster a culture of experimentation.

Airbnb

Launched as Air Bed and Breakfast, Airbnb has now become a pillar of the shared economy. It helps property owners to share their properties on a rental basis with hundreds of millions of potential guests around the world. It creates value for both the guests and the hosts. For the guests, it provides access to different travel accommodations and experiences that are challenging to discover on traditional platforms. It helps hosts to turn spare space or short-term vacancies into extra income. In return, Airbnb charges fees for bookings.

Airbnb was quick enough to understand the shifts in consumer behavior and disrupted the traditional hospitality business that has been around for decades. The key ingredient to the Airbnb business model is addressing human needs that were not being met. Airbnb's disruptive innovation transformed the entire hospitality industry and led to the creation of a cottage industry of short-term-rental start-ups such as Roomorama, Love Home Swap, and Stay Alfred, among many more. The new entrants are trying to take this bold idea to the next level by adding twists to it.

Airbnb has created an in-house innovation and design studio to find the new ideas that will move it beyond its current services. It wants to take social innovation to the next level by connecting refugees with housing. One can see tolerance and empathy in Airbnb's ambitions. Its refugee efforts represent the company at its very best on this front. An empathetic idea can convince people who are not interested in sharing their homes for money to patronize Airbnb.

Lessons Learned:

- Show empathy for customers.
- Encourage the concept of shared economy.

Alibaba

Alibaba's success is the result of its continuously launched platforms to meet the ever-growing needs of its customers. Instead of merely being an e-commerce platform, Alibaba makes it easy for sellers to do business and provides a positive purchasing experience for buyers. Since its inception, it has gone on a spree of expanding its core business to many different domains, such as advertising services, logistics networks, financial services, and mobile terminal services. Alibaba was initially founded in an apartment in Hangzhou in 1999. The use of the internet in China was growing, and by 2003 it had reached eighty million users. Recognizing the growth of the internet, Alibaba launched Taobao.com, and shortly afterward, Alipay and Aliwangwang were launched to augment the purchasing process of Taobao. Alibaba launched another platform called Alimama to facilitate advertisement transactions. And then in 2008, Tmall was launched as both B2C and C2C platforms. Alibaba adapted big-data technologies as part of its strategy and founded the Alibaba Cloud to strengthen its commitment. To facilitate mobile payments and global consumer presence, it then launched Juhuasuan, AliExpress, and the mobile Taobao app.

Alibaba's desire to create more value for customers according to their needs is leading the company to challenge traditional transaction patterns and to explore new ways of doing business. Alibaba creates a unique business opportunity by providing services to small enterprises and individuals. Customers who are loyal to the company were first attracted by its free admission and its charges based on services in marketing and technical support. With an innovative credit model of online certification to verify a customer's identity information, Alibaba can filter out any illegal transactions as sellers are supervised on the platform at all times. Alibaba's offerings, which help sellers to maintain positive interactions with buyers, create a comfortable purchasing environment, and provide a positive online customer experience, are leading users to engage more often on its platforms.

Alibaba relies on innovation to drive its growth. It is investing heavily in innovation to unlock new revenue streams aside from its core commerce segment. One of these innovation efforts led Alibaba to develop an artificial intelligence–based voice-controlled virtual assistant called Tmall Genie.

Lesson Learned:

- Innovate continuously.

Amazon

Started as a seller of paper-based books, Amazon constantly innovated horizontally and competing with its own business model constantly and disrupting itself. It extended itself to the partners without spreading itself too thin by finding ways to integrate them into its infrastructure and then selling that integration as a service to others. The Kindle e-book reader, Amazon Prime Video, the extended marketplace of individual resellers, the offering of warehousing and fulfillment services to its reselling partners—most of Amazon's business models were launched competing against its existing business models. Based on traditional perception, offering an e-book reader would be in competition with Amazon's core paper-based book business, but it showed courage in launching the Kindle. It made Amazon the leader in sales of digital content in the e-book market, which is valued at $1.6 billion. Similarly, Amazon competed with its own DVD sales by launching Amazon Prime. None of these self-competing initiatives have diluted the company's overall position. Amazon was also successful in making use of its own challenges.

At one point in time, Amazon technology teams were finding it difficult to maintain and deploy code frequently. To overcome these challenges, it came up with the innovative idea of Amazon Web Services, which later became an industry icon. The company that was started as an online retailer is now a powerhouse in cloud computing. Other innovations include Amazon's voice-activated Echo devices, Fire TV, Fire Tablets, and physical retail with Amazon Books and its Go convenience store pilot.

Amazon's success is driven by courageous leadership and an innovative culture that is hospitable to experimentation. It encourages talented engineers to experiment with their ideas for potential services. To facilitate this, Amazon has created a small team to experiment with the idea and find out if it is viable. They call it a two-pizza team, meaning the team should be small enough to be fed with two pizzas. The goal is to come up with a minimum viable product. By doing this, Amazon can offer the product to customers as quickly as possible and get their feedback so as to avoid wasting time working on products that don't serve the needs of real customers.

To encourage the diverse benefits of technology, there should not be a standardized set of rules and restrictions in selecting suitable technology. Amazon is following this rule. It is encouraging its teams independently to adopt whatever technology makes the most sense for the product. This concept emulates the best characteristics of a start-up mind-set at bigger companies. Amazon Go is the best example. It uses cameras and other sensors to track the customer's every step and detect when the customer takes an item off a shelf. Restrictions on the use of specific technologies would not have allowed this to happen. Innovations in order fulfillment are crucial to Amazon's success. A large number of automated fulfillment centers, which run using the technology picked up by the acquisition of Kiva Systems, are essential to this success.

Lessons Learned:

- Innovate continuously.
- Encourage a culture of experimentation.
- Have the courage to take significant risks and think beyond the borders.
- Onboard and integrate even competitive partners into the strategy, and offer the result as a service.
- Turn your own difficulties into opportunities by building products and helping other organizations overcome similar difficulties by offering those products as a service.
- Disrupt yourself by competing with yourself.
- Adopt agile innovation to make a series of smaller successes, mounting to a bigger success.

"Turn your own difficulties into opportunities by building products and helping other organizations overcome similar difficulties by offering those products as a service."

Google

What distinguishes Google from the other innovators is that Google does not rely on a single innovation strategy. Instead, it has built an innovation ecosystem based on numerous innovations. It is a massive powerhouse, with an array of products starting from a search engine to autonomous cars. At Google, product managers focus on customers' needs; researchers follow the path of science; and engineers work 20 percent of the time on projects based on their passions. However,

Google's cores strength relies on its ability to integrate all these innovative activities into one portfolio seamlessly. It requires a real entrepreneurial spirit deeply embedded into the organization's vision, which takes more than a streamlined operation.

Traditionally, innovation is treated as a linear process of research, development, demonstration, and deployment. Each step in the process acts as its own silo. This traditional perception of innovation does not work to disrupt the organization or the market. Google created a structure where every step works as a tightly coupled feedback loop. For example, the research teams and product management teams work hand in hand to identify fruitful research areas and translate them into a vital product.

Google established a practice literally in every field, where employees can spend 20 percent of their time working on projects that interest them. This concept aligns employees with their passions. People will not blindly pick up what it is interesting to them. They stretch their thinking to go to the extremes and explore the possibilities beyond the conventional boundaries. Some of Google's most popular products, such as Gmail and AdSense, originated from this practice.

Working freely does not necessarily mean that Google employees have to work independently. Working in collaboration with others creates synergy. For example, getting closer to the real needs of users gives them an opportunity to innovate further. Rather than working alone or with a small set of like-minded scientists in the lab, the scientists interact closely with users and data teams, the latter of whom possess the information about users, collaboratively, which helps them to get broader ideas. This is how Google encourages people to foster collaboration among teams.

Google gains access to breakthrough research through an active partnership with the scientific community. It funds several academic research projects and invites top scholars to spend sabbaticals at its headquarters every year. It offers scientists laboratory space with some of the best computing architectures in the world and the opportunity to continue to publish openly. Also, Google continuously acquires early stage start-ups that are launched as a result of academic research. One of Google's freshly acquired start-ups is DeepMind.

Lessons Learned:

- Innovate continuously.
- Encourage a culture of experimentation.
- Give employees the opportunity to use their passion and come up with creative ideas.
- Implement a strategy to build moon shots to expand the vision.
- Keep things simple and focus on customer experience.

"Give employees the opportunity to use their passion and come up with creative ideas."

Uber

Founded as UberCab in 2009, Uber launched its mobile app to the public in 2011. Through the use of a mobile app on smartphones, Uber created a shared economy and a network of drivers and users, and transformed the entire transportation industry. Initially launching the app in select cities, the company expanded to several cities across the United States gradually, eventually making its way overseas. Like Airbnb, Uber opened doors for similar participants to enter the growing market.

The culture of the legacy cab industry pretty much gave the cab owners a free hand in setting fair rates and charges. The riding public, with limited options of alternatives, had no choice but to bear the transaction costs. Uber removed these transaction costs for customers reserving a car through its mobile app.

Automobiles incur certain maintenance costs such as insurance and aging of tires, and the value of the automobile depreciates with age even if it is left to sit in a garage. The concept of the shared economy involves turning assets that are either unused or underused into resources that are profitable. Uber addressed this issue with its innovative shared economy concept and also provided additional income to drivers who prefer to work part time in their regular jobs. Uber simplified the process of the contractual relationship with the driver.

The drawback facing the legacy cab industry was its low-tech communications network. Uber was able to tap into this opportunity. Technology has been known to be able to break down entry barriers, and the widespread reach of the internet helped Uber to expand to cities all around the world. The development of a mobile app was a just-in-time best strategy that Uber employed, and with the rate of smartphone usage increasing among everyday users, Uber started conducting critical transactions over these mobile devices. Uber was able to take full advantage of the concept of collaboration. The use of GPS technology for matching drivers and their cars with passengers and tracking the trip was only possible because the technology was high-end. GPS-enabled real-time matching decreases the interval between the original request time and the pickup time, as the app is capable of matching the request with the driver who is closest to the requested location. Scheduling the desired pickup time certainly lessens the hassle of having to reserve the ride later during a busy time.

Lessons Learned:

- Encourage shared economy.
- Have the courage to take significant risks and unleash the potential of technology.

Tesla

From a traditional perspective, it is difficult for a new start-up to break into an industry that is more than one hundred years old. Tesla proved this notion wrong by breaking into the automobile industry with a disruptive idea. By coming up with electric vehicles and self-driving technologies, Tesla proved that a start-up could disrupt the market.

Tesla's disruption is making the incumbents move more quickly to adapt to the changing conditions and is also encouraging others outside the car industry, such as Google and Apple, to take a share in the disrupted market.

What is the key ingredient behind the success of Tesla? Creative thinking in the use of technology, the courage to take risks, commitment to rapid iteration, treating car development as software development instead of commodity manufacturing, computerization, connectivity, novel design, and automation are the crucial drivers behind Tesla's disruption. Tesla's policy of relentless innovation has mobilized competitors, fueled innovation, and popularized electric vehicles.

Tesla Motors was founded by Martin Eberhard and Marc Tarpenning, who obtained the funding from multiple sources. PayPal cofounder Elon Musk invested more than $30 million in Tesla and served as chairman of the company beginning in 2004. It released its first car, the Roadster, in 2008, surprising observers with 245 miles on a single charge and with performance comparable to that of many gasoline-powered sports cars. Elon Musk took over as CEO in 2008. In 2012 Tesla stopped production of the Roadster and focused on its new Model S sedan with three different battery options. The Model S had its battery underneath the floorboard to provide extra storage space in front. The vehicle also had improved handling with its low center of gravity.

The use of software to control some of the features of the car, including a touch-screen dashboard interface and over-the-air updates, shows how Tesla is thinking more innovatively than incumbents. Just like a software product, a Tesla car can be updated with new features remotely every few months and can also undergo some repairs remotely.

Tesla is disrupting itself by entering into the energy sector as part of its commitment to developing renewable battery technology. This is another bold step to encourage technological development to protect the environment, which hopefully will contribute to a positive change in the climate. There is no doubt that Tesla has contributed to the transformation of the automotive industry. Tesla's success demonstrates the importance of innovation in any business and shows that the leadership should have the courage to take bold risks and make big promises.

Lessons Learned:

- Have the courage to take significant risks and unleash the potential of technology.
- Think extreme, and bring the extremes to the mainstream.
- Do not be afraid to fail.
- Contribute to a positive climate.

"Think extreme, and bring the extremes to the mainstream."

Farmers Business Network

The agricultural sector is one of the lowest-rated industries for potential innovation and disruption. There are not many companies in the agricultural sector that are intensely focused on creativity and innovation. In the USA, independent family farms are the backbone of the rural economy. However, their incomes are more volatile due to low crop prices and high input prices. Farmers Business Network (FBN) was founded with the intention of helping farmers. By joining FBN, farmers become a part of a community of more than twenty-five hundred farms spanning millions of acres. FBN levels the playing field by networking farms together and enabling transparent national access to manufacturer-direct prices on farm inputs. By providing farm analytics, democratizing farm information, and enabling procurement services, FBN gives independent farmers the tools they need to make a profit.

In a traditional business, input vendors often use complicated bundling, rebates, and loyalty programs that can make it frustratingly difficult for farmers to compare prices and shop around. FBN works directly with manufacturers to source the lowest-priced products and passes those savings along to farmers. With the technology that is made available everywhere, FBN can publish prices online so that they are sufficiently transparent to members at all times. Farmers are using smartphones and tablets, and the availability of faster internet is gaining a foothold in rural areas as well.

Farmers can use the system efficiently to access the data that is collected from thousands of farmers and millions of acres across the country. FBN was innovative in using these advancements in infrastructure. The FBN repository is built on Amazon Web Services. The cloud-computing platform pools and processes data such as seed and chemical prices, field sizes, and crop yields to give participating farmers a holistic view of how their operations stack up against others'.

Lessons Learned:

- Have the courage to take significant risks.
- Unleash the potential of technology, and use it in every corner of the world.
- Encourage a shared economy.

4.4 Core Principles of Innovation

Following are the core principles of innovation:

- Do not penalize customers by taking advantage of their emotions.
- Do not ignore changing conditions in the industry, even if they are not immediate threats.
- Have the courage to disrupt yourself by having the courage to compete with yourself.
- Do not ignore the founder's mentality.
- Do not plan a strategy around tiny goals.
- Meet customer expectations by making the platform open to further innovations.
- Develop a product that is useful to a broader spectrum of people.

- Do not fall in love with a creative invention forever. Creative things can quickly become outdated in a rapidly changing world.
- Develop the product strategy that meets the changing behaviors of customers.
- Adopt agile innovation to achieve a series of smaller successes, mounting up to a bigger success.
- Let the community contribute to the platform if it is open to the community.
- Build products based on purpose and not on available talent.
- Make the customer experience simple and straightforward.
- Start complementary innovations, as these sometimes become core products.
- Ignite creativity by finding the passion in people.
- Transformation should be centered on the core ideology or product.
- Engage employees at all levels to contribute to innovation.
- Show empathy for customers.
- Encourage the concept of shared economy.
- Innovate continuously.
- Encourage a culture of experimentation.
- Have the courage to take significant risks and think beyond the borders.
- Onboard and integrate even competitive partners into the strategy, and offer it as a service.
- Turn your own difficulties into opportunities by building products and helping other organizations overcome the similar difficulties by offering those products as a service.
- Give employees the opportunity to use their passion and come up with creative ideas.
- Create a strategy to build moon shots to expand the vision.
- Keep things simple and focus on customer experience.
- Think extreme, and bring the extremes to the mainstream.
- Do not be afraid to fail.
- Contribute to a positive climate.
- Have the courage to take significant risks.
- Unleash the potential of technology, and use it in every corner of the world.

4.5 Types of Innovations

4.5.1 Incremental Innovation

Companies make regular improvements to their existing products, services, or processes to please users, improve productivity, and gain a competitive advantage. These changes are performed iteratively and incrementally. However, the magnitude of changes implemented through incremental innovation is not large enough. Incremental innovation may help a company to maintain its market position temporarily. Incremental innovation can be classified as a tactical innovation rather than a strategic innovation. It is also referred to as survival innovation.

Through incremental innovations, companies maintain the status quo but also optimize the status quo to a small extent. Incremental innovation gives companies a safe harbor, as there aren't many unknown factors in the process. However, companies fail to withstand the storm when a new entrant comes up with a disruptive business model. Nokia was providing incremental innovations to phones for an extended period, but those changes could not save the company from a disruptive product, the iPhone, that came from Apple. Optimizing the existing solutions for existing customers does not meet the expectation of future growth of the company and sometimes confuses the markets. Such solutions do not meet user expectations, who oftentimes have waited a long time amid much marketing hype. Indeed, those incremental changes make the product more complicated without offering substantial meaning to the users.

Customers do not care whether the product is crucial for the survival of a business or not. They expect something new that can solve their problems and help them make progress in their lives. If there is a better solution from other companies, they do not mind switching to that company. As Jeff Bezos once said, "Our customers are loyal to us right up until the second somebody offers them a better service."

Incremental innovation is not cheaper either. It requires enormous amounts of time and commitment to set up innovation labs, build innovation teams, and bring in design thinking methodologies. Some incumbents struggle with incremental innovation even after making unprecedented efforts because the culture and consumers' mind-sets block agility and adaptation. Those incumbents' business models are focused on exploitation, perfection, and protection of the status quo rather than on experimentation.

In a traditional business, there is not much need for rapid innovations. However, as the world is changing faster and innovation is accelerating faster than expected, the corporate culture must change to accept failure and be ready to face risks. Since innovation is associated with uncertainty, it does not make sense to set fixed goals up front and analyze only existing markets. This prevents companies from discovering new opportunities.

Even if companies are willing to innovate, employees may not like to take risks because they feel uncomfortable with uncertainty. Employees should see change as an opportunity, not as a threat. A business with a culture of experimentation can handle risk easily and travel through times of uncertainty and failure. An environment where new perspectives are always dismissed is not an environment that is right for innovation. Apple disrupted its own iPod business in favor of the new iPhone. True innovation radically destoys the status quo.

Incremental innovation may be considered as a starting point of innovation, something that starts to budge the stagnation.

4.5.2 Breakthrough Innovation

As we discussed in the previous section, incremental innovation will not make a company thrive in a fast-changing market because incremental innovation is not true innovation. Companies that innovate incrementally cannot jump-start growth. The type of innovation that is one level up from incremental innovation should be able to save companies in a perfect storm. For that to happen, companies must come up with breakthrough products. Breakthrough innovation requires courage to challenge the status quo, as it directly impacts profitability in the beginning. By creating a balance between the profitable short-term programs and the long-term benefits, companies can embrace breakthrough innovation. From a traditional perspective, most companies are focused on short-term profits and thereby miss the potential for breakthrough innovation.

Breakthrough products and services have the potential to open up a new consumer base for the business or change the way existing customers perceive the organization. This will create a competitive advantage over one's competitors. Breakthrough innovation will bring sustainability to the company and will create a brighter future for the people. It is not the only thing needed for either of those two things to happen, but it is vital to both. Breakthrough innovations require patience. The combination of flexibility and tolerance of uncertainty can help to develop a radically new product or service that can create a whole new market space.

In order to deliver a product that can truly impact the lives of consumers, companies have to put traditional marketing strategies on the back burner. Traditional marketing strategies include speed to market, the probability of quick return, and a profitability mind-set, among other things. A mind-set that puts possibility over profitability can unleash the innovations that can transform the organization. One example of breakthrough innovation is Microsoft Office 365. Microsoft has redefined its business model by offering Office as a monthly or annual subscription, a move from the traditional way of selling it as a product.

4.5.3 Disruptive Innovation

While incremental innovation allows for survivability to some extent, breakthrough innovation has the potential to change the direction of the company. However, neither of these two things will help an organization to withstand the storm of market disruption.

New entrants come up with business models that challenge the business models of incumbents. The core advantages to the new entrants is that they are fresh, they do not have any obligations to existing customers, and they are ready to take risks. Profit is not their immediate concern as the interest of stakeholders does not govern them, at least in the beginning. While established businesses focus on improving products and services for their most demanding customers, new entrants may gain a foothold at the extremes of the market spectrum. After proving themselves in the area where they gain an initial foothold, these new entrants will slowly move into the mainstream market.

Start-ups learn how to use the potential of innovative technologies and build the business models to offer their products and services to the incumbent's overlooked customers at a lower price. The lower prices do not mean low quality; they mean that the start-up is offering its products at low prices, forgoing profits. Then the product steadily moves into the mainstream, disrupting the market without compromising on the quality and price that drove the early success. The products and services from start-ups may appear inferior to the incumbent's customers. This is mainly due to the usage habits consumers have developed with the incumbent's products. Because of this, customers are usually not prepared to switch until they know that the products will have a positive impact on their lives. This type of innovation is called disruptive innovation.

People do not switch to new products just because they are of low price and high quality. While these two factors have some impact on consumer selections, disruptive innovations make a broader impact on economic and social aspects. Social impacts make people switch to those disruptive products and services.

Elon Musk's Tesla Motors' electric car is the best example to demonstrate market extremes. It started at the top end of the market, and after proving its success there, Tesla is now offering Model 3, which is affordable to mainstream customers.

Another version of disruptive innovation is a paradigm shift. In a paradigm shift, the innovator brings a disruptive business model directly to the mainstream market. The best example is Uber. It did not start at the high end or the lower end of the market. It did not target the people who use public transportation or drive themselves. It targeted customers who already use cabs to build a position in the mainstream market but in a limited number of cities and subsequently expanded the services globally.

Figure 4.1 provides four pictures showing different market streams.

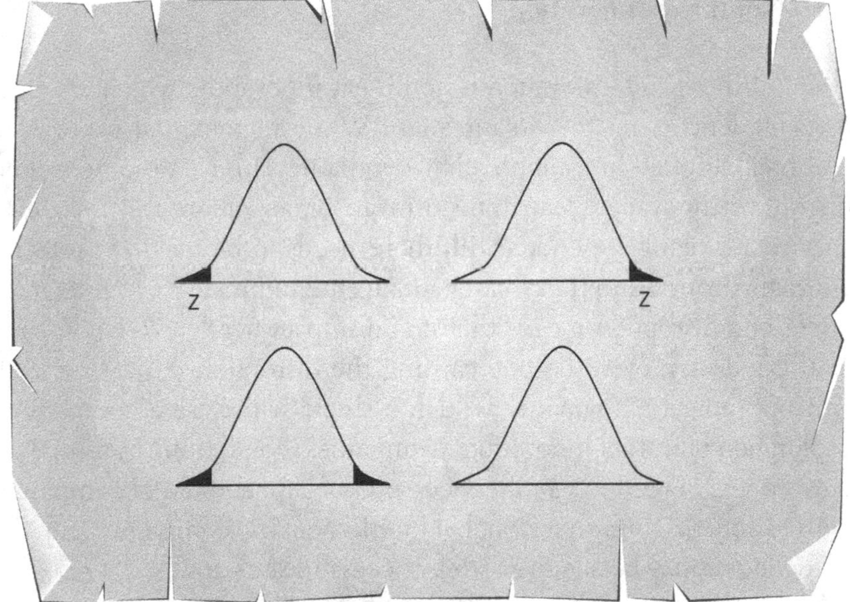

FIGURE 4.1. Four different market streams

Disruption is contagious, meaning even those companies that are immune to incremental and breakthrough innovations from their competitors will not be immune to disruptions that occur in the markets. Disruptive innovations by digital agents such as artificial intelligence, robotics, cognitive computing, and the Internet of Things are bringing diverse business organizations together. This type of convergence is happening between widely different companies that may have not even heard of each other a few years ago. This is an opportunity for an organization to expand the scope of its business.

Disruptive innovation is the fundamental force behind transformation. Disruptive innovations will transform the business model, the organization, the customer experience, and the quality of life for people in society. Consider the subscription model used by Netflix, charging a subscription fee to the customer in exchange for continued access to the product or service. Then there is the freemium model of Spotify and LinkedIn, where users do not pay for an essential service but pay a fee to make use of the full spectrum of offerings.

4.5.4 Nonlinear Innovation

The fourth type of innovation is nonlinear innovation, which serves as invisible fencing for the organization. While incremental innovation and breakthrough innovation allow companies survive to some extent, disruptive innovations can transform an organization and help it to survive a prolonged period. Still, there needs to be fencing protect a company from disruption that occurs in the industry. The contagious effect of a disruption means that it can impact nearly every company in the industry, even the one causing the disruption. Shielding itself will not protect a company, as such a shield will close a company to exploration of further innovation. Companies should think beyond their current line of products and services and look for additional companies with diversified cultures. Such complementary companies can be launched or may be acquired from successful start-ups.

Such innovation will embrace constant disruption in the industry and serve as invisible fencing. Therefore, the key for a business to thrive in the rapidly changing business environment is to exponentially contribute to the disruption.

Companies like Yahoo have indeed disrupted the industry at some point in time but have failed to defend themselves from the other disruptions that occurred in the industry. Companies will fail to protect themselves if their primary focus is value creation, which only benefits a select group of stakeholders, rather than continuously trying to improve the lives of people in society.

Continuous disruptive innovation that is achieved through "invisible fencing" innovation focuses on creating tremendous value in the long term, achieving a meaningful period of sustained value creation, and continuously changing the lives of people in society and the ways companies conduct the business. This means that value creation should not be measured purely by way of quantitative factors such as shareholder returns but should also be measured in qualitative terms such as long-term gains and impact on people's lives.

Two examples of companies that practice continuous disruption through invisible fencing are Facebook and Google, which are continuously launching moon shots and acquiring potential disruptors. Invisible fencing innovation will result in more comprehensive innovation that brings new and unexpected products and services to customers and transforms business models and other valuable outcomes.

4.6 Design Thinking for Innovation

Design thinking is a methodology used to solve the complex problems that draw upon empathy, imagination, intuition, ideation, and systemic reasoning, to explore possibilities for a desired design and outcome that benefits the users. Design thinking is not problem focused; it is solution focused. However, it does not expect the solution to be created in one shot. It is more experimental and iterative. Design thinking solves problems by way of design. Design thinking can be applied to designing tangible things such as products and also intangible things such as services, processes, and business models. It can be used to solve problems in several fields such as business, social services, politics, education, and engineering.

As discussed in earlier sections, innovation is associated with risks because of the uncertainty and unknown factors accumulated by rapid changes in customer behavior, disruptive technologies, hyperconnected systems, shifting economic winds, and increased social connectedness. The transformational leader must have the courage to take risks and should know how to overcome these risks to discover new opportunities.

Design thinking can help an organization to minimize risk at every step of the innovation process.

> "Business opportunities come from the risk of uncertainty and unknown factors accumulated by rapid changes in customer behavior, disruptive technologies, hyperconnected systems, shifting economic winds, and increased social connectedness."

Design thinking is best for nonlinear problem-solving. Business models that use linear problem-solving attempt to define everything up front and then implement the solution in a systematic way. While design thinking is also very systematic, it is more like nonlinear thinking, where we can uncover the problems and then find the solutions to those problems. Linear thinking is best for value capture, whereas nonlinear design thinking is best for value creation.

Traditional analytical thinking alone cannot help people to discover solutions to the challenges faced during innovation. Analytical thinking will help to solve any problems that are predictable, linear, and well-defined. These types of problems typically arise over an extended period. The uncertainties and complexities that arise in the innovation process are mostly unpredictable, nonlinear, chaotic, and ill-defined.

Solving problems in the innovation process requires a different approach that involves a better understanding of the situation and the why factors behind the business goals, collaboration, empathy, an understanding of customers' pain points, ideation, and experimentation. The approach should utilize quantitative and qualitative research that focuses on the why rather than on the how. By understanding why people do what they do, one can anticipate the future, discover customers' unmet needs, and align these with the business goals.

Any product must satisfy the conditions of desirability, feasibility, and viability. Desirability tells us how the product is suited to the needs, emotions, and behaviors of the users. Feasibility tells us if the design is technically possible or if it requires technology to be invented. Viability tells us if the design fits the existing business model or if it will create a new business model. Design thinking is not about making an immediate profit, as it is a nonlinear, long-term process. However, it will help to maintain balance among desirability, feasibility, and viability.

"Solving problems in the transformation process requires a different approach that involves a better understanding of the context and the purpose, collaboration, empathy, ideation, and experimentation."

Nobel Prize laureate Herbert Simon outlined one of the first formal models of the design thinking process in his seminal text on design methods, *The Sciences of the Artificial,* which was published in 1969. Simon's model consists of seven major stages, each with component stages and activities, and was most influential in shaping some of the most popular design thinking methodologies.

According to Herbert Simon, the seven stages of design thinking are as follows:

- Define
- Research
- Ideate
- Prototype
- Choose
- Implement
- Learn

There are several versions of the design thinking methodology in use today. Some of them are custom made based on the nature of the industry and on consumer need. Each version may have a different number of stages ranging from three to seven. However, they are all based on the same principles described in Simon's model. According to the Hasso-Plattner Institute of Design at Stanford, the leading university in teaching design thinking, the five stages of design thinking are as follows:

- Empathize
- Define
- Ideate
- Prototype
- Test

Design thinking is a structured framework that facilitates an understanding of the problem and embraces innovation in ways that contribute to organic growth and add real value to customers. The design thinking cycle involves observation to discover unmet needs within the context and constraints of a particular situation, framing the opportunity and the scope of innovation, generating creative ideas, testing, and refining solutions.

Design thinking will help to minimize uncertainty in innovation by engaging users through a series of prototypes to learn, test, and refine concepts. Design thinking methodology relies on customer insights that are gained from real-world experiments instead of analytics drawn from historical data.

Design thinking is not quick magic that makes the innovation process succeed all the time. Design thinking needs the right people in the process at all the stages to ensure that user perspectives are considered from the very beginning to the end. Transformational leaders must encourage collaboration between consumers and employees who have good observation and intensive questioning skills. Design thinking teams should contain critical contributors who can inspire people and draw insights for meaningful change. The right type of design thinking values a cross-functional approach to nurture a range of possible alternatives to discover new opportunities.

Design thinking is not about visual design; it starts with identifying areas for innovation and generating fresh ideas to design the experience that ensures efficient human interaction with a product or service.

Businesses fail in design thinking when the problems are viewed only through data-driven lenses. Design thinking requires a mind-set that starts with empathy for the user in order to gain insights and to combine those insights with what is technologically feasible and economically viable. Consumers and their experiences mainly drive the change.

If we treat data as the only key input, believing that a problem lies in the system or process, we will end up forcing incremental improvements to said system or process. With design thinking, we can minimize the uncertainty and risk associated with the process of innovation. Design thinking will become a powerful tool if the problems are seen through the right lens by the right people on the team in a world where customer expectations are rapidly changing.

Based on the level of complexity involved in most organizations, and based on the level of thinking that needs to be applied for idea generation, my view is that there are six stages in design thinking, as follows:

- Empathize
- Define
- Idea divergence
- Idea convergence
- Prototype
- Evaluation

Let us now explore each stage of design thinking in detail.

4.6.1 Empathize

The first step in problem-solving and designing an innovative product, service, or process is gaining an empathetic understanding of the problem. From the chapter "Igniting Creativity," we learned that empathy is the ability to look outside ourselves, walk in someone else's shoes, see with someone else's eyes, and think with someone else's mind to feel what someone else is feeling. Empathy allows us to set aside our assumptions about the world and gain insight into users and their needs. This phase involves consulting people; finding out the areas of concern through observing; understanding users' experiences and motivations; and immersing ourselves in the physical environment to gain a deeper understanding of the problems to be solved. Doing these things will shift the mind-set from "What do we have in store to offer to the customers?" to "What is empathetic to the customers?"

Designers should capture a significant amount of information to give contextual meaning to the solution, whether the solution is a product, a service, or a process. In traditional problem-solving where we use analytical thinking to solve people's problems, we ignore the reasons why people do what they do. Alternatively, in some places, people use focus groups to understand the needs of potential customers. However, most focus groups fail to assess the unmet needs of customers, because it is difficult to know what people are missing until they experience it. We cannot find what the customer wants in the traditional way of questioning and interviewing. It is hard to get creative ideas about a product or service that does not exist yet through plain interviewing of customers. This is because the workarounds mostly influence our habits and we are unconsciously forced to avail ourselves of a less than optimal solution. This makes us incapable of telling focus groups what we want. Moreover, we are skeptical of things that do not exist because they are not familiar to us. And since market research is done over the telephone, it is not able to gain insights into people's problems, as people are accustomed to working around the problem. Focus groups could easily give one hundred ideas to make improvements to the traditional cell phone, but they could not have given the idea of the iPhone. Analytical reports based on market research cannot predict what is going to be successful.

"In traditional problem-solving where we use analytical thinking to solve people's problems, we ignore the reasons why people do what they do. On the other hand, empathetic observation allows us to set aside our assumptions about the world and gain insight into users and their needs."

Empathetic concern will lead to game-changing ideas and proactively invent the future on behalf of the customers. Empathetic concern augments anecdotal observation, interviewing, and listening to help us see the world differently and discover new opportunities faster than our competitors do, and long before customers even recognize them.

"Empathetic concern will lead to game-changing ideas and proactively invent the future on behalf of customers."

Rational or analytical thinking fails to capture people's emotions. Emotions drive people's purchase decisions. Even what appears to be rational to consumers in a traditional perception is not what is usually grounded in nonrational impulses and feelings. So, if we can experience the feelings that they feel, then we can simulate the emotions within ourselves and design products and services in that emotional context.

What are the best practices to be empathetic in an organization?

Every one of us has empathy embedded within us. It is one of the natural characteristics that humans have. People are kind observers and listeners. However, over time, our brains are trained, whether consciously in structured learning or subconsciously from past experiences, to make judgments on the things that we observe. Sometimes, our brains act quickly and rush to make judgments, ignoring the broader context.

Empathy comes by way of immersion, that is, through the direct experience of others' lives, contexts, and environments. To immerse ourselves in other people's experiences profoundly and meaningfully, we should put aside our knowledge, opinions, and worldview temporarily, no matter if we are experts in the related matters.

There are many qualities, characteristics, and traits that lead one to develop empathy, which helps us to form a broad and accurate understanding of users. These qualities, characteristics, and traits are described below:

- An egocentric view of things and rigid opinions will hurt the drawing of meaningful context. We need to put aside our egos and become aware of the feelings of others. Humility can help us abandon our preconceived ideas and biases. Moreover, it motivates us to understand the needs, wants, and goals of other people.

- We need to practice the kind of listening that blocks out conflicting inner voices and allows others to resonate, which will help us uncover profound meaning and experience. We should also listen to what is not being said.

- The more in-depth observations will help us to interpret nonverbal expressions, body language, and the environment. If we want to connect with the users on a deeper level, we need to observe their body language, their facial expressions, and the positive and negative signs that come from these.

- The why–what–how method described in chapter 2 will help us while observing people. With this method, we start with concrete observations: why the person is emotional about certain things, what is happening in the background, and how the person is doing what he or she is doing

- We need a strong sense of imagination to see through another person's eyes.

- We need a strong sense of care and a desire to help and provide assistance. This will motivate us to gain a better understanding of the problem.

- Curiosity will help us to dig deep into unexpected areas and explore all aspects of people's lives.

- We should use questioning and interviewing, without losing the context, to probe deeper into others' emotions and behaviors. To make the most out of the interviews, we should group the questions thematically and create a smooth flow between the themes so that the interview flows naturally.

By applying the qualities, characteristics, and traits described above in the empathizing stage, we should be able to break down the complex concepts and problems into smaller components and document the details. After following the above process, analyzing and conducting relevant research, and becoming an expert on the subject from both the business context and the customer context, we can align the business goals with people's needs.

4.6.2 Define

The define stage is the second stage of design thinking. We use the empathizing stage to document the insights gathered by applying empathy. During the define stage, we take that information and synthesize it to define an actionable problem statement with a strong point of view. It helps to organize, interpret, discover connections and patterns, and make sense of the insights gathered.

The define stage will attach the purpose to the information we have gathered and bring clarity and focus to the design space. Putting together the analysis and research showing the cause and the point of view will help designers to come up with great ideas to establish features, functions, and any other elements to incorporate into the product, service, or process.

As discussed in earlier sections, innovation is associated with certain types of risks. Some of these risks usually arise from uncertainties. Defining these uncertainties in a problem statement will help the design team to break them into groups and solve them iteratively and logically. We will get the answers to unknowns based on what has been designed so far in an iterative process. That is the beauty of the iterative process of solving problems.

Uncertainties are of three types:

- Unknown knowns
  These are the contexts with a clear cause-and-effect relationship that is easily understandable with extra effort.

- Known unknowns
  These are the contexts that have clear cause-and-effect relationships, but few people know the contexts. This means we know where to get the answers.

- Unknown unknowns
  This is the category into which most problems are classified. As we travel along the path of innovation and transformation, we will discover the problems and the answers. The things that are designed to address the point and the problems that are solved to address the point will show the direction to the unknowns in the journey of problem-solving.

Design thinking is an iterative process by nature. By classifying the problems into the right category in the define stage, the designers know how to decide on the iterations for the experiments. The clarity of the problem is most important in a purpose-driven innovation, and ambiguity in the context can have a ripple effect on the overall process of innovation.

The goal of the define stage is to achieve clarity on the context, form the point of view, and frame the challenge in such a way that it will be open for exploration of the ideas to find the desired solution. A strong point of view will illuminate the right challenge to address based on an understanding of the people and the problem space. A focused problem statement tends to yield some ideas without compromising on quality.

The aspects of the define stage map to two of the factors in the why–what–how method:

- The section "Point of View" will map the why.
- The section "Framing the Challenge" will map the how.

Point of View

Each challenge in the define stage must have a strong *point of view*, as this serves as the spirit for problem-solving. The point of view should make the problem statement human-centered. The point of view should provide a focus, inspire the team, and guide the innovation efforts. The point of view should create a sense of possibility and optimism so as to encourage team members to generate ideas during the ideation stage.

"The point of view serves as the spirit for problem-solving and provides a focus, inspires the teams, and guides the innovation efforts."

The define stage serves as a foundation for the next stage of design thinking, which is ideation. So, the goal of the problem statement is to explore as many ideas as possible for the solution. If the problem statement says that we need this solution for this problem, then it will eliminate the possibility of generating ideas. Instead, the question should be framed in such a way that it opens up the challenge so as to gain more ideas. There is a difference between clarity of context and clarity of solution. We should have clarity on the context and should maintain some kind of ambiguity in the solution-finding process as to open the door to several types of ideas.

Framing the Challenge

The next step after preparing the point of view is to frame the challenge by asking ourselves, "How might we?" By doing so, we are admitting that we do not know the answer yet and need a collaborative approach to find one. The "How might we?" question will spark the imagination of all team members and will align with the core insights and user needs that have not yet been met.

For example, if the point of view is "Young people need to eat nutritious food to thrive and grow healthily," then the question should be something like "How might we make healthy eating something to which young people aspire?"

The three words in "How might we?" have three different purposes, as follows:

- *How* suggests that we do not yet have the answer and we are open-minded.
- *Might* suggests that we need to explore ideas for multiple possible solutions.
- *We* suggests that we are going to make a collaborative effort.

4.6.3 Idea Divergence

The next stage in design thinking is ideation using the concept of idea divergence. The point of view that was formed and the challenge that was framed during the define stage will serve as the foundation for the idea divergence stage. Framing the challenge in the format specified in the define stage will spark creativity in people and will help them to come up with the most relevant ideas to solve the problem. While the goals should be to generate original creative ideas, the adaptation of ideas used by other groups will also be helpful. So, idea divergence should focus on both creativity and adaption of existing ideas from elsewhere.

Brainstorming, which was covered in detail in the chapter "Igniting Creativity," can be applied to the design thinking ideation stage. Collaboration and diversity are the two pillars for brainstorming to foster divergent thinking and idea generation.

The most valuable resources in an organization for generating ideas are its members, whether they are from senior management, architecture, analytics, user experience, business, or any other division. In the context of the ideation stage, we should alter the definition of stakeholder and make everyone who is involved in the process a stakeholder.

At the beginning of the session, the leader must present the outcome of the define stage, which is to determine the point of view and to frame the challenge. The goal is to get as many ideas as possible. We never know from where the ideas will arise, so it is best to give everyone the opportunity to speak about their passion and the subjects that are interesting to them without losing the context of the problem.

When we bring various people onto the team, we will find it is quite common for different people to think in different ways. That is the main reason why we should bring them onto the team. The brainstorming session should adopt a culture where all siloed thinking can be linked to the context of the challenge. The leader must create a collaborative culture to energize the team, to promote creativity, and to make the environment more productive and joyful.

The idea generation part of the structured brainstorming process should follow certain inspirational, motivational, and positive thinking norms. These norms include, but are not limited to, the following:

- Provide an open environment that encourages everyone to participate.
- Everyone should feel that they have contributed to the solution.
- Create an environment where the brain may get creative. Providing plenty of writing space and utensils, selecting a conference room with a great view, and so forth will create a joyful environment.
- Motivate people to think divergently.
- At this moment, the ideas do not have to be realistic. The feasibility and viability of the ideas should not be discussed.
- Encourage people to come up with ideas even if they seem a bit crazy. Crazy ideas sometimes spark more new ideas.
- Divergency does not mean to transcend the line of sight altogether. To improve productivity, whenever there is a feeling that the team is completely deviating from the problem context, steer the team toward the stated challenge.

- Avoid criticizing or rewarding ideas during the brainstorming session.
- Avoid judgment during the brainstorming session, as it hinders idea generation and limits creativity. Judgment creates fear of rejection in the team members and unnecessarily filters out the good ideas.
- Defer the evaluation part to the end of the session.
- When one member gets stuck with an idea, the other members' experience should take the idea to the next stage.

Some people are a bit hesitant to talk about their ideas in meetings. The leader should provide a different mechanism that is preferred by such people. One suitable mechanism, for example, is a brain dump. A brain dump is a way of sharing knowledge about a particular subject, moving it from the brain to some other medium, such as computer or paper.

Sometimes ideas are sparked based on what exists already. Providing the details on how people are currently doing something, even if only a few, can provide a baseline to spark ideas. This technique is called reverse engineering.

Derived knowledge can help ignite ideas. So, if possible, discuss how others in the industry are attempting to solve the problem. This can feed more relevant information to the brain in order to get more ideas.

4.6.4 Idea Convergence

The next phase is to discuss, short-list, and prioritize the ideas. This is where convergent thinking comes into the picture. At this stage, conflict can take place among the ideas, which can hinder the innovation process when people do not understand one another. Fostering a healthy process requires bringing all the team members together and getting a comprehensive set of ideas, whether they are analytical, intuitive, conceptual, experiential, social, or values-driven. A brainstorming group should encourage its cognitively diverse members to respect each other's thinking styles.

During the discussion phase, the leader should encourage the cognitive differences and preferences of the team members. And team members should not be rigid in their ideas or operate within narrow cognitive boundaries.

Applying techniques such as value proposition and fitting these in with iteration can help to short-list and prioritize the ideas. Value proposition is a technique that explains what benefit we provide to the users and how we will relieve the pain expressed by users and observed during the empathy phase.

After mapping the value proposition to the idea, the next step is to assess the difficulty level. Based on the level of difficulty and its logical connection to the other ideas, the team can decide which iteration of experimentation the idea will fit in with.

The goal of the idea convergence thinking session is to come up with a short list from the vast list of ideas and prioritize these short-listed ideas to get ready for the next stage in design thinking, which is prototype. In other words, some of the ideas can be filtered out before the team even experiments with them.

4.6.5 Prototype

The next stage in design thinking is prototyping the idea. Not even the linear thinking approach can produce the optimal solution in just one phase. Any product development will have multiple phases. So, it is quite evident that design thinking, which is nonlinear, should not expect the optimal solution to be built after one trial.

That is the primary reason why we should have a stage in design thinking dedicated to prototyping and encouraging experimentation. Experimentation comes in the form of iterations. Iteration is a cycle of building something, testing it, improving it, and resting it. Within this cycle we can embed the second stage, which is ideation, in order to improve the quality of ideas based on the findings from the prototyping stage.

The goal of the prototyping stage is to identify the best possible solutions for the problems identified during the idea convergence stage. The solutions are implemented one by one. The prototypes are either accepted or suggested for improvements based on feedback received from the stakeholders and users. Building something to show how the ideas will be implemented will make it much easier for stakeholders to understand and will allow the teams to build more prototypes.

Design teams can start with low-fidelity prototypes such as paper mockups or sketches and then move on to create higher-fidelity prototypes, spending more energy and time.

In order to minimize the risk associated with the process of innovation, the prototype team should choose specific features of the product by grouping them logically and produce a number of inexpensive, scaled-down versions of the product. Prototypes must be shared with and tested on all the relevant people, even with those people are outside the design team.

The prototype will suppress any fear of failure. We should be prepared to fail, as failure is expected in innovation experimentation. This is because the steps involved in prototyping are associated with several assumptions. One of the goals of prototyping is to validate the assumptions made during the ideation stages. There is no concept of failure in innovation. In each iteration, we either succeed or learn. The opportunity to learn will make us more adaptable and will provide an opportunity to use this experience in later iterations. This is the way to maintain the courage to take risks in innovation and to mitigate those risks. The smaller the iteration, the faster we fail, and then we can learn quickly and reuse the experience. We should create a model that is demonstrable. If we cannot explain how the solution works, then we will find there are holes in the idea. Moreover, coming up with the explanation presents an opportunity to learn.

There is a wrong perception in many organizations, especially among the teams who are new to design thinking, that prototyping is a waste of time and resources. Even though we have to spend time on prototypes with some degree of probability that they will be thrown away, creating prototypes allows us to move faster in the long term. The small amount of time that we spend on prototyping will help us save a great deal of time in the future. This is because failing early is better than failing in the end.

The focus of the prototype team must be on the usability of the product rather than on the quantity of product features. Say that we have added many features, making the product bulky. If it is not usable by the user, then there is no point in developing the prototype. Usability is determined by how easy it is to use the product and if there is a real benefit from the product even if it is minimal. If there is no minimal benefit, then the product is meaningless even if 90 percent of the features have been implemented.

There is always room to add more features and make the product more complex to meet the needs of a broader range of people. When we try to overload the early stages of a product, it will create more stress and anxiety for people, as it takes some time to get adapted to the new product. People will fail to complete the work using the product if their cognitive loads reach a certain level. This will give the impression that the product has failed even if the product is successful in reality. Therefore, the unnecessary features of the product must be deferred unless they are blockers for other features.

In this stage, the design team must prototype several alternatives, even using one idea, and should not discount the possibilities until they are thoroughly tested. Developing alternatives can lead to even more ideas and provide an opportunity to merge a few solutions into a better and more successful product.

Design teams should not fall in love with what they have prototyped. There is an emotional bias effect that will not let designers throw away the whole or part of the prototype they designed.

After going through several iterations of prototyping, the design team will have a better idea of the problems and constraints inherent within the product. They will have a better perspective on how real users would feel when interacting with the end product.

There are several methods used to develop the prototype, depending on whether the prototype is a product, a service, or a process. And there are a variety of tools available for all these scenarios.

The storyboard is a technique used to develop prototypes for nontangibles, which are not products but types of services, processes, or business models.

Storyboards visually express user interactions through the use of the art of narrative to focus on a user's experience of using the service. Storyboarding is derived from the film industry. A storyboard is a series of drawings or pictures put together in a narrative sequence.

4.6.6 Evaluation

The evaluation stage is the last stage in design thinking. This stage is often referred to as the testing stage in other versions of design thinking, but the testing of a prototype in design thinking requires methods that go beyond traditional testing. Therefore, in my version of design thinking, it is called evaluation.

The evaluation stage is the most difficult of all the stages. Since users are accustomed to the existing products, they need new features in order to get excited. As discussed in earlier sections, people are used to using old versions of products and will continue to do so even if they feel pain, as the brain creates patterns based on the experience. The truths gleaned pass through some criticism in the early stages. Indeed, criticism is the most crucial part of evaluation in that it provides valuable feedback. The rule of thumb is that the designers should design as if they know that they are right and take the prototype to the evaluation stage thinking that they are wrong. The primary goal of the evaluation stage is to generate user feedback related to the prototype in order to gain a deeper understanding of the users, and then feeding the evaluation back into most stages of the design thinking process. Criticism can lead to insights that change the way the problem is defined, and it may generate new ideas in the idea stages and eventually lead to an improved version of the prototype in the next iteration.

It is easy to deal with people who accept everything during the evaluation stage, but that acceptance may end up adding only a little value to the design thinking process. User feedback is critical to understanding what users need in order to carry out specific activities and make the iterative process successful. Therefore, the critics are the most valuable resource to the design thinking process.

The same techniques such as observation and interviewing that are applied during the empathize stage can be applied in the evaluation stage. That is why it is called an evaluation rather than testing.

For the most effective results, the evaluation must be carried out within a real context of the user's life. So, if the prototype is a tangible object, the users should take it with them and use it as part of their regular routines. If the prototype is a service prototype, then it is essential to simulate a realistic situation by having users take on a role.

Designers should show all the alternatives that have been developed and ask the users to compare them. This will suppress the bias level in the user's mind.

During the prototype demonstration, designers should avoid overexplaining. The goal is not to sell the prototype to the users, but to gain understanding and feedback. Overexplaining can create some biases in the minds of users and lead to less valuable feedback.

In summary, the evaluation stage is an opportunity for the designers to learn, go back to the empathize phase, redefine the problem statement, get new ideas, and build an improved prototype. The evaluation stage is what triggers the next iteration in the design thinking process.

4.7 Lean Innovation

A lean process is centered on a "build, measure, learn" feedback loop. The goal is for companies to build a minimum viable product (MVP), or a scaled-down version of a product or service with the core features that make the product work to serve as a guide for future development. By placing an MVP in users' hands, companies can quickly discover what's working and what's not and iterate based on the feedback. Then they can eliminate waste and build a product based on what customers want.

Henry Ford first introduced the lean process in 1913, in the manufacturing process, to reduce assembly time for a single vehicle. By reducing the time, money, and human capital required to build a car, Ford made automobiles more accessible to the public. Toyota later replicated Henry Ford's original principles as the basis for developing the Toyota Production System.

Lean process is based on the principle that 20 percent of a product's features will deliver 80 percent of the benefits to users. Lean innovation identifies the features that are most important, rapidly develops a minimum viable product based on those features, tests it with customers, and repeats the process until the core product is competitive. Lean innovation can fit well into corporate cultures, especially in the field of engineering, which is focused on process-improvement programs such as Six Sigma.

The lean innovation approach is somewhat related to the design thinking process in that it incorporates design thinking principles. As we discussed in an earlier section, design thinking principles are valuable to gain empathy for users and come up with a solution addressing the user's problems, needs, emotions, and feelings.

Lean innovation provides a scientific approach to developing products or business models that shorten the development life cycle by adopting a combination of hypothesis-driven experimentation, iterative product releases, validations, and feedback. This methodology is good for start-ups as building products or services iteratively to meet the needs of early customers can reduce the risks, reduce the amount of initial funding, and help avoid failure. Lean does not merely mean spending less money; it is about spending money in the sequence of iterations, meaning that if failure is unavoidable, then the company should fail cheap.

Many start-ups fail because they begin with an idea for a product and spend months or years focusing on perfecting it without ever showing the product to prospective customers. So, they do not get an opportunity to learn if the customers are interested in the product or not. A start-up fails when it learns from the customers in the end that they do not care about the idea.

The lean innovation approach eliminates the uncertainty for start-ups by providing tools to test a vision continuously and by implementing a process and methodology for the development of a product.

The experimental nature of the lean innovation methodology will help to build a sustainable business around a set of products and services. This allows firms to look for early adopters, adding the resources to each further experiment and eventually building a product. By the time the product is ready for distribution, it will already have established a customer base.

The build–measure–learn feedback loop of the lean innovation methodology will help start-ups to test a fundamental hypothesis about the product, a strategy, and/or business growth. It also helps start-ups by asking the questions they should study and pointing out the problems they need to solve along the way. It will also tell if a start-up is moving the drivers of the business model or not and indicate the time to pivot or make a necessary course correction.

Lean innovation is focused on increasing efficiency by capturing customer feedback early and often and minimizing waste in the product development cycle. The process prioritizes experimentation over elaborate planning and celebrates continuous, incremental improvement.

The core principles of lean innovation are as follows:

- Apply customer-centric design thinking to identify new opportunities.
- Develop, prototype, learn about, and validate the product with fewer resources.
- Eliminate waste, make incremental improvements, and break the barriers that hinder innovation.

Many organizations are embracing lean innovation whether they are start-ups or well-established large organizations. In other words, lean innovation may not be the best innovation process, but it is a more efficient learning process. The learning will have the most significant impact on the revenue from new products. Creating a better environment for learning is the spirit of lean innovation. It focuses on the most critical product attributes. And rapid cycling of trial and error in the real-life competitive environment ideally accumulates critical knowledge at a rapid clip.

4.8 Agile Innovation

Transformation projects, whether they are focused on developing a new product, implementing a new service, introducing a new process, or reengineering the existing operations, often pose a challenge to an organization. The challenge comes from rapid changes in the market, less time to monetize, and the reduced life span of products and services. The more challenging the environment, the more opportunities it presents. An environment with VUCA (volatility, uncertainty, complexity, and assumptions) is indeed an asset to innovators, allowing them to come up with the best innovative solutions to these complex problems.

The traditional flow of operations involves doing a vast amount of research spanning across months, developing the whole project once, testing it over an extended period, and making a big announcement once it is ready to launch. However, the problem is that the solution may not have been defined explicitly in the beginning, and it may not be possible to have clarity. If it is such a simple solution, then there won't be much room for innovation. The goals in the transformation process must be ambitious and far-reaching, and therefore the solution should not be defined up front. Alternatively, the problem itself sometimes may be undefinable.

The latest developments in innovation and transformation projects lead transformational leaders to follow agile methodologies, in which high-performing cross-functional teams work toward a common goal such as customer-centric vision, real-time decision-making, rapid iterations, and end products that can be released quickly and refined continually.

The key aspects of agile approaches are as follows:

- Cross-functional teams
- Disaggregation of complexity
- Continuous improvement
- Collaboration
- Rapid customer feedback
- Mitigation of the risk of failure

The cross-functional teams include representatives from all the groups required, such as business, technology, and consumer groups and testing teams collaboratively working together toward a customer-centric vision.

Agile approaches will help disaggregation of complexity by defining a minimum viable product or service and delivering it to the customers in only a few months. A joint working session typically ranges from a week to two weeks and is typically called a sprint, with each sprint contributing to a logical unit of work. These sprints occur recursively, facilitating continuous improvements to the products. Agile approaches are not just limited to software development. One-week to two-week sprints are mostly applicable to software development, but depending on the field and nature of the project, the sprint length can be customized. Sprints can be applied virtually in any field and for any project magnitude or length. The sprint is based on a principle of achieving smaller successes and using those successes to energize future developments and mount a sequence of smaller successes to achieve bigger success.

Encouraging collaboration and daily interactions among teams helps to identify and remove roadblocks early, reducing the delivery time and minimizing the risk of failure. The agile approach helps teams to become self-sufficient and self-managed. It offers people the tools and processes to do their jobs productively. If the team learns from the feedback that the iteration is not good, then they can easily fine-tune the product in the next iteration. That means it is better to fail early and cheap if failing is unavoidable. The agile approach creates an environment of continuous learning.

There are several versions of agile methodologies, including the following:

- Scrum framework
- Kanban
- Extreme programming

While each agile methodology has its own importance depending on the context, for the purpose of general understanding, scrum framework will be discussed in detail in *The Art and Science of Transformational Leadership.*

4.8.1 Scrum Framework

Scrum is a framework developed by Ken Schwaber and Jeff Sutherland to develop, deliver, and sustain complex products. The scrum framework was developed based on three pillars called scrum principles:

- Transparency
- Inspection
- Adaptation

Transparency: Scrum provides common standards to foster transparency in the development and delivery process to ensure that the aspects of the process are visible to those responsible for the outcome.

Inspection: The scrum framework provides the components to facilitate user inspection to detect any undesirable variances and provide feedback.

Adaptation: The iterative working session provides an opportunity to make the necessary adjustments if the inspectors detect any aspects of a process deviating from acceptable limits.

The scrum framework is made up of the following components:

- Scrum teams
- Scrum events
- Scrum artifacts
- Scrum principles
- Scrum values

Each component serves a specific purpose. Scrum is founded on empiricism, which asserts that knowledge comes from experience. Scrum aids in controlling risk by employing an iterative, incremental approach to optimize predictability. The rules of scrum framework serve as the glue for the teams and govern the relationships and interactions among them.

Scrum framework can be used in virtually any industry and for any product or service. For years, it has been used in software development, hardware development, embedded software development, construction, engineering, government, marketing, and processes to manage organizational operations. Because market complexities are increasing year over the year and since there is tight integration between business and technology, scrum will play a proper role in managing the complexities iteratively and delivering the end products or services. The beauty of scrum is its small team sizes. Jeff Bezos calls it the "two-pizza team" size; the smaller individual teams are highly flexible and adaptive. The smaller teams collaborate and interoperate and target release environments.

Scrum teams, events, artifacts, principles, and values are further broken down as listed below.

Roles in a Scrum Team:

- Product owner
- Scrum master
- Team member
- Scrum of scrum master
- Agile coach

Scrum Events:

- Product increment planning
- Sprint planning
- Daily scrum
- Product demo
- Sprint retrospective

Scrum Artifacts:

- Product backlog
- Sprint backlog
- Epic
- Story
- Subtask
- Sprint
- Product increment

Scrum Principles:

- Transparency
- Inspection
- Adaptation

Scrum Values:

- Commitment
- Courage
- Focus

- Openness
- Respect

4.8.1.1 Scrum Artifacts and Events

Let us discuss how the requirements of the product or service are broken down into logical units called scrum artifacts.

Product Backlog

As the word *agile* suggests, the agile methodology is very flexible in breaking complex product or service requirements into smaller essential components and pieces. The scrum framework calls these components and pieces a product backlog. Here the word *backlog* refers to the concept that, in a continuously innovative world, the product will not take a concrete end shape and will continue to evolve—and therefore it will continue to undergo changes that will be implemented iteratively.

Product backlog is one of the artifacts of scrum. Product backlog is an ordered list of requirements for any changes to be made to the product. The list may start as small but will evolve as the product evolves and changes dynamically to identify the user needs, competitor products, and product usefulness. Product backlog exists as long as the product exists. The product owner is responsible for maintaining and prioritizing the backlog so that the most valuable requirements are added first.

The requirements in the product backlog are divided into multiple types: epics, stories, and subtasks. The product backlog is different from the product road map. The product road map will not contain detailed requirements and stories.

Story

Stories are at the heart of scrum. The story represents the smallest piece of product functionality that is intended to be added. The story describes who, what, and why. The how is divided into the subtasks, into which each story is broken down. Therefore, the subtask is the smallest piece of the work from the implementation point of view, and the story is the smallest piece of the requirements from the functional point of view.

The story is a description of the feature from the perspective of the user who desires the new capability. It takes a structured format:

As a <Role>, I want <Goal> so that <Reason>.

- The user is the one who uses the feature.
- The goal is what the user wants.
- The reason is why the user wants the feature.

Let us write one story for example:

As an analyst, I want to be able to see a new feature in the reporting dashboard to help me to decide to execute a trade.

Here the user does not necessarily have to be an end user. During product development, there may be many requirements that are not directly visible to the end user but that may be visible to the people who develop those features. So, an internal team member can also serve as a user of those stories.

Anyone can write the stories. It is not necessary for only the product owner to write the story. However, it is the product owner's responsibility to maintain and prioritize the stories. The stories are usually written during a release planning workshop. The stories do not represent the full-fledged documentation of the overall project. There is a misconception that the agile methodology does not require documentation. Some products that are heavily regulatory oriented needed a full-fledged master business requirement document either at the inception or during the evolution along with product development. The requirements can be taken from the master document and translated into stories.

Epic

The story cannot add any significant value to the product independently. Rather, it is the epic that adds incremental value to the product. An epic is a logical unit of stories. Epics somewhat resemble stories, but they often consist of a complete workflow for a user. It is a big-picture story. An epic is a big story that can be broken down into smaller stories. While it is standard practice to write the epic first and then break it into multiple stories, it is sometimes possible to first come up with the stories and then group them into epic by connecting the stories based on their relationships with an value to the user.

Following are some reasons why epics are needed over stories:

- The story may not add any value when it is delivered alone.
- The subtasks that make up the story may be too complex.
- The proposed work may have dependencies on other work.
- There are more unknown technical or business elements at work.
- The work estimation may be difficult without a further breakdown.

To better tackle some of the complexities and unknowns, the big story will better serve as an epic made up of multiple stories. And sometimes there may be different types of users who can provide more insights into the big-picture work. In that case, the individual users will help to provide the inner details. The individual stories may have an implied workflow, in which case the attention of multiple users is required to provide feedback and sign off on the work done. Each story paints a more in-depth picture of what is happening in the system and helps users to understand complexities and deal with the unknown factors. This is one of the ways to minimize risk using the agile approach.

The other reason why we need the epic is related to the implementation point of view and not necessarily related to value and workflow. The estimation of effort for each story is made by assessing the story points by having discussions with the team members. The rule of thumb is that any story that requires more than thirteen story points must be broken down into multiple stories. While it is true that the effort is going to be the same whether there is a bigger story or a smaller story, smaller stories are useful for tracking purpose and psychological point of view. Breaking the stories into smaller pieces will cause their completion status to produce better metrics and improve predictability. Having a bigger story will result in the story's sitting in the dashboard for many days, with the risk of its being carried it forward to the next sprint. A healthy dashboard not only helps to build the momentum but also encourages stakeholders to see the progress of the team.

Sprint

A sprint represents a time box of typically two weeks' worth of work with a set of epics and stories adapted for implementation. The subset of product backlog is added to the sprint, which is called a sprint backlog. A sprint represents a unit of work that has the potential of validating and receiving feedback. The work delivered at the end of the sprint may not be eligible to deliver to users but will help users to review and provide feedback. Each sprint will have a begin state and an end state and multiple events in between.

Scrum events during the sprint include the following:

- Sprint planning
- Daily scrum calls
- Product demo
- Sprint retrospective

The scrum master is responsible for facilitating all these events.

Sprint Planning

Sprint planning is a collaborative session aiming to discuss and elaborate on the stories produced during the sprint backlog. This is the time when each story is broken down into subtasks and the team discusses how to implement the subtasks. Each task will be discussed in detail to assess the associated risks and dependencies. If it is determined that a subtask needs further clarification or if it does not fit into the current sprint, then the corresponding subtask or whole story will be moved back to the product backlog. The sprint officially starts when everyone on the team agrees about the feasibility of the sprint and the countdown starts toward completion.

Daily Scrum

The daily scrum is typically a fifteen-minute call or meeting where all the team members provide updates and discuss any roadblocks and dependencies. The goal of the daily scrum is to ensure that there will not be any roadblocks to perform the work at least for the next twenty-four hours. The daily scrum is conducted consistently at the same time each day to develop a culture of collaboration.

Product Demo

The product demo, also called a sprint review, provides an opportunity for the users and all team members involved in the process to inspect the increment. The development team, along with the product owner, demonstrate the work performed during the sprint to the actual users. This is a way of reviewing the work, ensuring that there are no significant deviations from the desirables, and making adjustments accordingly for the coming sprints. This is also a way of minimizing the risk of failure.

Sprint Retrospective

The sprint retrospective is an opportunity for the scrum team to discuss what went well with the sprint, what went wrong, and what can be done better to improve the development process. This retrospective is different from the product demo in that the product demo gives an opportunity to receive feedback on the product functionalities, whereas the retrospective facilitates the receiving of feedback from the development team itself on the how factor. The sprint retrospective is a tool that facilitates continuous learning.

The sprint is officially closed at the end of the sprint retrospective, and the team is ready to start the next sprint with a sprint planning session.

Product Iteration

A product iteration is an actual unit of work that is viable to deliver to users or customers. The work that was developed in multiple sprints, spanning across several epics and stories, is grouped into a deliverable unit of work and is deployed to the production team for official use. This is the stage at which the work is transformed from a useful state to a usable state.

Product iteration is also called a product version or product release. Each product iteration consists of several sprints, typically three to five.

Each iteration starts with product iteration (PI) planning. During PI planning, all the stakeholders involved in the process, such as business users, product owners, scrum masters, and the development team, come together collaboratively, adopt a set of epics and stories, discuss in detail, and plan the work. For a PI of five sprints, the duration of PI planning is typically two to three days. Depending on the complexity and size of the project, the overall team may span across multiple scrums, having multiple scrum masters. Therefore, the presence of the scrum of scrum master is mandatory during PI planning.

This is the time when the epics are confirmed, ensuring that an epic will not spread across multiple iterations. PI starts with business users and product owners reading out big-picture goals for entire sprints, giving the business context, and explaining the value the PI will add to the product. The product backlog, which exists all the time, is reviewed, and a set of relevant epics and stories is identified. The prior backlog grooming may have informally discussed possible epics and stories for the PI. Therefore, the team may already have a very good idea about the probable items for the PI.

It is not necessary to use any agile tool during PI planning. Traditional whiteboards, sticky notes, notebooks, voting cards, and video conferencing facilities are widely used during PI planning. The relevant epics, stories, and other factors such as risks and dependencies are later ported into any adopted agile tool.

Epics and stories are moved back and forth between the scrum teams depending on the relevancy, team capabilities, team velocity, and any other dependencies.

Each member of the scrum team talks about the complexities and unknown factors in the epics and stories. Story points are assigned with the consultation of all the scrum members and after taking a vote among all the team members.

PI planning is different from product backlog grooming and sprint planning. PI planning is big-picture planning aiming to develop a viable product increment with the potential to add value to users and the business.

During PI development across multiple sprints, constant feedback is received from users at the end of each sprint, the corresponding members of the scrum test the changes according to quality assurance standards, and the users test for acceptance, which will eventually be deployed in production after the PI is concluded. This last is planned according to the cycle.

The hierarchy of product functionalities during a given product iteration cycle is as follows:

Product iteration → Sprint → Epic → Story → Subtask

4.8.1.2 Scrum Teams

Scrum framework defines a set of roles for the team members. It also defines a set of values that each member must maintain regardless of the role they play. These values are commitment, courage, focus, openness, and respect. It is believed that these values will help promote the scrum pillars of transparency, inspection, and adaptation.

The scrum framework encourages the scrum teams to be self-organizing to accomplish the goals rather than being directed by a leader outside the team. Scrum teams deliver product features iteratively and incrementally utilizing constant feedback received from the user groups.

The scrum team consists of the following roles:

- Product owner
- Development team member
- Scrum master
- Scrum of scrum master

In addition to the above roles, an organization sometimes employs an agile coach, at least during the initial period of new agile development.

Product Owner

The product owner is responsible for maintaining and growing the product backlog. The product owner does not have to be an end user or customer. He or she is part of the scrum team representing the group of business users whose purpose is to understand the requirements. Epics and stories can be written by the product owner or other relevant people, but it is the product owner who owns the list and prioritizes the epics and stories. By collaborating with other members of the scrum team, including the scrum master, the product owner understands the nature of the work and part of the implementation details and seeks to optimize the value of the work the team performs. The product owner manages backlog grooming sessions, which are informal scrum meetings to ensure that the epics and stories have enough breadth and depth and that they are visible, transparent, and evident to all. During the product backlog grooming session, the product owner ensures that the team understands the epics and stories and are ready for the PI planning workshop. The product owner helps during the acceptance testing and with getting the story to the completion state. The product owner must have enough commitment and support from the organization to succeed.

Development Team

The development team consists of people who are involved in developing and delivering the epics and stories. The scrum framework does not recognize any exclusive member titles; everyone is simply called a development team member. This does not mean that the team cannot have specialists such as architects, quality assurance professionals, and business analysts. These types of members may be on the team, but everyone is simply called a member of the team from a structural point of view. The stories may be assigned to a certain person based on the skill that such person possesses. However, accountability belongs to the team as a whole. The different skills that the members bring can create synergies when working in collaboration.

Scrum Master

The scrum master is responsible for making sure that everyone on the team follows the scrum principles and values and for helping everyone understand scrum theory, practices, and rules. The scrum master's role is different from the traditional project manager's role. The scrum master's leadership abilities should help the team to become self-organized. The scrum master facilitates the sprint planning, daily scrum calls, product demo, and sprint retrospective and coordinates testing activities. He or she works collaboratively with all the stakeholders during the PI planning, clears any obstacles faced by the team members, and creates an environment where the team can efficiently address the unknown factors and dynamics. While it is the responsibility of the product owner to manage the product backlogs, it is the scrum master's responsibility that the team breaks these down effectively into subtasks to implement the stories successfully. The scrum master ensures that the product owner is efficiently engaged during the development process to provide necessary guidance on a daily basis. The scrum master protects the team members from outside interruptions and distractions.

Scrum of Scrum Master

If the product scope is more significant and if one team is not sufficient to handle the development, then the organization may deploy multiple teams, either at the same location or a different location. While each team will have its own scrum master, it is standard practice to deploy a scrum of scrum master to foster the collaboration across the scrum masters and teams and to play a more prominent role in overall development. All the scrum principles and values apply to the scrum of scrum master as well.

Agile Coach

The agile coach teaches the scrum framework and rules to the teams so that they may adopt the agile culture in their organization.

4.9 Blend of Design Thinking, Lean, and Agile

The process of innovation is truly successful when we apply the power of design thinking, lean approach, and agile methodology together. Design thinking powers the ideation and experimentation phase, lean approach fosters the learning environment, and agile methodology helps to break down the complexities and deliver iterative success.

5

Organizational Cultural Transformation

5.1 Barriers to Transformation

The organizational culture is the spirit that guides everyone involved in the process, whether verbally or nonverbally. Culture is the collective mind-set of expectations, experiences, philosophy, values, underlying beliefs, and assumptions that spark inspiration in people. This spirit contributes to the unique social and psychological environment of an organization. The spirit influences how people behave, how things are done, and how things are managed on a daily basis.

"Culture is the collective mind-set of expectations, experiences, philosophy, values, underlying beliefs, and assumptions that spark inspiration in people."

Because the dynamics of the global environment are changing rapidly, customer expectations are also changing rapidly. In order to cope with this fast-changing environment, organizations need to be transformed from their current state. Organizational transformation comes from a shift in the mind-set of an organization's members. When the organization plans transformation initiatives, it will receive three kinds of responses from its members, as follows:

- Some people welcome transformation instantly. In other words, people get inspired by the purpose and vision.
- Some people welcome the transformation with certain incentives. In other words, people get motivated by rewards.
- Some people resist the change.

Start-up companies usually move fast by embracing the disruptive innovations resulting in the disruption of industries. Also, several incumbents are currently transforming themselves to protect themselves and to take part in improving the lives of people in society. The larger incumbents find it difficult to react to the changes happening in the industry and find it challenging to bring any innovative products and services or to adopt innovative products and services. With cultural shifts, an organization can mobilize all its members to take part in the transformation process. There are several reasons for the lag in adopting innovations.

Traditionally, some of the larger incumbents have relied on vendor products to carry out their business operations. Therefore, a change in management is perceived as moving from one product to another, one technology to another, and one process to another. This type of change in management brings only limited and known changes to the organization, though these changes are quick enough to show results.

Transformation, on the other hand, is evolutionary rather than revolutionary. It will not show results quickly. Though specific innovations have the potential to disrupt or create new markets, they are put on the back burner if they are compared with pedestrian projects through a standard budgeting process. The type of leadership that recognizes only short-term results cannot create an environment where creativity and innovation thrive and cannot embrace transformation. Transformation is not about replacing or developing one product, and innovation is not about making money right away. The transformation journey will introduce several frameworks, impacting the existing networks and channels and engaging customers in creating value for the organization. It will open up a number of new revenue sources that will contribute to the organization's profit.

> "The type of leadership that recognizes only short-term benefits cannot create an environment where creativity and innovation thrive and cannot embrace the transformation."

While the incorrect legacy revenue model is one of the barriers to transformation, there are several other barriers pertaining to the organization's and employees' mind-set. In summary, these barriers to transformation include the following:

- Organizational silos (physical or behavioral)
- Resistance to change
- Rigid culture
- Lack of courage to take the risks
- Legacy business models

Let us now discuss how an organization can overcome each of these barriers.

5.2 Collaborating the Silos

One critical aspect that contributes to the success of any innovation or transformation is collaboration. Collaboration is a big challenge at larger organizations because of the presence of silos, whether real or virtual. Even in organizational units where silos do not exist in reality, the people's silo mentality creates some virtual silos within the organizations. This issue is a blend of structural and cultural issues.

In our rapidly changing world, it has become more important to bring diverse minds to the table than in the past. As business is increasingly becoming cross-functional, silos create some unnecessary obstacles for organizations, preventing them from moving forward.

The organizational structure is the framework providing guidelines for managing the business operations. There are two types of organizational structures found in the business environment: centralized and decentralized.

In a centralized organizational structure, a few top individuals typically develop the company's vision and mission and set directions for managers and other employees to follow when achieving the goals.

Start-ups and small business organizations often use a centralized organizational structure since the founders are usually responsible for creating the organizational structure, which typically reflects the founder's personality, management style, and characteristics. Start-ups and small organizations are adaptable to innovations. In such innovative companies, the power stays with the innovative teams. The synergy comes from working together and doing things in unusual ways.

At the same time, the centralized organizational structure in a larger organization can suffer from the adverse effects of layers of bureaucracy. These businesses often have multiple leadership layers stretching from the top to the frontline operations. Business leaders responsible for making every decision in the organization will require more time to accomplish tasks, which can result in slow business operations.

In a decentralized organizational structure, the leaders create the units and define the precise lines of responsibilities to the unit heads. The incentives are structured based on meeting specific goals. Heads of each unit work very hard to try to meet their targets. In this kind of system, each head becomes independent and eventually makes the unit highly independent. By doing this, the organization becomes a collection of independent silos. Decentralized organizations engage a variety of experts to run various operations. A diversified management team helps to ensure the organization has the resources to handle various types of business situations. The power stays hierarchical. While the hierarchies are created with a clear purpose and positive thinking, they sometimes take different directions because of unhealthy power struggles. More often, the hierarchical units develop internal politics and exhibit a lack of coordination with one another. Moreover, those units are relatively low in dynamism and often seem to be risk-averse. The leaders, who are required to move toward innovative thinking, find it a challenge to give up their power.

Sharing the decision-making and involving more minds will actually create more synergies and power. If leaders are serious about taking a company to another level and preparing for future markets, they have to disengage from the power struggles. Decentralized organizations can struggle with multiple individuals having different opinions about a particular business decision. Because of this, these businesses can face difficulties trying to get everyone on the same page when making decisions.

Both the centralized structure and decentralized structure can lead to a siloed structure as they induce some barriers over time, either virtually or really. The virtual barriers are referred to as behavioral silos. These silos can occur anywhere in the organization, but they are most commonly found at the operations level. Silos are the most prominent barriers to transformation. They are the result of outdated business approaches and do not work in the dynamic economy. Despite the uptick in technological advancements, these structural and behavioral barriers can impede communicating a shared vision for transformation.

Behavioral silos at the operations level can bring transformation and growth to an abrupt halt. It takes years for behavioral silos to develop and become entrenched in the corporate culture. Organizations must transform operational behaviors at all levels. The challenge is how to break down behavioral silos and prepare an entire organization to embrace transformation. Indeed, this challenge cannot be addressed overnight. Through a series of steps and in an evolutionary way, organizations can carefully disrupt their business operations. Organizations can break down behavioral silos and embrace the path to transformation by making healthy changes to corporate culture, getting all units involved in the transformation, and keeping the communication channels open.

The solution to overcome the shortcomings of both centralized and decentralized structures and to destroy physical silos is to merge the two and induce collaboration. This will result in a less centralized and less decentralized structure, fostering a culture of trust and relationships.

Transformational leaders cultivate collaboration within the organization, which requires that these leaders transform themselves from the command-and-control style of leadership to collaborative leadership. By empowering teams to work across functional units with the autonomy to make real-time decisions, organizations can move forward amid the ever-changing business landscape.

The mind-set that restricts specific departments from sharing necessary information with others in the same organization will lead to silo mentality, which in turn leads to behavioral silos. This type of mentality will reduce trust and morale in the overall operations and will contribute to the demise of a productive culture.

Complex tasks need to involve larger teams. As the size of a team increases beyond a certain threshold, the tendency to collaborate decreases. In the right environment, large teams can achieve high levels of cooperation, but creating such an environment requires thought and sometimes investment in the capacity for collaboration across the organization.

Challenging tasks that businesses are facing today require the input and expertise of people with diverse views and backgrounds to create cross-fertilization and spark insight and innovation. Unless the environment is healthy, diversity can create problems. The factors that inhibit collaboration include age, educational level, and tenure, among other things. The higher the diversity of background and experience, the less likely the team is to exhibit collaborative behaviors. The responsibility to increase diversity and strengthen the organization's ability to perform complex collaborative tasks resides with the transformational leadership.

Teams collaborate thoroughly when the top leadership invests in supporting social relationships and demonstrates collaborative behavior themselves, what is called "leading by example." This means that the executive teams must be engaged and sit at the forefront, steering the vehicle.

The leadership must formulate the purpose and vision and share them with all levels of employees. The purpose inspires and motivates people. This was discussed in the chapter "Purpose-Driven Vision." Before sharing the purpose and vision, there must be an executive buy-in and core understanding of the organization's long-term goals, objectives, and key initiatives among the leadership team. Such actions encourage trust, create empowerment, and break the leaders out of the "my unit" mentality and move them into the "our organization" mentality. Once the leaders' mentality is changed, it is essential that all members of the leadership teams work together to achieve the common goal.

When the leader shares the responsibility with the people and also shares the vision with them, the people walk with the leader along the path to reach the destination. Shared vision transforms the company from "my company" to "our company." It brings coherence to diverse activities. It allows diverse people to work together. The shared vision helps employees to see their purpose in the workplace. The shared vision strengthens the slogan "Together we can do it," which will drive employee engagement and attract the best talent.

"By empowering teams to work across functional units with the autonomy to make real-time decisions, organizations can move forward amid the ever-changing business landscape."

In addition to managing diversity, the factors that influence the creation of a collaborative culture include the following:

- Right thinking
- Incentive system

- Relationships
- Trust
- Influence
- Transparency

Several forms of wrong thinking include, but are not limited to, the following: First of all, many people think that they need to solve problems on their own without reaching out to others. This is because either they think that reaching out for help will make others feel that they are less competent or they think that they are higher in status. A transparent process defining when to reach out for help and how other people should respond to such requests will reduce the ego issues. People should know that helping each other, especially when it is needed, accelerates the process of solving problems and making decisions. People think that sharing knowledge will make them less powerful and less valuable to the organization. Indeed, sharing knowledge will expose them to many aspects and make them more powerful. Sharing information generously gives others the ability to act confidently and take responsibility for initiating change.

The incentive structure is another factor that makes a culture less collaborative. In a unit-focused incentive structure, people give preference to reaching their own targets and as a result feel pressured to do their own work. They may not have enough time to respond to requests from other units.

One of the results of a tall structure to an organization or organizational unit is hidden competition that is created by people within the units. This results in less collaboration, which happens especially when multiple people are seeking to hold on to responsibility so as to avail themselves of opportunities. From their point of view, they want to add more value to the organization. However, in reality, this action dilutes the net value of the organization because of the redundant processes. The fewer number of silos, with flat organizational structures within each silo, the fewer levels of management, with more people reporting to a single leader. This will help with fast, reliable communication, increased collaboration, and faster decision-making.

Collaborative leadership is about breaking down silos and building trust-based cross-functional relationships. This requires a shift in thinking about who is on the team. Instead of viewing the team as a unit of only direct reports, the leader must learn to embrace a horizontal team consisting of peers. However, leading a horizontal team requires influence and healthy relationships. Leading outside the area of one's responsibility and accountability is the hallmark of collaborative leadership.

"Collaborative leadership is about breaking down silos and building trust-based cross-functional relationships."

The flat structure requires fewer leaders but expects everyone on the team to behave as a collaborative leader. This allows individuals to take more responsibility, which gives them increased accountability for decision-making and the power to initiate change. This is the right choice for an organization, as many people within the organization want to become leaders and expect to take on the responsibility to lead.

Letting go of control and sharing power gives others the opportunity to develop their leadership skills. Transformational leaders must focus intensely on the development of collaborative leaders at all levels of the organization by allowing everyone to act as a leader. The best way of developing leaders with less investment and embracing collaborative leadership is to give people leadership experience and make them lead outside their comfort zone.

It is imperative to recognize that overcollaboration can cost an organization a lot. In an overcollaborative environment, people spend more time on meetings, sharing ideas, and having conversations with the people they like without having a strong reason to do so. When managers involve too many people in every single decision, the outcome will suffer because of the prolonged decision-making time. The fact is that not every decision requires the entire department to be present for discussion and debate. Some decision-making processes cannot include other members because those members do not possess the necessary information on account of confidentiality agreements.

5.3 Removing Change Resistance

As discussed in the previous section, silos create barriers to communication. Even within the silos, people prefer to work independently with a silo mentality and a highly competitive spirit. This is one of the most significant challenges that transformational leaders face when attempting to foster collaboration among the people within an organization. Success is not possible without changing the behavior of the people throughout the organization.

There are several other reasons why people resist the change, as follows:

- People fear that any administrative or technological changes will result in their role being eliminated or reduced.
- For some people, the reward is more important. The reward will motivate them to support the change over the long term.
- The change process involves a lot of unknown factors. A large number of unknown factors will create fear among people.
- If the change effort is taking place in an environment where most of the people working with the change process mistrust each other, then the program will see only limited success or will fail ultimately.
- Because of organizational politics, certain people with an organization sometimes try to prove that a decision is wrong regardless of its authenticity and value. Also, some people think that they will lose some power in the organizational restructuring.
- Changes deal with many uncertainties. Some people do not like to deal with uncertainties.

- The change process requires more work, and people are often overloaded mainly because of the inevitable unanticipated glitches in the middle of change.

- Lack of competence is another reason. Change in organizations requires changes in skills, and some people think that they will not be able to make the transition very well.

Recent developments in cognitive science can help the transforming organization take into account the physiological nature of the brain. This research helps us to understand why some people resist certain types of changes. It explains why many organizational change initiatives fail. We discussed the neuroscience of creativity in chapter 3. Here let us discuss the neuroscience of leadership.

Organizational change provokes a feeling of physiological discomfort even when it is in the organization's best interests to change. This feeling is closely related to human working memory and its relationship to conscious attention. When the brain senses something new, the working memory takes that new information and matches it against the old. This activates the prefrontal, cortex which is an energy-intensive part of the brain.

The routine activities that we perform on a daily basis are performed in the basal ganglion without our consciously paying attention. The basal ganglion is sometimes referred to as the habit center of the brain. The activities performed in this part of the brain require much less energy compared to those of the working memory. This is because over time, with training and experience, the brain makes specific patterns and links everyday actions with these patterns. These basal ganglia can function without conscious thought. The working memory, on the other hand, can hold only a limited amount of information at any one time and tries to reject any new information. The repetitive activities get pushed down into the basal ganglion, freeing up the processing resources of the prefrontal cortex. Trying to change hardwired habits requires much attention.

Trying to alter routine behaviors sends out persuasive messages to the brain that something is wrong, which causes the brain to reject the new thought process. Change thus amplifies stress and discomfort. This is what any strategic or organizational changes that appear new make people feel uncomfortable and thus cause them to avoid the change.

Many change programs underestimate the challenges inherent in implementation. One of the goals for a change program is to establish trust in the members and then convince them of the value of the change. When leaders act like coaches, instead of command-control leaders, then it is easier for the people to digest the desired goals, which causes the brain to make the pattern easily and quickly.

Flexible thinking that welcomes change can be practiced simply by paying attention. In the brain, neurons communicate with each other with electrochemical signaling driven by the movement of ions such as sodium, potassium, and calcium. These ions travel a very short distance through channels within the brain, that distance being about a single ion wide. Paying attention to any specific activity repetitively over time makes the brain keep the appropriate circuitry open and alive. These circuits then eventually lead to stable physical changes in the brain's structure. This means that paying continuous attention to a given activity reshapes the patterns of the brain. Among the implications is that practicing a specialty every day helps people to think differently and makes them feel no pain when coming up with a diverse set of ideas. It also makes them welcome change.

Perceptions play a crucial role in adjusting to a new environment. Expectations play a role in forming perceptions. Large-scale transformations require a different perception. Therefore, the mental maps that relate expectations to perceptions require some kind of event that causes people to change their attitudes and expectations more quickly than they usually would. Repeated, purposeful, and focused attention can lead to long-lasting personal evolution. Useful insights need to be generated from within.

The moment of insight is well-known to be a positive and energizing experience. This is what helps people fight against the internal forces that try to keep change from occurring, including the fear response of the amygdala. The neural networks are influenced moment to moment by genes, experiences, and varying patterns of attention.

There are several levels of resistance. While new ideas usually encounter resistance from the majority of people, they are still acceptable to some early adopters. Once these people are on board and begin to feel comfortable, the people with the next level of resistance start giving the new thing a try. As each threshold is passed, the next group becomes more likely to adopt the new idea. That is how disruption happens.

5.4 Redefining the Culture

The organizational culture is vital to the success of any transformation initiative. As has been discussed in several parts of *The Art and Science of Transformational Leadership*, transformation deals heavily with VUCA (volatility, uncertainty, complexity, and assumptions). The traditional way of thinking and behaving that is successful in a low-risk environment does not fit well with the initiatives that are associated with VUCA factors. Transformation deals with strategies, architectures, systems, processes, and technologies that are radically different from their traditional peers. Without adopting the fundamental principles that are needed for the success of transformational initiatives, the initiatives are likely to fail.

There is a strong correlation between employee performance and inspiring organizational culture, as the culture will influence the behaviors that matter most.

To transform the culture, leaders should transform themselves first according to the "lead by example" philosophy. Because the organization's culture is built on the pillars of emotion and influence, the executives who work within the organization can accelerate positive change. When positive culture and strategic priorities are in sync, employees can draw energy and increase the momentum to gain a competitive advantage. Culture is not something that can change overnight. Since culture deals with work habits and emotional responses, it cannot be borrowed from other organizations. Since culture is not tangible to define, change is not measurable easily. However, it can be observed easily. As it is with any transformation, the cultural shift must be steady and gradual. Without the involvement, cooperation, and feedback of the members, transformation initiatives cannot gain momentum. People at all levels—leaders, managers, and employees—must support the cultural shifts.

Transformational programs should not completely ignore the traditional business goals of larger organizations. The goal is to maintain a balance between the business goals and the agility that is needed for transformation.

In the hyperconnected world of business, more dots to be connected are involved, increasing uncertainty and creating much more fear in the workplace. In some cases, innovation and transformation can lead to an unknown state. So, the fear factor is not about the fact that something will be lost but about the unknown state. This requires every organization to have an entrepreneurial spirit and to take responsible risks. It requires transformational leaders to have the courage to embrace transformation. The rewards that courage returns are customer and employee happiness and improved quality of life for people within society. The sense of fear makes people maintain the status quo. It blocks an organization's ability to move forward. Fear keeps millions of individuals from reaching their potential. Transformational leaders must create a courageous culture where people can think creatively, present innovative ideas, and challenge the status quo. Employees should not be afraid to escalate certain matters, especially if they are affecting the customer and/or the work environment. It takes courage for employees to communicate the message to senior management that clutter and toxins need to be removed from the organization's culture.

"Fear keeps millions of individuals from reaching their potential."

As the transformation process is associated with risks, some failures at various stages of innovation are common in the business world. Even if the founders and key stakeholders have a tolerance for failure, the same is not true of most employees. Employees want a perfect track record, and therefore they feel uncomfortable with failure. The organizational leadership should take necessary steps to ensure that teams feel empowered.

It is evident that a courageous culture amid a transformational project management office should take specific fundamental steps. These are as follows:

- Embrace intuition.
- Implement a fail-fast strategy with idea experimentation and agile development.
- Be proactive.

In the case of start-ups, entrepreneurs have the willingness to go outside their comfort zones for something they believe in to come up with disruptive ideas. These entrepreneurs-cum-leaders have the courage to create a vision and make the tough decisions required to achieve the vision. They have the flexibility to make corrections as the culture of their business evolves.

"To be a successful entrepreneur, you must have the willingness to go outside your comfort zone for something you believe in and come up with disruptive ideas."

In the case of large incumbents, the culture is well matured. The people at all levels already feel comfortable with the current practices. However, the current practices of the culture cannot last forever and will likely become irrelevant at some point in time.

Undoubtedly, leaders who are trying to change the status quo will face challenges. First of all are the challenges that come in the form of criticism. Transformational leaders should be ready to face and manage criticism. Challenging the status quo and facing criticism takes an extraordinary amount of courage. Leaders who do this have to be creative thinkers and passionate leaders who are not afraid of failure.

The transformational leader should make everyone in the organization think like a leader regardless of their title. Titles will not help people to achieve goals. They only let other people who those with the titles are. If such people are not doing justice to their titles by exhibiting poor leadership qualities, then the titles have no meaning. A courageous environment will foster innovation and make people learn, adapt, and flourish. As discussed in the earlier section "Neuroscience of Courage," courage is developed over time through practice. In risk-averse cultures, people take risks only if those risks are assessed and found to be safe to assume. By cultivating a culture of courage in which people feel secure enough to move outside their comfort zones and take risks, organizations achieve an extraordinary result.

"By cultivating a culture of courage in which people feel secure enough to move outside their comfort zones and take risks, organizations achieve an extraordinary result."

As discussed in an earlier section, the things that make people feel fear are not necessarily real threats. Unknown elements are behind most fear. When there are unknown elements, people sometimes feel fear because they do not yet have answers to all their questions. Exploring the space beyond the known area will lead people to get the answers they seek. People should show the courage to go beyond industry boundaries and conventional wisdom to seek solutions to unconventional challenges. Transferring the control and responsibility to the team and giving them the chance to lead will give them the courage to take risks. Transformational leaders must hold their employees accountable and responsible but not make them victims or blame them for failure. Room for failing can be created by employing a framework that minimizes the cost of failure. This is the key to the "fail fast and cheap" strategy. Not every risk is worth taking. The fail-fast strategy will encourage people to let go of unwanted risk quickly.

"Not every risk is worth taking. Failing fast and cheap will encourage people to let go of unwanted risk quickly."

Traditional project management office (PMO) practices need to be transformed radically to foster a culture of courage. The traditional project management offices operate within a governance structure that requires detailed business cases, substantial evidence for the expected returns, and reduced levels of risk. In a risk-averse cultures, the chances of getting approval for innovation projects are low, exposing a business to real risk that could ultimately be avoided.

The modern transformational project management office should incorporate a risk-taking culture by reframing the governance structure that supports design thinking and agile development. Both design thinking and agile development are critical to implementing innovative initiatives and managing risk with courage. In a traditional project management office, once risks are identified, innovation often stops. However, a clear-eyed view of risks balanced against benefits can create an environment where innovation is nurtured rather than killed. The transformational project management office governance framework should encourage a business model based on both value creation and value capture instead of merely relying on value capture. The decision of whether or not the budget should be extended should be made based on whether the results of the experiment are aligned with the organizational strategy.

Research and development programs and employees' commitment to the organization's mission will go to waste if the business is not managed with courageous leadership. It requires bold decisions and a renewed entrepreneurial spirit to build a great global company.

Some organizational leaders lack courage because they focus too much on managing to reach their financial goals. They avoid making risky decisions because they fear failure and think that the mistakes may make them look bad in the eyes of their critics.

Divergent thinking leads a person to explore the areas beyond conventional borders. As discussed in the chapter "Igniting Creativity," divergent thinking, an essential aspect of creativity, is the ability to come up with several answers to the same question. To explore things divergently beyond the usual scope, one should break the rules. That means one should step outside the box, leaving all previous experiences, mind-sets, and attitudes behind, and start to see things from an entirely different perspective. Outside-the-box, unfiltered, unbiased thinking, openness to suggestions, and willingness to empathize with others' feelings will open the gates to a flood of ideas.

"To be successful transfromational leader, one should step outside the box by leaving all past experiences, mind-sets, and attitudes behind and start to see things from an entirely different perspective."

Although the human brain is well adapted to respond to risk, it is not so skilled at sorting out which current risks to worry about. The problem is that our emotions make lightning-fast assessments about risk without giving our brains a chance to think. This causes the brain to focus on loss aversion as it tries to protect us from harm. That means the brain becomes hyper-analytical. It recalls past instances of failure to keep us safe, which will make us become demotivated and less inclined to take any action. Loss aversion is more powerful than greed. The reward pathway that releases feel-good chemicals when we do something novel overrides loss aversion and encourages risk-taking. By cultivating a more human-centered and compassionate approach to leadership, one becomes a more courageous leader. The risk-averse environment drives people to make decisions based on the fear of what could go wrong when deviating from the commitment instead of on the hope of what could go right and empower us and others.

Missed opportunities lead to regrets. For example, Nokia could have innovated to dominate the smartphone market, and Yahoo could have sold to Microsoft much earlier. Courage makes a leader challenge conventional wisdom and imagine new possibilities, making innovation and transformation possible.

Jeff Bezos has courageously led Amazon from an e-commerce bookseller to a device producer. Courage comes from caring genuinely about achieving a shared vision.

"Outside-the-box, unfiltered, unbiased thinking, openness to suggestions, and willingness to empathize with others' feelings will open the gates to a flood of ideas."

No readily available framework guides leaders to embrace cultural transformation. However, there are a few basic principles that any organization needs to adapt, as discussed throughout *The Art and Science of Transformational Leadership*. These principles will help when developing governance methodologies tailored to transformational programs.

What are the primary principles that contribute to a healthy organizational culture? They are as follows:

1. Define the purpose statement and articulate it to everyone involved in the process. Purpose statements should exist at all levels of the transformation program, including the top level, and should describe why the transformation is needed and what is needed at every sublevel.
2. Create the vision statement articulating what the desired state is, and set the course to reach the desired state.
3. Foster creativity among all employees. Encourage all employees to exhibit curiosity and observation.
4. Enable innovations by way of creativity and experimentation.
5. Adopt design thinking to foster a culture of experimentation.
6. Foster collaboration to create synergies.

7. Initial funding for a product should be based on a good idea and an underlying cause, not on endless rounds of analysis.
8. Prepare employees to take responsible risks.
9. Adopt a fail-fast strategy, and do not punish people for failures.
10. Make everyone think like an entrepreneur, which will make them intrapreneurs.
11. Encourage empathy in designing the products and services.
12. Encourage faster decision-making and approvals.
13. Adopt agile development approaches.

5.5 Embracing the Courage to Take Risks

Courage and the mechanism to embrace the courage will be discussed in chapter 7: Courage to Take Risks.

5.6 Transforming Business Models

A business model is defined as a way of creating and capturing value by business organizations. It is a system where various features interact, often in complex ways, to determine business success. The economic benefit of transformation cannot be quantified using traditional revenue models. Transformation indirectly creates much value, yielding the slow long-term benefit. The traditional revenue model relies on the equation Revenue = Price × Volume. This model works best if the goal is to replace an existing product or to develop a new product. Most innovations are difficult to explain in terms of return on investment. A business model is required when a company is undergoing transformation. Business model transformation will be discussed in chapter 14.

6

Inspiring People

6.1 Inspiration and Motivation

One of the most important traits for any leader to possess is the ability to inspire people. Inspiration sparks passion in the leader, passion fuels the purpose, purpose drives the vision, and vision makes the leader think creatively and innovatively to embrace the desired transformation. Inspiration awakens the person to think beyond experiences and limitations and seek out new possibilities.

"Inspiration sparks passion in the leader, passion fuels the purpose, purpose drives the vision, and vision makes the leader think creatively and innovatively to embrace the desired transformation."

The word *inspiration* comes from "in spirit." That is, inspiration comes from within. Sometimes we use the words *inspire* and *motivate* interchangeably. Though they may seem related, they are indeed as different as *push* and *pull*. The word *motivate* is derived from *motive*, or *moto*, which is an external force that makes us perform tasks. Motivation pushes us to work through stressful situations to achieve the result. That means a result motivates us. For example, a well-defined reward motivates people to undertake certain activities. On the other hand, inspiration pulls us toward something that stirs our hearts, minds, or spirits. Inspiration is an energy that is buried deep in the unconscious. Several things help to draw that energy out. It can be a person, an event, an environment, a movie, or a book. These things may not explicitly ask us to do certain things, but we draw inspiration from them and act on our own. They give us the positive energy to develop passion. When we are tuned into the spirit, we are drawn to do whatever feels best. Motivation is external, whereas inspiration is internal. This does not mean that motivation is a negative factor. It gives much energy to people and pushes them toward a goal. It keeps on reminding the person what he or she is supposed to do.

"Motivation and inspiration are as different as push and pull. Motivation pushes us to work through stressful situations to achieve a result. Inspiration pulls us toward something that stirs our hearts, minds, or spirits."

Inspired people think in an unconventional manner and achieve unusual things. It is not about self-interest as many people commonly think. A desire for money or status does not drive inspiration. The goal takes hold of a person. The time investment prepares the person for inspiration and yields the return that the individual desires. We do not need external motivation if we are filled with inspiration. Inspiration fuels people, transforming a concern into a possibility and transforming the way we think about our capabilities. When we are void of inspiration, it is a reward system that will motivate us and move us forward, toward a defined end state.

"Inspiration awakens a person to think beyond experiences and limitations and to seek out new possibilities."

The priority for the transformational leader is to inspire employees to become infused with energy, passion, and commitment and connect them with the direction and mission. Inspired employees perform well and are more productive. Historically inspiration has been treated as a supernatural or divine power. While this may be true, the latest research and developments in neuroscience show that inspiration can be activated to have a significant effect on relevant outcomes.

"Inspiration fuels people, changing a concern into a possibility, and transforms the way we think about our capabilities."

Organizations will see a real breakthrough in creativity and innovation when employees are inspired instead of merely engaged. Inspired employees will, in turn, inspire those around them to strive for higher heights. Organizations invest millions of dollars in leadership training to enhance the soft skills that inspire, motivate, and create a positive environment. However, most of these training initiatives do not show any noticeable results. A little one-hour or two-hour session during a busy time will not help people pay attention or focus.

"Organizations will see a real breakthrough in creativity and innovations when employees are inspired instead of merely engaged."

How to inspire people? While specialized training can give a high-level idea of inspiration and motivation, there are practical ways to spark inspiration in people, as follows:

- Share the clear purpose of the activity.
- Bring out the passion in people.
- Share the vision.
- Encourage people at all times.
- Lead by example.
- Follow ethics and principles.
- Expect the highest contribution from the team.
- Challenge the team to show courage.

- Care for people.
- Share the power
- Sharing the credit.
- Foster team integrity.

Purpose and vision were discussed in an earlier chapter. However, we will discuss them here in the context of team building. Courage will be discussed in chapter 7.

6.2 Purpose and Passion

Most people want to know why they are doing what they have been asked to do. They care less about the how. This is a problem for certain talented people who have well-advanced technology skills and exhibit proof of concept with the potential to develop disruptive products. When they approach investors for funding, they fail to explain why the product needed. While the investors are more interested in knowing why it is being developed, the people who actually develop the product keep discussing how they are doing it. The dreams of prospective entrepreneurs who have good ideas come to an end when they fail to inspire investors by neglecting to openly communicate the benefit of the idea. Similarly, employees want to understand the benefit. It is not about how much they receive in compensation. The soft matters like the purpose will boost their productivity. They will get more excited when they know that the initiative is going to have a direct impact on the lives of people in society. Human biology instills us with the desire for a sense of purpose and meaning in the work we do, beyond the monetary reward, either in professional life or personal life.

Transformational leaders should enlarge the context for employees so that they can see *why* they are doing what they are doing through a bigger lens and reframe their role, not only in the context of how it contributes to the organization but also in the context of how it serves society at large.

> "Human biology instills us with the desire for a sense of purpose and meaning in the work we do, beyond the monetary reward, either in professional life or personal life."

When people know that they are valued and their work is valuable, they will approach the challenge with greater tenacity than they otherwise would. Knowing the purpose brings out the passion in people. Having a purpose makes people develop a passion for new things. If there is one word that describes something that a successful leader can work on over and over again without getting bored, that word is *passion*. A passion is something that people enjoy the most and want to continue doing for the rest of their lives. Passion fuels the creative and innovative fire. Passion encourages people to undertake new challenges, engage in creative thinking, participate in ideation sessions to develop new skills, and solve the problems in a challenging environment. It is the intangible component and the most underrated trait that explains why some people and teams can stick with their plans and achieve higher levels of success. Successful people in the present day and throughout history have had a deep source of energy and a passion for what they do. When building teams, the leaders attract talented people who are passionate about what they do. Passionate people listen to their hearts, work hard, and trust their intuition. Passionate people believe that without following their passion, life would be without color, joy, or meaning. Passionate people, overall, do live happier and better lives than the average individual.

> "When people know that they are valued and their work is valuable, they will approach the challenge with greater tenacity than they otherwise would."

Passion makes people growth oriented. It is evident that the passionate leader leads significantly different from his or her peers who are less passionate. Passionate leaders maximize the energy of the team with their high mentoring skills and make the team more dynamic and valuable. The passionate leader displays confidence, and this confidence creates value for them and the team. Passionate people have a stronger desire and curiosity to understand everything about the industry in which they work, which will put them ahead of the game and cause them to be in demand. Passion is an essential ingredient for leaders in delivering high-quality products and services, motivating employees to have a positive outlook, and embracing a positive culture and results. Passion sparks happiness. Passion drives people toward change. They get excited when they see new things. That is why some leaders like to facilitate change and why some leaders like to see change.

Passionate people do things differently, as follows:

- They start their days early.
- They always have their passions on their mind.
- They get excited more than the average person.
- They digest negative emotions.
- They get emotional more than the average person.
- They are willing to take more responsible risks.
- They devote their lives to their dreams.
- They surround themselves with their work.
- They talk about their projects.
- They tend to be either pushing ahead full throttle or are entirely still.
- They always think positively about the future.
- They connect the past and future with the present.

Let us discuss some of the neuroscientific aspects of passion. Two things that help create passion are exploration and connection. The brain has two neurotransmitters called dopamine and oxytocin that reinforce exploration and connection. When we explore challenges, the brain releases dopamine, which gives us a sense of pleasure and increases our motivation. Dopamine drives our passion. Passion makes people explore more. When we connect with other like-minded people, the brain releases oxytocin. Oxytocin makes people empathetic and generous. These two behaviors will, in turn, reinforce the release of oxytocin.

As we repeat the process of exploration and connection again and again, these two neurotransmitters are released more and more. Because the brain is plastic in nature, it forms patterns over the time. The brain becomes better adapted to pursuing passion more effectively. Passion changes the brain, and then the brain makes the person pursue more passion and get results faster.

The inspiration sets the purpose, and the purpose makes the person explore and connect, generating dopamine and oxytocin to drive the passion and providing the sustained focus required to fulfill the dreams.

6.3 Shared Vision

As discussed in the chapter "Purpose-Driven Vision," transformational leaders must have a vision for the organization. However, this is not enough; leaders must also share that vision with other leaders across the organization and communicate it accordingly. By sharing the vision organization-wide, founders and top-level leaders ensure that the founder's mentality is upheld and make all other leaders feel ownership of the entity. Sharing the vision is as important as creating the vision.

Because of the nature of transformational projects, and especially in the case of larger organizations, there must be a vision at every project level. While this is aligned with the corporate vision, the goals and strategies for different parts of the organization can vary slightly. Moreover, they are more specific to the work being performed.

By thinking ahead and looking into the future, leaders design a strategy and create a culture that can withstand change and any potential volatility encountered along the transformation journey.

Shared visions are created with the involvement of key people such as direct reports who are associated with the process. The vision helps the team understand how the leader envisions the future, and then the team can help the leader to create the goals, so together they can manifest the end goals of the vision. The best way to lead people into the future is to connect them to the present through a shared vision. Sharing the vision means sharing the responsibility and goals so that people come together to travel along the road of transformation.

"The best way to lead people into the future is to connect them to the present through a shared vision."

So how does a shared vision inspire people? When a leader gives a speech without sharing the vision, anticipating that the people will get inspired, the people may stand up and say, "Yes, we are with you," but later sit back down and wait for the leader to take the action.

On the other hand, if the leader shares responsibility with the people and also shares the vision with them, the people will walk with the leader along the path to reach the destination.

Shared vision transforms the company from "my company" to "our company." It brings coherence to diverse activities. It allows diverse people to work together. A shared vision helps employees to see their purpose in the workplace. A shared vision strengthens the slogan "Together we can do it," which will drive employee engagement and attract the best talent.

"If the leader shares responsibility with the people and also shares the vision with them, the people walk with the leader along the path to reach the destination."

6.4 Encouragement

Encouragement is a process and one of the must-have qualities for leaders. Encouragement focuses on an individual's strengths and contributions. It drives people's motivations and brings out the best in them. When people are encouraged, they feel valued.

Business magnate Richard Branson once said, "When you lavish praise on people, they flourish; criticize, and they shrivel up."

Indeed, some people within an organization, regardless of their titles, make a positive difference. It is social nature that people want to be involved in challenging activities. People feel accomplished when they are encouraged to be part of challenging activities. Still, many people have great talent but lack the ability and courage to face challenges. Encouragement helps them to take risks and move toward positive change.

"People feel accomplished when they are encouraged to be part of challenging activities."

For transformational leaders, it is crucial to have an understanding of human behavior and how people are motivated. Encouragement gives positive energy to people. Many people, either in the workplace or elsewhere, feel that they need an encouraging leader to be around when they need a lift. A few words can have a powerful lasting impact to drive better commitment. When leaders make people feel more valuable, capable, and motivated, people reach their potential, and their lives change for the better.

Many people feel rewarded when they are assigned challenging tasks. As we know, not all rewards can be monetized, but many rewards are more valuable than money. Playing a role in solving challenging problems, whether in an organization or society, is one such reward.

"When leaders make people feel more valuable, capable, and motivated, people reach their potential, and their lives change for the better."

It is not always necessary to micromanage the whole organization. And anyway, a leader does not have enough time to do so. A leader should focus on fostering a more engaged, trusting, and productive environment. This can be done by identifying the people with better leadership qualities and encouraging them to take the initiative. Transformational leaders who have influential leaders on their team can delegate some tasks without having to worry about how they will get done or who will do them.

Trusting people and giving them the opportunity to make some meaningful decisions will bring out their leadership qualities and improve their productivity. Assigning them tasks outside their comfort zones gives them the opportunity to build confidence. With this confidence, they will learn to seek answers on their own.

Transformational projects require a lot of flexibility and agility in the business environment. Traditional projects have more formal and rigid rules, which create walls to innovative thinking. It is evident that a positive environment fuels creative minds, the give-and-take of others, experimentation, and risk-taking. Creativity and innovations depend on a great deal of freethinking and the freedom to play. In an environment where freethinking is encouraged, creativity flourishes.

Other Factors That Inspire People:

- In reality, people want to contribute more than what is expected of them. Increasing their expected contribution will inspire people.

- Caring for people authentically, treating them well, and interacting with them with pleasure will inspire people. People get inspired when their leader listens to the people around them and shows that their ideas are worth hearing,

- Minimal room for politics and gossip in the workplace.

- Sharing the credit for good things with the entire team, and taking the blame for the bad things.

- The leader talking about the people who have inspired him or her and using quotations from the books.

- Instead of telling the people exactly what to do by giving precise directions, the leader should empower them to be their best.

In summary, inspiring leaders take a particular interest in people, talk about their hopes, dreams, and interests, and help them to feel engaged and to thrive.

6.5 Leading by Example

To transform an organization or any assignment that a leader is undertaking, the leader should transform herself first by leading by example. The leader should act as a role model for the transformation. Leadership is not merely a title. Some of the most celebrated leaders in history, like Mahatma Gandhi and Steve Jobs, led by example. Leading by example requires leaders to commit and live a life that reflects their leadership message.

"To transform an organization, the leader should transform herself first by leading by example."

Mahatma Gandhi once said, "You must be the change you wish to see in the world." Gandhi established the methodology of nonviolence to drive the freedom movement, and he followed that methodology throughout his life.

Steve Jobs led by example by following his passion. Jobs once said, "People with passion can change the world." Steve Jobs's passion for music led him to transform Apple into the dominant technology company.

When Jobs returned to Apple, he had an idea for a product that would help people to consume music digitally. Within a few years of his return back, Apple designed, developed, and sold over three hundred million iPods and ten billion tracks via the iTunes Store.

Since an organization's culture is built on the pillars of emotions and influence, executives who work with these pillars can accelerate positive change. When positive culture and strategic priorities are in sync, employees can draw energy from them and accelerate the momentum to gain a competitive advantage. The leaders who lead by example seek answers required for empathy and sense their own success and failure. By having an in-depth and broader understanding of the industry and the business, a leader can work alongside the team.

Leading by example serves as both mirror and window in that it helps leaders to reflect on themselves continuously and make course corrections. It also practically demonstrates to the people how they should behave and act. That is what makes reciprocity so powerful. The organizations must have tools and mechanisms to track lead-by-example examples that occur inside the organization and incorporate these as an essential leadership development metric. Exploring the better ways of leading by example is central to a healthy culture of leadership development.

The "lead by example" principle is not just limited to the leaders of an organization but also applies to the organization itself. Organizations must demonstrate to their customers that they are doing what they are asking their customers to do. When companies say one thing to the customers but do another themselves, they erode trust. Let us take a simple example: a company that advertises that it is a pioneer in digital transformation projects and helps customers to implement their digital capabilities. To make the customer believe, first the organization should show them what digital capabilities they have in place. A company that is using legacy technologies from a decade ago in a traditional manner cannot ask their customers to grant them their business.

6.6 Principles and Ethics

Principles and ethics help leaders a great deal in problem-solving, decision-making, and making judgments. Principles and ethics are somewhat related, but indeed they are different.

Principles are a set of laws that serve as a foundation for an entity or a person. They are centered on society, individuals, systems, philosophy, and more. They can even be scientific and engineering related. In the case of the business world, principles guide entities in devising strategy and making decisions.

Ethics, on the other hand, are principles related to morals. With this in mind, the ethical leadership culture is a work environment that is governed by the principle of fostering morals rather than power. Ethical leaders will not use their power over people but will share the power among people. Ethical leadership engages in ethical conduct based on what is right or wrong for members of society.

While traditional leadership or transactional leadership is based on rigid rules, there is a need to alter those rules in the case of transformational leadership to make the journey more agile and adaptable. This does not mean that transformational leaders should violate the rules. It means that during the journey, leaders should adopt ethical leadership, which will shield them from any angular deviations by following ethics. Ethical leadership will guide a leader to make changes to the rules that benefit the organization and the broader society. This is the reason why some transformational leaders encounter critics who state that transformational leadership is unethical. Critics claim that transformational leadership is based on emotions rather than reason. They also claim that it violates the principles of an organization and manipulates the organization's followers. Altering the rules based on what is right and wrong should not be considered unethical.

One of the best parts of transformational leadership that inspires people is the leader's respect for ethics. Critics of transformational leaders fail to assess the positive aspects of transformational leadership. Some of the positive aspects are inspiration, motivation, the courage to take risks, and willingness to disrupt the industry to bring about radical positive changes to people's lives.

True transformational leaders inspire society by serving as moral agents and expanding the freedom to work toward a noble cause and ethical outcomes. The transformational leader uplifts the morals of his or her followers by sharing rewarding visions of success and empowering them to convert these visions into realities.

"True transformational leaders inspire society by serving as moral agents and expanding the freedom to work toward a noble cause and ethical outcomes."

Transformational leaders expect ethics-based behavior from everyone in the workforce, not for convenience but to make the difficult transformational initiatives successful. When there are no principles set explicitly, the people involved in the transformation journey should, at a minimum follow these principles:

- Employees should assume ownership.
- Strategic perspective should be aligned with the purpose, vision, and mission.
- People must be self-accountable for their behaviors.
- There must be a focus on respectful behavior that builds high self-esteem in everyone.
- Maintain integrity.
- Build trust.

6.7 Inspirational Lessons from Transformational Leaders

Several famous personalities from history transformed either industry or the country, or even the world. Some of them are Mahatma Gandhi, Martin Luther King Jr., Thomas Edison, Stephen Hawking, and Steve Jobs. Their life stories continue to inspire the world.

Mahatma Gandhi

Mahatma Gandhi was a believer in nonviolence. Noninjury to any form of life was his belief, and he never sacrificed it, not even during his political career. The weapon of Satyagraha was to him nothing but the recognition of God and his attribute of love. Gandhi refused to be violent despite many provocations. When a fanatic Afghan tried to harm him, he was bold enough to forgive the fellow because he was a fool who could not distinguish between justice and injustice. Gandhi forgave the man who threw a bomb at his prayer meeting at Delhi because the fellow was a madman and could not judge his action according to his conscience.

Martin Luther King Jr.

The following famous quote from Martin Luther King Jr. stands well for transformational initiatives:

"The ultimate measure of a man is not where he stands in moments of comfort and convenience, but where he stands at times of challenge and controversy."

King's famous speech "I Have a Dream" implicitly tells us that the dream is more significant than the goal. His actions showed the importance of his beliefs and philosophy. He continued practicing nonviolence throughout his life amid death threats, assaults, and more than twenty arrests. He called for people to stand in the light of creative altruism rather than amid the darkness of destructive selfishness. The dream reminds organizational leaders that just transforming an organization is not enough; the organization should help to transform communities, nations, and the world.

Thomas Edison

There is a famous quote from Thomas Edison, "Our greatest weakness lies in giving up. The most certain way to succeed is always to try just one more time."

Giving up is what has stopped many people from changing the world. There are so many people in history who gave up when they were very close to success. Edison failed several thousand times before he invented the light bulb. Many people criticized him, saying that he was wasting his time, but the ultimate results were more than one thousand patents, including one for the light bulb and another for the phonograph.

Stephen Hawking

Stephen Hawking has an exciting inspirational life story. One of his famous quotes reflects his life story:

"However difficult life may seem, there is always something you can do and succeed at."

Hawking was diagnosed with ALS disease at the age of twenty-one, but he decided not to give up and to do his best for as long as he lived. Having to sit in a wheelchair and speak through a synthesizer, he had overcome an obstacle doctors never thought he would, living for forty-eight years with ALS. Surprisingly he became an exceptional role model. Moreover, he continued to give his best to the fields of cosmology and quantum gravity, discovering things about black holes, creating a theorem of general relativity, et cetera.

Steve Jobs

Steve Jobs is another inspirational person who transformed his company and several other industries simultaneously.

> "The people who are crazy enough to think they can change the world are the ones who do."
>
> —Apple's "Think Different" commercial, 1997

In 1985 Steve Jobs was ousted by Apple, the same company that he had cofounded in a garage in 1976. He returned to Apple in 1997 when Apple was close to bankruptcy. His passion, simplicity, intensity, and extreme emotionalism transformed Apple. He was serving the company even when he was battling his final illness. There are several inspirational aspects that anyone in business can draw from his life. Real lessons from Steve Jobs have to be drawn from looking at what he accomplished. After Jobs returned to Apple, he reviewed an array of computers and peripherals and several versions of them that the company was producing. He first applied simplicity to the list of products and asked the team to focus on just four types of products in matrix, customer, and pro in both desktop and portable formats. He took an extraordinary interest in cutting the clutter and released the iPod with a simple interface, which was indeed a turning point for Apple. Steve Jobs believed that the best way to achieve simplicity was through a productive ecosystem that helps to integrate hardware, software, and peripheral devices seamlessly. Such a system made more complex tasks such as making new playlists simpler by allowing the iPod to have fewer functions and buttons. Steve Jobs's passion was to build an enduring company where people are motivated to make great products. Everything else, including profit, was secondary to him. That passion drove the company to become the most profitable.

Steve Jobs did not believe in focus groups, as he thought that customers do not know what they want until they have seen it. However, he was able to see from the customers' eyes and think from their minds and introduce exciting products. Caring about the customers does not require continually asking them what they want. The intuition we develop can help to serve them better. Steve Jobs could push people beyond their comfort zones and do the impossible. He inspired his team to change computer history with a small fraction of the resources used by significant incumbents. Steve Jobs inspired the people at Apple, exhibiting the desire to envision an overarching strategy on the one hand and focusing on the minute details of product design on the other hand. He inspired society by combining the humanities with science. He connected the dots among humanities, sciences, creativity, technology, the arts, engineering, and more. There are excellent technologists, and yes, there are better artists. However, there are not many people with these combined skills. Steve Jobs was able to bring out people's skills in a way that jolted innovation, as he had an intuitive feel for business strategy.

7

Courage to Take Risks

7.1 Why Be Courageous?

"Courage is the ability to confront fear, uncertainty, or intimidation." The process of innovation and transformation deals with VUCA (volatility, uncertainty, complexity, and ambiguity). We cannot see opportunities in the absence of VUCA. With this in mind, transformational leaders should be happy when they encounter VUCA so that they can transform the environment into a more meaningful and healthy one. However, to deal with these factors requires courage. Courage makes innovation and transformation possible. Courage leads a person toward unconventional thinking and outside-the-box thinking. Skilled people must take risks to solve significant problems and innovate.

"Courage leads a person toward unconventional thinking and outside-the-box thinking."

With traditional project management methodologies, the risk is typically managed by the framework RAID (risks, assumptions, issues, and dependencies) that helps to document how risks are mitigated and managed. RAID requires creating a governance system that monitors the risks and indicates when those risks need to be escalated to senior management.

Commonly, there is a high magnitude of risks and a high number of known and unknown factors in innovation and transformation projects. From the knowledge point of view, these factors are classified into three types, as follows:

- Known unknowns
- Unknown knowns
- Unknown unknowns

We encounter many situations of unknown unknowns, meaning we do not know what is not known. That is what makes leaders fearful.

7.2 Neuroscience of Fear

What makes people have fear despite their experience? Are courage and experience directly related? Let us look at the neuroscience of fear.

As we discussed in the section "Neuroscience of Creativity," the brain is divided into three principal parts: the neocortex/cerebrum, the cerebellum, and the brain stem. Each part focuses on its own specific tasks. There is another crucial system buried within the cerebrum called the limbic system, which is also called the emotional brain. The limbic system contains the thalamus, hypothalamus, amygdala, and hippocampus.

The original part of the brain is called the reptilian brain, which we inherited from prehistoric reptiles. The reptilian brain is very basic, focused on the need to survive and containing the fight-or-flight response. When faced with a threatening situation, reptiles either fight for survival or run away to hide. The part of the brain called the limbic brain is the domain of the emotions, formerly associated with parental responsibilities. The reptilian brain and the limbic brain make up the unconscious mind.

The other part of the brain, called the neocortex, is unique to mammals. The neocortex is the thinking part of the brain and is responsible for planning, constructing ideas, and making logical decisions. The neocortex is the conscious mind.

While the whole brain is responsible for emotions, the two active areas that play a vital role in generating fear signals are the brain stem and limbic system, especially the amygdala, which is part of the limbic system.

The limbic system's responsibility is to respond to stress by filtering and assessing danger signals with the help of the hypothalamus. These emotional responses are often called the fight-or-flight response. Under a condition of threat, the body prepares for fight or flight by releasing adrenaline and increasing blood supply to the muscles without being consciously aware of this.

As the level of the threat increases, the neocortex of the brain naturally shuts down and lets the limbic system do whatever it unconsciously needs to do to ensure the best chances of survival as quickly as possible. It redirects the hypothalamus to begin producing extra cortisol and adrenaline to motivate and produce movement in the body to better respond, whether that means fighting or fleeing.

The hypothalamus continues to produce cortisol and adrenaline either to subdue the threat or flee successfully. After the initial reflexive reactions, the amygdala starts getting input from the prefrontal cortex, which is involved in the planning phase of the response. While the amygdala is fully developed at birth, the prefrontal cortex does not fully develop until early adulthood. That is the reason why children do not always make rational decisions and cannot always control their emotions.

Fear comes directly from the unconscious reptilian brain. People remember events that create strong emotional feelings, especially negative emotional feelings. The unconscious mind tries to compare the current and perceived future events with past events. The amygdala has a role in fear, but it is responsible for detecting and responding to threats and only contributes to feelings of fear indirectly. Consciously activating the more analytical part of the brain is the key to controlling runaway fear and anxiety.

7.3 Neuroscience of Courage

"Courage is resistance to fear, mastery of fear—not absence of fear." When people try to take on a challenge, they come encounter fear of failure, fear of the unknown, and fear of loss. People are not be able to continue unless they overcome the reptilian brain's fear with neocortex logical thinking. This is the way leading to larger possibilities and achieving one's potential. Courage is a cognitive ability that can be strengthened through neuroplasticity. One can build and strengthen courage through the right behaviors and exercises.

The core elements of courage are a willingness to act in the face of uncertainty and the ability to manage fear to maintain the ability to act. Consistently performing certain mental exercises with a clear focus to build courage can strengthen these core skills.

In business and social life, the fear does not come from real survival threats like a pouncing tiger. It comes from fear of failure, uncertainty, risk, and being vulnerable. Managing fear means honestly confronting the source of that fear.

Courageous leaders do their homework to recognize their fear-based patterns, and then they reframe their fear-based thoughts to reboot their mind-set and get ready to be resilient in the face of failure.

Instead of letting fear control us, we can consciously be emotionally present and remain mindful during uncomfortable confrontations. When we repeatedly confront and face down our fears, we can destroy their influence on us, further strengthening our courage.

The neurology of courage involves a competition between the amygdala, which drives fear, and the neocortex, which acts to suppress biological fear responses. Neurologically, cognitive activation of neocortex can suppress and shut down the amygdala response. What activates the neocortex?

The ability to picture the positive results that will come from the mission increases the ability to act. In case of uncertainty, focusing on *why* we are doing what we are doing can have magical results on our ability to act.

"The ability to picture the positive results that will come from the mission increases the ability to act."

The courage to fail in order to succeed is key to the courageous leader. We may have moments of bravery in our lives. Routinely recalling and reliving those moments activates and strengthens the neural patterns associated with bravery and helps us begin to see ourselves as brave. When unexpected problems suddenly threaten to overwhelm us, retreating to the divine safety within will make us feel courageous. At any given moment we have all the courage necessary to overcome any seeming difficulty. In the face of difficulties, one should never allow courage to become paralyzed and should uproot fear from within by effectively concentrating on courage.

7.4 Building a Culture of Courage

In the hyperconnected world of business, there are more dots to connect and more actors getting involved, increasing the level of uncertainty and creating much more fear in the workplace. In some cases, innovation and transformation can lead to an unknown state. So, the fear factor is not that we will lose something but that we are entering a state of unknowns. The current business climate requires every organization to have an entrepreneurial spirit and to take responsible risks. It requires leaders who have the courage to embrace transformation. The rewards that courage brings are happiness of customers and employees and improved quality of life in society.

A sense of fear makes the people maintain the status quo, and it blocks an organization's ability to move forward. Fear keeps millions of individuals from reaching their potential. Transformational leaders must create a courageous culture where people can think creatively, present innovative ideas, and challenge the status quo. Employees should not be afraid to escalate matters, especially if they affect the customer and work environment. It takes courage for employees to communicate the message to senior management that clutter and toxins need to be removed from the organization's culture.

"Fear keeps millions of individuals from reaching their potential."

Given that the transformation process is associated with risks, some failures at various stages of the innovation process are common in business. Even if the founders and key stakeholders have a tolerance for failure, the same is not true of most employees. Employees want a perfect track record; they feel uncomfortable with failure. An organization's leadership should take necessary steps to ensure that teams feel empowered.

It is evident that there are specific fundamental steps that a courageous culture in a transformational project management office should take. They are as follows:

- Embrace intuition.
- Implement a fail-fast strategy with idea experimentation and agile development.
- ➢ Be proactive.

In the case of start-ups, entrepreneurs come up with disruptive ideas and are willing to go outside their comfort zones for something they believe in. These entrepreneurs-cum-leaders have the courage to create a vision and make the tough decisions required to achieve that vision. They have the flexibility to make corrections as the organization's culture evolves.

> "To be a successful entrepreneur, you must have the willingness to go outside your comfort zone for something you believe in and come up with disruptive ideas."

With large incumbents, the organizational culture is well matured. Employees at all levels feel comfortable with current practices, which may have shown success in the traditional way of doing the business. However, the current practices cannot last forever and may become irrelevant at some point in time.

Undoubtedly, leaders who try to change the status quo will face challenges. First of all, challenges will come in the form of criticism. Transformational leaders should be ready to face and manage criticism. Challenging the status quo and facing criticism takes an extraordinary amount of courage. Leaders who are criticized have to be creative thinkers, must be passionate, and must not be afraid of failure.

> "By cultivating a culture of courage in which people feel secure enough to exit their comfort zones and take risks, an organization achieves extraordinary results."

One should step out of the box by leaving all previous experiences, mind-sets, and attitudes behind and should start to see things from an entirely different perspective. Outside-the-box, unfiltered, and unbiased thinking, openness to suggestion, and willingness to empathize with others' feelings will open the gates to a flood of ideas.

> "To be a successful transformational leaer, one should step outside the box, leaving all previous experiences, mind-sets, and attitudes behind, and start to see things from an entirely different perspective."

Courage makes a leader challenge conventional wisdom and imagine new possibilities, making innovation and transformation possible.

Jeff Bezos has courageously led Amazon from an e-commerce bookseller to a device producer. Courage comes from caring genuinely about achieving a shared vision.

"Outside-the-box, unfiltered, unbiased thinking, openness to suggestion, and willingness to empathize with others' feelings will open the gates to a flood of ideas."

7.5 Fail-Fast Strategy

As we move on to design thinking and the agile approach, it would be wise to reframe emotional failure as "feedback." Doing this will enable people in an organization to adapt, respond, iterate, pivot, and develop a culture of experimentation. Mistakes are not bad at all. They are the inevitable consequence of doing something better.

Failure unconsciously invokes a series of reactive responses resulting in a range of irrational cognitive distortions such as disappointment, confusion, and shame. This will make people feel violated and disappointed, instilling a fear of being fired and of being disregarded for promotion. This will further result in their running away from new ideas and solving the problem, ultimately leading to negative consequences. Failing early is better than failing in the end. The transformational leader should create a safe environment where employees are allowed to fail so as to protect new ideas and the employees who are working on them.

"The transformational leader should create a safe environment where employees are allowed to fail in order to protect new ideas."

No business organization wants to fail. Businesses want to serve customers better than their competitors do. However, there are some occasions when failure is necessary. Innovation is impossible without intermittent failures as innovation is based on the scientific method, involving the steps of developing a hypothesis, testing it, and finding out if it is valid. Sometimes ideas will fail because of technical failures, unaccounted contingencies, or unknown variables, but these things can be rectified by trying alternative approaches. Implementation failure does mean that the idea has failed.

The process may encounter repeated failures but allow those who are working on it to get closer to figuring out what will really work. Failing fast means failing cheaply. A culture of experimentation also needs to be created at the individual level so that brainstorming, risk-taking, and experimentation become part of every process in the organization.

Leveraging failure requires transformational leaders to provide a safety net so that doing something wrong does not turn into a disaster for the organization.

7.6 Proactive Leadership

Some believe that it is an unpredictable environment that makes people feel fear, whereas the truth is that the more uncertain the environment, the more opportunities there are. A leader who masters the skill of leading people and the organization should be able to capitalize on the opportunities that arise from uncertainty. The transformational leader who is flexible and persistent in the face of setbacks should also be able to react strategically to environmental shifts. Navigating through an unpredictable environment and making people feel courageous requires the leader to think strategically.

The actions that help the transformational leader include the following:

- Anticipating
- Challenging

- Interpreting
- Decision-making
- Aligning of interests
- Learning

Anticipating

The organizations that are poor at detecting ambiguous threats and opportunities on the periphery of their business fail to innovate and ultimately disappear. Transformational leaders should remain constantly vigilant, honing their ability to anticipate by scanning the environment for signals of change.

Challenging

In a rapidly changing business environment, the only constant is change. Questioning the status quo, as well as challenging one's own and others' assumptions and encouraging divergent points of view, will help leaders to see the problem through many lenses to determine which action to take.

Interpreting

In an environment with lots of uncertainties and unknowns, it is entirely possible that even the right challenges will result in conflicting information. Instead of expecting favorable inputs, leaders should be able to synthesize all the input they receive and recognize patterns. They should also push through ambiguity to seek new insights.

Decision-Making

Leaders face criticism for their decisions in an unpredictable environment and during uncertain times. People in an organization insist on multiple options so that they do not become prematurely locked into a final decision. However, in a critical time, decision makers may have to make tough calls with incomplete information yet by following a disciplined process that balances rigor with speed, considers the trade-offs involved, and takes both short-term and long-term goals into account. Transformational leaders must have the courage of their convictions, informed by a robust decision-making process. To achieve this, they should have a higher acceptance rate and develop confidence among their people based on their own consistent behavior and sound decision-making.

Aligning of Interests

Because stakeholders have disparate views and agendas, it is challenging for the transformational leader to achieve buy-in amid an uncertain environment. With active research, proactive communication, trust, and frequent engagement, the transformational leader should be able to find common ground to achieve buy-in among stakeholders. The transformational leader must combat the two most common complaints in organizations—"No one ever asked me" and "No one ever told me"—by identifying critical internal and external stakeholders, mapping their positions on the initiative, and pinpointing any misalignment of interests.

Learning

Knowledge makes people feel courageous. Promoting a culture of inquiry, curiosity, and observation helps the people in the organization search for the lessons amid a series of past successful and unsuccessful outcomes. Encouraging people to study the failures of their own team and other teams in a constructive way to find the hidden lessons will make them fearlessly prepare for unexpected outcomes.

8

Collaboration for Synergy

8.1 Collaborative Work

According to Dictionary.com, *synergy* is defined as "the interaction of elements that when combined produce a total effect that is greater than the sum of the individual elements and contributions."[1] A collaborative culture will energize teams, promote creativity, foster innovation, and make the environment more productive and joyful.

Collaboration does not mean a group of people working together. Instead, it is the ability to think together and solve complex problems. Traditional management practices are not modeled to transform organizations. Most of the practices are devised to execute a well-tested strategy. Collaborative leadership, on the other hand, is a defined process where various shareholders work together constructively and share the responsibility for problem-solving and decision-making.

Collaboration is a process whereby individual people do not come together naturally but instead come together based on the vision created by the leader. Collaborative leadership is very much required in a business where the problems are so complex that no one person

1 Dictionary.com, s.v. "synergy," https://www.dictionary.com/browse/synergy?s=t.

or unit has either the information or the power to make decisions. A collaborative process will open the doors for innovation.

Togetherness improves the design process by doing the following:

- Helping people understand the problem that needs to be solved
- Utilizing past experiences
- Bringing together diverse areas of expertise
- Suppressing biases.

Let us look at each of these critical elements and see how we can use collaboration to mitigate some of the worst effects they can have on design.

Understanding of the complex problem can fall short if certain necessary information is lacking, and this may not be realized until the shortcomings surface. Collaboration encourages each team member to contribute to the shared understanding and bring a unique perspective. The team becomes stronger with this type of pooled knowledge.

Past experiences can certainly help people succeed in the future. Having done something well in the past is a good indication that a person will do well in the future.

However, in a rapidly changing business context, past experiences can create false assumptions because of the patterns forged in the brain. Working collaboratively with pooled knowledge and previous experiences will encourage other members to challenge the assumptions made by any one team member.

Reinventing the wheel is never a good idea unless someone gets an idea of how to use the wheel in unconventional ways. Likewise, a collaborative team needs to find ways to use everyone's area of expertise instead of just relying on the expertise shown in past successes. Each team member may have unique perspectives and understandings. Solving problems together with cross-functional teams will help an organization make better and more-informed decisions about which solutions to explore further and which past explorations not to repeat.

Before challenging any idea or assumption, it is best to be aware of any biases. While it is easy to spot the biases of others, it is tough for the one to spot his or her own biases. Team members build some form of emotional attachment to their creations, and letting go of these can be hard. Working collaboratively will remove some of the common pitfalls related to biases and save the team from leaving them unchallenged.

As discussed in the chapters "Igniting Creativity" and "Organizational Cultural Transformation," there are several ways of bringing collaboration into the organization. Some of those approaches are as follows:

- Breaking down physical silos
- Breaking down behavioral silos
- Cocreating
- Brainstorming

Regardless of how we bring collaboration to an organization, there are certain traits that the leaders and everyone on the teams must practice to make the collaboration experience healthy and to create synergies, unleashing everyone's full potential. These traits include, but are not limited to, the following:

- Relationships
- Influencing
- Listening
- Trust
- Integrity
- Transparency
- Communication
- Delegation

8.2 Relationships

Collaboration is not necessarily limited to working together within the organization. It applies to cross-organizations as well. Transformational leaders must understand how other leaders are currently solving the problem in question. One of the goals of the transformational leader should be to think in different ways and generate more and more ideas, which in turn bring forth a difference of opinion, shared insights, and learning. While we learn more from our own experiences, it is helpful to learn from the experiences of others in the same field or outside the field. Attending workshops, summits, conferences, and conventions will connect leaders with more-experienced mentors and with people who are more influential and knowledgeable in any specific area. The cross-fertilization that comes with connections and the ideas that are openly discussed and shared through the network and open platforms develop new opportunities, innovations, and solutions to common problems.

One of the arts that strengthens relationships is social engineering. Social engineering makes discussions more pleasant. These discussions help to build relationships, and relationships help a person to grow as a leader. Relationships that extend beyond the organization are invaluable to acquiring knowledge. These relationships sometimes lead to cocreation, co-innovation, or joint-development agreements. When others understand the innovations effectively through presentations at relevant summits or conventions, doors will open for the collaborative team, giving partners insights into how to commercialize the innovations further.

In larger organizations with many thousands of employees, relatively few will have the opportunity to interact physically with others. People are spread across the building, across cities, and sometimes across countries. Traditional business interactions were centered on documents such as email, reports, and spreadsheets. However, in today's hyperconnected business world, structures are less rigid, and the rapid growth of mobile devices in the workplace has resulted in the use of any device, anywhere and anytime a person so chooses.

The human element is still critical to fostering relationships, building trust, and enhancing collaborative interactions within the organization. To bring the human element to the physical and virtual environment and to create a more comfortable and engaging environment for collaborators, an internal social network is vital. Realizing the importance of relationships to in-house collaboration and cross-organizational collaboration, several organizations are investing an enormous amount of money into fostering collaboration innovatively and building and maintaining social relationships throughout the organization. Building virtual atriums and conference theaters is an example. With the development of sophisticated digital network channels and virtual theaters, people can fill virtual boards with photos of groups, departments, and countries showing people working together. This brings the mechanics of internal communication to unprecedented levels.

8.3 Trust

Trust is one of the traits that inspires and motivates people. In a culture where trust is embodied throughout the entire organization, people are more productive and willing to collaborate more. Trust makes the environment more enjoyable and removes or reduces stress levels. What makes a meaningful difference for transformational leaders is the ability to build a culture of trust.

"In a culture where trust is embodied throughout the organization, people are more productive and willing to collaborate more."

Often leaders assume that trust comes from a title or nameplate. But trust is earned through a number of things such as abilities, morals, values, principles, ethics, consistency, relationship building, integrity, and commitment. Trust requires that what is spoken be aligned with what is being done. Trust cannot be built overnight. It is a steady and slow process.

Human brains reject strangers by default. This is because people are afraid of the risk of being exploited. Through conscious awareness, the brain can seek the right balance between strangeness and interaction.

Constant interactions help both parties see value in each other. With interaction, one can perceive that the others are capable, caring, ethical, and consistent in their behavior, which will help to give the signal to the brain that the others are to be trusted.

As discussed in earlier chapters, the neurotransmitters oxytocin and dopamine play a vital role in building trust. Oxytocin signals that a person is safe to trust by reducing the natural fears we have about strangers. Oxytocin increases emotional connection with others. Empathy motivates people to help others, including strangers. Stress causes heart rate and blood pressure to spike and reduces the ability to connect with others. A culture of healthy social relationships even at the workplace makes people become more compassionate by tuning into empathy. Building an organization's culture, and engaging in leadership practices that help to promote the release of oxytocin in the human brain, builds trust among colleagues.

Several characteristics that contribute to trust are as follows:

- ➢ Openness to sharing relevant information broadly with people throughout the organization.
- ➢ Clarity, which makes people feel confident. Clarity of purpose, vision, mission, expectations, and daily activities fosters trust among people.
- ➢ Group discussions, which stimulate the release of oxytocin and build trust among team members.
- ➢ Confidence in those who are capable of delivering things.
- ➢ Little things that are done consistently, which builds up a high level of trust and produces better results. Great leaders consistently do the small but most important things first.
- ➢ Social recognition and appraisal, which causes the brain to release oxytocin.
- ➢ Putting faith in those who will go the extra mile.
- ➢ Caring, which will build relationships with colleagues, serving as the foundation for trust.

8.4 Influencing

In the command and control leadership style, tasks are achieved mostly by way of command. Authority gives commanding power to the leaders. With transformational leadership, the style should move from command-control to collaboration. This is not just limited to organizational leadership but is evident elsewhere. Collaboration is an integral part of transformational leadership. While authority is still needed in specific contexts, such as taking responsibility and designating accountability, the way leaders achieve things should shift toward influence and away from command.

What is influence? Influence is the ability to affect others' actions, decisions, opinions, and thinking. On the one hand it is about fostering compliance among people, and on the other hand, it is about getting a commitment from people to accomplish goals and tasks. Why do leaders need to influence others? What do people gain from leaders by being influenced? In traditional leadership, people often think that influencing is the best way to make people listen. This is a wrong perception. The core idea of influencing is to help others achieve more. The leader's motivations and strengths should influence others' ability to accomplish their goals. In other words, the leader is someone who influences the hearts and minds of others to improve their conditions. Influence is one of the core characteristics of the transformational leader. The foremost thing that influences people is to gain a deep understanding of people. This is very much required because by nature people want to protect themselves first. And if people think that the leader's strengths are not aligned with the leader's life, then the leader will quickly find resistance.

By having a clear understanding of employees' social and cultural life, the leader will be able to speak their language and get synchronized with them. The leader will gain an understanding of their needs and understand what to do better to fulfill their needs. Sometimes influence can be mutual, which in turn can strengthen the leader's vision. Leaders who misuse their influence can cause lasting damage to an organization.

Having influence means more than just having power. It is about taking charge and understanding emotions and nonverbal signals.

People with power tend to talk more, interrupt others, and drive the conversation. However, collaboration is not driven by power. A logical and intellectual appeal can make an argument for the best course of action based on benefits to the organization. Positive emotions and passion can win over the person in authority.

The leader's emotional appeal can connect the goal to the appealing vision, causing others to respect and follow him or her. A cooperative appeal builds a connection between the leader and other people, thereby increasing the influence of the leader.

"Having influence means more than just having power. It is about taking charge and understanding emotions and nonverbal signals."

8.5 Listening

The Dalai Lama once said, "When you talk, you are only repeating what you already know. However, if you listen, you may learn something new."

Listening is one of the most underrated leadership traits, especially in the world of collaboration. Listening will help to avoid conflicts and to solve any conflicts that do arise. Even though people do not have to agree with others' opinions all the time, it is essential to keep the doors open for the perspectives of other team members. Through active listening, one can understand the views and perspectives of other people.

Active listening will encourage team members to speak regularly and openly about conflict, resulting in a more transparent work culture.

As discussed in the chapter "Igniting Creativity," hearing and listening seem to be the same on the surface, but they have significant differences.

While these two activities involve the use of ears, there is more of a mind process involved in listening. In other words, sounds are perceived by the ears, and the brain understands the sounds by paying full attention to the meaning behind them. Listening is the process of diligently hearing sounds and interpreting the meaning of those sounds.

Active listening influences our lives. Active listening makes a conversation a positive experience for the other party.

Leaders make others feel supported through active listening. It fosters a safe environment in which issues and differences are discussed openly. Active listeners capture ideas and restate issues to confirm that their understanding is correct. It helps to observe nonverbal cues, such as facial expressions and gestures. It helps leaders to empathize and validate those feelings in a nonjudgmental way. Through active listening, feedback flows smoothly in both directions, with neither party becoming defensive. Poor listening might make a person an excellent debater, but it does not make a person a good leader.

8.6 Integrity

> The supreme quality of leadership is unquestionably integrity. Without it, no real success is possible, no matter whether it is on a section gang, a football field, in an army, or in an office.
>
> —Dwight D. Eisenhower

Integrity is defined as "adherence to moral and ethical principles; soundness of moral character; honesty."

Leaders with integrity maintain the highest ethical standards and expect the same from others. Leaders should keep their promises. There is no obligation to make promises, but once the leader makes a promise, he or she must fulfill that promise without fail. It is an integral part of collaborative leadership to treat everyone with respect and fairness.

Leaders often encounter tough situations when faced with a loyal employee. If a person is loyal to the leader, this does not mean that the leader should encourage the person to make mistakes. By playing a coaching role, the leader will get an opportunity to correct the person, however loyal that person may be, without compromising his or her ethics. That makes the leader more integral. In other words, when it comes to loyalty vs. integrity, integrity takes precedence.

Integrity is a state of mind and is associated with several traits and characteristics of leadership, such as the following:

- Straightforwardness
- Commitment
- Honesty
- Authenticity
- Accountability
- Trust
- Reliability
- Humility
- Genuineness
- Generosity
- Kindness
- Intuition

8.7 Transparency

Transparency is an essential trait to fostering a culture of collaboration within an organization. As has been discussed in several sections of *The Art and Science of Transformational Leadership*, in most cases, transformation deals with VUCA (volatility, uncertainty, complexity, and ambiguity). While the shared purpose and shared vision make people feel that they are sharing the responsibility, transparency should go beyond the shared purpose and shared vision. Transparency fosters trust between the leader and employees. Transparency keeps leaders honest. Transparency is required for all organizations regardless of size or the industry and regardless of the nature of the initiatives undertaken.

Sharing information builds trust, generates learning opportunities, leads to smarter decisions, and speeds up organizational growth.

- Transparency provides employees the context for making better decisions.
- Transparency eliminates gossip.
- Transparency builds trust, loyalty, and morality in an organization.
- Transparency empowers people to participate in conversation and decision-making.
- Transparency makes people feel ownership.
- It moves the people from darkness to light.
- It speeds up an organization's growth.

Often, some leaders think that transparency makes them less authoritative. This is an entirely wrong perception. People are tired of surprises. People face several issues in problem-solving that deal with unknown factors. People observe that their leaders also experience the same problems, or else they are just kept in the dark. It is not only in problem-solving that transparency is required. Transparency is needed in every facet of an organization, unless the matter being dealt with is restricted or there is some other reasonable business justification. People want to know precisely who the decision makers are, who is responsible, and who is accountable.

Transparency is a way of engaging employees. Transparency leads to effective collaboration, greater creativity, faster problem-solving, and improved performance. It serves as a motivational tool.

"Transparency leads to effective collaboration, greater creativity, faster problem-solving, and improved performance."

Being transparent does not mean opening the floodgates of information and data for public viewing. Providing a clear road map, a strategy, context, commentary, and clarity around information will help people feel confident.

Transparency involves inviting and encouraging people to ask questions and then delivering honest answers. Understanding the context of a difficult situation will help a team better empathize with any hard decisions the leader will need to make in time. Some of the mechanisms that help to foster transparency are brainstorming sessions, design thinking, and agile methodologies. These help a team know what is happening around it.

8.8 Delegation

When it comes to transformational leadership, delegating work to other leaders is an art form. We have discussed engaging others and sharing the responsibility with other leaders to foster a collaborative work culture. However, there are specific tasks that cannot be delegated quickly, and there are specific tasks that must be delegated. In case of tasks for which leaders see challenges in delegating, the solution is "leading along with," in other words, walking alongside the team. This means that instead of delegating the work as an example of outsourcing, the leader walks along with the leader, resulting in reduced effort. By bringing in the right talent and putting together a team, transformational leaders can use the "leading along with" process, thereby reducing their day-to-day efforts.

Undoubtedly, transformational leaders cannot do everything on their own. In cases where work has to be delegated, the transformational leader must ensure that the charge leaders are capable, are committed, and can take responsibility and accountability. The transformational leader provides vision and ongoing direction and ensures that the charge leaders are harmonious and productive. Transformation affects almost every aspect of a business. Transformational leaders must have the ability to inspire all their people with a deep understanding of the purpose and mechanics of the business, as well as have expertise in transformation.

Regardless of the above, the transformational leader, or even the organization, should never outsource the core competencies. Core competencies are a competitive advantage for the leader or the organization. It does not mean distrusting people.

Examples of tasks that can be delegated are as follows:

- Adding business value
- Executing streamlined projects
- Learning practices

Examples of tasks that can be delegated by leading along with:

- Shared vision
- Mission
- Customer-centric actions
- Inventions and patents
- Key hiring decisions

Examples of tasks that can never be delegated:

- Those related to the core vision
- Crisis management
- Team building
- Those related to core values
- Those related to ethics
- Appraisals

9

Commitment for Fulfillment

9.1 Commitment

Commitment is the most powerful tool that can help a leader stay on the path to the vision. In a rapidly changing, hyperconnected business world, a leader can quickly lose sight of this. When markets become too competitive, business leaders find it challenging to respond efficiently when they are implicitly or explicitly committed to their vision, or the predecessors' vision, or the founder's mentality.

"Commitment is the most powerful tool that can help a leader stay on the path to the vision."

A commitment refers to "any past or present action that binds the leader or an organization to a future course of fulfillment." Here the action can be a pledge, a business agreement, a customer-centric business model, employee benefits, or a self-declared clear statement about the future.

Commitments are essential to people both in personal life and professional life. They are the means by which a company secures the resources and attracts the talent that is required to move forward and grow. Commitment will also serve as a competitive advantage. For example, if a well-established organization makes a promise that it is going to introduce a disruptive product, it can make competitors rethink their plans if they are in the early stage. At the same time, an open promise serves as a motivational tool for the people involved in developing such a product. It gives them a clear sense of focus and helps them prioritize their actions. This will create positive energy in people, inspiring them to proceed despite hardships, setbacks, and challenging situations.

The most robust commitments, primarily in the form of talent and investment, can bring like-minded companies together to work collaboratively and cocreate a product. A company may have the best talent but lack the investment. On the other hand, some companies may have the investment but lack the talent. The proven track record of each company in fulfilling the commitment, can bring two companies together and allow them work together to create synergy. Also, many marketing partners like to work with companies based on their commitment. Commitments also convince customers that it is worthwhile for them to continue being customers of those organizations.

Whether in public life or organizational life, there are several areas where the leader and organization must respect commitments. These commitments do not have any ranking or order; all of them are equally important. They are as follows:

- Founder's mentality
- Purpose
- Vision
- Social responsibility
- Ethics
- Principles
- Customer focus
- Employee satisfaction
- Investment

- Public pledges
- Public assertions
- Explicit contracts

These commitments are potent weapons that help leaders manage an organization's life cycle. At the same time, past commitments can become roadblocks for needed transformation. Since commitments prescribe specific future actions, they can potentially limit a company's flexibility. For example, if the organization commits to a particular technology, this can prevent the organization from gaining the benefits of well-advanced technologies that have just emerged. Open promises can sometimes reveal the strategic avenues of an organization to its competitors.

In the journey of evolution, a company's original identity may become counterproductive, requiring leaders to transform the business through a set of new models and commitments that contradict earlier ones. The transformational leader must have the ability to manage commitments efficiently and prevent commitments from turning into liabilities.

Indeed, many leaders or organizations are not clear about the context of their commitments. Not every past or present action should be treated as binding. For examples, the past or present ways of doing things to achieve goals aligned with the vision may become outdated in light of present or future business conditions. Deviations from collective action mainly related to the how factor should not be treated as an unfulfilled commitment. Rigid, outdated rules, silo structures, hierarchies, and behaviors should not be seen as commitments. This means that there are both real and pseudo commitments.

"To transform an organization, leaders should take bold actions to break and remake the pseudo commitments if they are seen to be roadblocks."

There is mounting pressure on leaders and organizations to reinforce commitments in the face of compliance and regulations. However, this does not mean that organizations should avoid innovation and transformation. For leaders who are comfortable with current processes and who want to maintain the status quo, it is easy to reinforce pseudo commitments. They use traditional compliance and regulations as excuses to support their agenda. None of the regulations insists on maintaining the status quo related to technology, infrastructure, operations, and/or business models. To transform an organization, leaders should take bold actions to break and remake the pseudo commitments if they are seen to be roadblocks.

Agility, flexibility, and adaptability are still relevant and must be allowed if people are to focus on the vision. The traits that help to reinforce commitment are as follows.

- ➢ Consistency
- ➢ Persistence
- ➢ Clarity
- ➢ Focus
- ➢ Responsibility
- ➢ Accountability
- ➢ Open-mindedness
- ➢ Flexibility
- ➢ Adaptability

9.2 Consistency

Inconsistency in behaviors and actions will lead to uncertainty. People prefer a predictable environment. People cannot trust their leaders if the latter are inconsistent in their behavior and attitudes. Consistency is an important trait not only for leaders but also for the organization. It is not just limited to behaviors, either. Consistency is needed everywhere, such as in planning, execution, rulemaking, and decision-making. It is critical especially for the mission of innovation and transformation. Leaders must communicate consistent messages to teams on critical issues and relentlessly follow up and focus only on those issues. In doing so, leaders should remain consistent with prior commitments.

One of the most demoralizing practices in the transformation process is putting an enormous amount attention and effort into a program for a short period and then abandoning the program by moving on to another attractive initiative. In a world of experimentation, unless we have tried the variations for a while and in a consistent manner, we cannot make the judgment of whether or not it is worth it to continue. Being consistent requires that leaders stick to the message no matter how difficult it is and focus their attention on achieving the goals.

Transformational leaders should establish a period of consistent experimentation before making a decision. Establishing the practice of recurrence helps people to adapt to the transformation initiatives. This is the reason why agile frameworks insist on daily scrum calls. Daily calls ensure that the development process is consistent. They create accountability. A business reputation cannot be built overnight. It requires a lengthy track record of success, and such a track record cannot be established by constantly shifting gears. Consistency makes the efforts more relevant. Customers also assign importance to a company's consistency in delivering innovations and value. People reconcile what is pledged or advertised with what is delivered. With consistent delivery, the organization can focus on promoting a positive image with the customer.

If leaders do not behave consistently, the people around them do not know what to do. Instead of proactively taking actions on their own, they have to waste energy on seeking direction from the leader. Even if they are sure of the action they should take, they will hesitate. Being consistent gives people moral authority. Trust is the foundation for leadership, and consistency is one of the ways of establishing trust. By defining the expectation, leaders can let people know what they can expect from them and what they themselves expect from the people. The key is to make the people aware of the leader's preferences and style so they can quickly adapt to them. If leaders make decisions that come at the expense of principles and justify their inconsistent actions, then people feel unsafe in the environment. Such inconsistency serves to dilute performance unconsciously. From the neuroscience point of view, inconsistency causes the amygdala to register a threat to one's safety, triggering fight-or-flight, reducing the executive function of the prefrontal cortex, and eventually inhibiting creativity.

"Trust is the foundation for leadership, and consistency is one of the ways of establishing trust."

9.3 Persistence

Persistence is a critical characteristic that transformational leaders, creative people, and innovators must possess. Leaders must persistently push ahead on the path to accomplishment in order to bring dreams to fruition. On the way to success, several things can knock down a leader. Leaders must be able to pick themselves up, dust themselves off, and return to the path. Transformational leaders are dreamers. More than that, they are doers. They cannot achieve anything if they are not persistent. They are committed to the constant pursuit of game changers.

Obstacles are common to the mission of transformation to realize the vision. Therefore, on the path toward the goal, leaders need to remain agile enough to make corrections but must be persistent to achieve the final goal. By trying out all the pathways, leaders can reach their goal. This means that the leader can easily adjust if one strategy is not working. Sometimes what we think of as failure is not a failure. In transformational leadership, people may fail several times, but they do not quit until they get things right, because they know in their hearts what they want. Even if there is a failure, leaders must have the courage to try again. The real failure is in giving up. Therefore, instead of giving up on the mission, leaders should consider redesigning the approach to achieve the final goals. There are always multiple avenues to reach the destination.

"Obstacles are common to the mission of transformation to realize the vision. Therefore, on the path to the goal, leaders need to remain agile enough to make corrections but must be persistent to achieve the final goal."

The best way to remain persistent is to fall in love with the cause and commit to lifelong learning. Persistence allows leaders to remain open to new ideas. Persistence causes leaders to seek new opportunities to move people toward the purpose, even if that means modifying the route or some of the details along the way. The core purpose of the mission will drive people to succeed. By identifying the deeper purpose behind the goal, by stating the why, leaders will be able to push through any challenging times. The best leaders proactively focus on pursuing game changers and are never satisfied with intermediate goals.

Intermediate failures do not indicate that the project will never work. Failure means that the person is one step closer to achieving the result. Abraham Lincoln failed in business, was defeated in a legislative race, lost a congressional race, lost a senatorial race, and failed to become vice president, but finally he was elected of the president of the United States of America at the age of fifty-two.

"The real failure is in giving up. Therefore, instead of giving up on the mission, leaders should consider reinventing themselves to achieve the final goals."

The transformational leader also needs to ensure that everyone on the team remains persistent. Generating higher levels of motivation will keep the team persistent. Transformational leaders must have the ability to deal with the naysayers, who at the first sign of failure will suggest that the team go back or stop. Transformational leaders should maintain persistence to keep the entire team moving forward, against their fears and doubts, when there are setbacks. Leaders should have the courage to stay the course, show the route to success, and boost people's confidence.

People follow the leader as long as the leader consistently demonstrates progress. They see what the leader does and assess the leader's capabilities and desires. When the leader starts showing doubt, then people start stepping back, and the mission becomes harder to take forward. That is why persistence is essential for leaders. It demonstrates and sets the tone of how leaders and the organization react when faced with adversity.

9.4 Clarity

Clarity adds incredible value to the mission to turn the purpose-driven vision into reality. Clarity is the fuel for vision. If people are not clear about the why, then how can they jump-start the vision? The duo of clarity and focus plays a vital role in strengthening various traits of leadership. Leaders need to have a clear understanding of what they want and how they will reach the vision. When leaders are clear about what they want, they can explain the vision to others so that they can understand the vision as well. Indeed, there will be uncertainties, complexities, and unknown factors in executing the mission. Being aware of these risk factors will give clarity to the mission and help to remove the roadblocks, hurdles, and obstacles. Clarity will give precise meaning to the purpose.

"Clarity adds incredible value to the mission to turn the purpose-driven vision into reality."

Often, leaders lose their teams because of mistrust and lack of strategic clarity. When a leader brings clarity to the table, the roles and goals will get aligned, and the team becomes one unit.

The trait that strengthens clarity is transparency. A transparent agenda creates an environment of clarity and builds momentum for the collective support of the mission.

In large incumbents where there is a large number of silos, there is misalignment within leadership across the silos that makes it difficult to define expectations clearly. Everyone wants to be successful. Without clarity, people will have no idea how they can make a difference. Transformational leaders need to bring clarity to the bigger picture to unleash the full potential of team members so they can achieve their own success in light of the vision.

The elements that bring clarity to a mission are as follows:

- Clear thinking
- Clear communication
- Clear conscience
- Self-awareness
- Reflection

9.5 Focus

Focus and clarity go hand in hand. While it is crucial to keep on searching for more extensive great ideas, it is equally important to focus on prioritized ideas and the steps to implement them. Not every idea is going to be a disruptor. Leaders need to focus on which ideas to bring to the table for implementation. The mission must be free of obstacles and roadblocks. The fact is that leaders cannot try to do everything at once. Identifying the easy parts of the mission, putting the right people on the right teams, and aligning them with the purpose will free up some time for the transformational leader and will keep him or her focused on removing the roadblocks to the challenging programs.

The real priority for leaders is to focus on what makes them uncomfortable. Instead of focusing on what the organization has been doing for decades, leaders must focus on how innovative ideas, new models, and modern technologies can take the organization to the next level.

From an organizational point of view, the leader should focus on himself or herself, focus on others in the organization, and focus on the broader world. A failure to focus on oneself leaves the leader rudderless; a failure to focus on others renders the leader clueless; and a failure to focus on the broader world leaves the leader blindsided. Leaders who can effectively focus on others will find common ground. These are the leaders for whom people want to work. Focusing on the broader world helps people to embrace change to improve the future prospects of the organization.

Indeed, that is the connection between creativity, innovation, and transformation. Creativity deals with self-exploitation, and innovation deals with exploration. Exploitation of one's self-advantage requires concentrating on the job at hand, and exploring new ones requires paying attention to others. Switching between exploitation mode and exploration mode requires a deliberate cognitive effort to disengage from the routine and roam widely to pursue new paths.

9.6 Responsibility and Accountability

Responsibility and accountability prove a leader's commitment to excellence. These two things are the tough parts of leadership and put the leader's abilities to the test. While these two words *responsibility* and *accountability* are often used interchangeably, there is a big difference between them. Indeed, they are very close to each other. If there is only one leader for the team with no hierarchies, then they both refer to the same thing. Whether we say that the leader is responsible for delivery or the leader is accountable for delivery, it is the same. The difference comes when there is delegation involved in levels of leadership. If the senior leader has another leader reporting to him and is given charge of the project, then both leaders are responsible for delivering the objectives, but the senior leader should be held accountability for the overall work. In a hierarchical leadership, the leader is both accountable and responsible. She is responsible for the duties she is assigned, and she is accountable for those duties that are delegated or transferred to other leaders. In other words, accountability is bidirectional in this case. Often in traditional leadership, leaders blame the team leaders for the things that went wrong, leaving them accountable. Unfortunately, this has become the standard practice in many places.

Transformational leaders should hold themselves accountable for change and should encourage their team leaders to hold them accountable in a hierarchical manner. The way they hold the responsibility is through influence. The trait of influence has been discussed in chapter 8: Collaboration. The way leaders should make the team leaders accountable is through inspiration and motivation. Transformational leaders should take accountability for the outcomes of their choices, behaviors, and actions in light of the work they have undertaken. Accountable leaders should behave like fixers instead of merely blaming others. Accountable leaders can question the decisions involved in the transformation process.

"Accountable leaders should behave like fixers instead of merely blaming others."

Responsibility is the stepping-stone for leaders to grow. Until leaders take responsibility, they cannot prove their leadership qualities. Even if the magnitude of responsibility is small, it makes a big difference for the leader's ability to grow.

"Responsibility is the stepping-stone for leaders to grow."

The traits that help a leader to become accountable are as follows:

- Honesty
- Responsibility
- Self-awareness
- Influence
- Inspiration and motivation

By being honest, leaders can put aside their pride and admit their mistakes. With honesty, leaders can self-develop a solution to resolve issues, conflicts, and challenges authentically and genuinely. Accountable leaders should understand that they are implicitly responsible for the work they are involved in. They should be self-aware of their limits and should neither undercommit nor overcommit. They should be able to influence people to achieve the goals the leaders are accountable for. Moreover, leaders should be able to inspire and motivate team leaders and encourage them to take accountability.

9.7 Flexibility and Adaptability

The two words *flexibility* and *adaptability* are another pair with close meanings like *accountability* and *responsibility,* but there are also differences. Flexibility means the ability to change plans to match the reality of the situation. Adaptability is the ability to be changed to fit into new circumstances. Both these traits are crucial for both the leader and the organization.

How do flexibility and adaptability help to maintain commitment? As discussed under the section "Persistence," obstacles are more common to the mission of transformation to realize the vision. Therefore, on the path to the goal, leaders need to remain agile enough to make corrections but must be persistent to achieve the final goal. This means that the leader should easily adjust if one strategy is not working. In other words, to achieve the final goals and fulfill the commitment, the leader needs to be flexible and adaptable to make due corrections to the plan. Flexibility and adaptability do not dictate that leaders change the vision but do suggest that the mission be changed to achieve the vision. Leaders must learn to face uncertainty and ambiguity as the new normal. Being flexible allows leaders to respond to unexpected events in an adverse situation. Adaptable leadership means being ready to be changed. From the organizational point of view, it is about the organization's readiness to be changed. An adaptive leadership style helps the leader to get adjusted to the changing business environment and to people's changing lifestyles. It makes leaders move away from their comfort zone of a singular leadership style.

"Being flexible allows leaders to respond to unexpected events in an adverse situation."

Indeed, transformation deals with change and adapting innovative methods. Adaptability is not new to leadership. However, one should not be confused about the difference between commitment and adaptability. A leader should be an early adapter rather than resist change.

In an era of VUCA, it is tremendously challenging to devise strategy. This is because the traditional approaches to devising strategy assume a relatively stable and predictable world. But today, strategies become obsolete quickly. A sustainable competitive advantage is no longer a valid case. The real competitive advantage comes from the second-order capabilities that foster rapid adaptation.

"Adaptability helps a leader to get adjusted to the changing business environment and to think outside the comfort zone."

10

Emotional Intelligence for Humanity

Emotional intelligence is the human ability to identify and manage one's own emotions and the emotions of others to solve one's own problems and the problems of society. Several unknown factors tagged with volatility, uncertainty, complexity, and ambiguity (VUCA) during the mission of transformation will create the uncomfortable feelings of tension, stress, and anxiety. These unknown factors can come in any form. We encounter them while we search for the solution to the problem, or they come in the form of resistance, which opposes change. If these emotions are not addressed, they can strain the mind and body. They can negatively impact a leader's performance. Emotional intelligence skills help leaders to manage uncomfortable emotions and enable them to tackle tough situations before things get worse.

Not all emotions are uncomfortable. There are positive emotions that make people act productively. Leaders who experience positive emotions are more likely to show empathy and kindness, which leads them to enhance their ability to assert themselves and establish new trends. Emotional intelligence is the art of accurately identifying emotions as they occur and relating them to the context without jumping to conclusions.

A leader who lacks emotional intelligence quickly makes conclusions with a confirmation bias. A confirmation bias entails gathering evidence that supports one's opinion and ignoring any evidence to the contrary.

Uncomfortable emotions negatively impact the way leaders deliver their messages. At the same time, purely positive emotions can make leaders stay in the comfort zone and cause them to be reluctant to take risks. Emotional intelligence is about employing both negative and positive emotions in all situations, addressing them efficiently, and using them to understand the problem and the reason behind the emotions in solving the problem in society.

"Emotional intelligence is the art of accurately identifying emotions as they occur and relating them to the context without jumping to conclusions."

The critical skills needed for transformational leadership that can be practiced to enhance emotional intelligence are as follows:

- Empathy
- Compassion
- Humility
- Kindness
- Generosity
- Mindfulness
- Resilience
- Self-awareness

Specific specialized skills such as active listening, observation, curiosity, and conflict resolution also fall under emotional intelligence.

10.1 Leading with Empathy

We have discussed empathy in the chapters related to creativity and innovation. Empathy is a crucial step in design thinking. Empathy is a human being's ability to sense others' feelings. Daily we learn many things. Not all of these things we learn come by way of the spoken or written word. There are many things that teach us. As it is said, one picture is worth a thousand words. Likewise, there is so much meaning behind emotions. With empathy, we can sense unspoken emotions.

Empathy is an essential tool not only for creativity and innovation but also for leadership. Empathy makes a leader distinguishable and effective. It is essential for all kinds of leadership, whether it is organizational leadership, business leadership, political leadership, or any other type of leadership.

Empathy makes conflict resolution friendlier by promoting constructive and connective relationships. It counters stress levels by calming down the bodily reactions. Empathy filters out toxic emotions from body and mind alike.

"Empathy makes conflict resolution friendlier by promoting constructive and connective relationships."

Empathy has a cumulative effect to it. This means that empathy drives a leader to assess the emotions of other people, making the leader most distinguishable. This elevated level of leadership will help the leader to take empathy to the next level, which will, in turn, increase his or her emotional intelligence overall. Empathy puts the leader in other people's shoes, helps him to see through their eyes and think with their minds. Leaders have multiple conversations on a daily basis with a range of constituents. These interactions collectively determine the ultimate success of the leader. Using empathy to understand critical constituents' concerns, frustrations, and feelings will make the leader think of the big picture and broaden his vision.

Recent research and developments in the field of neuroscience reveal that the brain is involved with two distinct types of empathies, as follows:

- Cognitive empathy, which is the ability to understand the perspective of another person and the forces behind that perspective.
- Emotional empathy, which is the ability to experience others' feelings by picking up on those emotions through verbal and nonverbal cues.

The rapid improvements in social connection among people and entities highlight the importance of empathy to the success of a business leader. They remind organizations to prioritize empathy across all departments, not just product development. Empathy will catalyze new growth, innovation, and employee engagement to drive profits and long-term results. In a world where all business leaders are gaining the same amount of knowledge rapidly, applying empathy will help some leaders gain knowledge in a way that other leaders do not. Empathy gives leaders the ability to reach beyond their comfort zones and connect with other people.

There are different ways that an organizations can benefit by practicing empathy.

1. Empathy transforms the work culture, which will improve the operating models.
2. Empathy helps in designing a business model that focuses on customers.
3. Empathy helps leaders to perform well in coaching, engaging others, and making decisions.
4. Empathy is correlated with ethics and compliance, and any compliance failure can prove costly.
5. Empathy can reduce the severity of any scandals.
6. Empathy can help improve social responsibility.

Can empathy be practiced? Why do some people lack the empathy? There are several reasons why leaders fail to show empathy in a way that needy people expect them to. Some of the reasons include the following:

- Anger
  Anger suppresses a person's ability to feel warmth for those around her. Taking a step back from emotional anger can give a person the ability to empathize with employees, customers, or any other people involved in the activities.

- Stress
  Stress kills happiness and causes conflict with the people with whom the leader interacts directly or indirectly. Leaders sometimes fall victim to stress. The ability to manage stress using the tools of emotional intelligence can help a leader thrive even under challenging conditions.

- Self-Protection
  People tend to give preference to taking care of their own matters, which limits how much time they spend on others.

Empathy is a way of gaining knowledge for business purposes. It does not mean the leader has to agree with the other person always, but it will help the leader to acknowledge that others have their own perspectives. A leader should stay away from making quick judgments and should take the time to understand other people's problems.

> "Using empathy to understand critical constituents' concerns, frustrations, and feelings will cause a leader think of the big picture and broaden his or her vision."

Empathy causes leaders to put their people at the heart of everything they do. In the case of organizational leaders, the people are employees. In the case of business leaders, the people are customers. In the case of public leaders, the people are the public. Four core principle elements move leaders toward empathetic thinking, as follows:

- Putting people first.
- Nurturing relationships.

- Leveraging technology to create a truly human experience.
- Creating a culture of reciprocal trust.

10.2 Compassion

Compassionate leadership means leading from both the head and the heart. According to Thupten Jinpa, a well-respected scholar and the Dalai Lama's longtime English translator, compassion is defined as "a mental state endowed with a sense of concern for the suffering of others and aspiration to see that suffering relieved." Compassionate leaders put others' needs before their own. In traditional leadership, there is a wrong perception that being compassionate means compromising on the output and profits. Compassion helps leaders to increase their approval rating and makes them more approachable. Increased compassion and understanding fosters trust in people and connects them with their leaders. Compassion does not mean that the leader agrees with whatever has been done by the people in the organization or on the teams. The leader can be compassionate and simultaneously not compromise on the performance of the people on the team. Leaders need to hold people responsible for the delegated tasks. Compassion does not mean that leaders should compromise on the responsibilities. A leader can be compassionate and simultaneously hold others responsible for not meeting high expectations. Compassionate leaders should not distinguish between top performers and low performers. By showing compassion, leaders can encourage people to achieve higher performance. Compassion boosts the energy levels of people within an organization and serves as a motivational tool.

According to Jinpa, there are three pillars of compassion, as follows:

- Cognitive Understanding
  Leaders should conceptually understand the problems, situations, and decisions their peers and employees are facing.

- Affective Understanding
  Leaders should understand people on an emotional level. Are the people feeling stressed out? Are they excited about the

projects they are working on? Do they feel like they are growing professionally, or are they feeling bored with their work?

- Motivational Connection
  The leader should create a sense that he or she wants the people to succeed.

Switching from "I" to "we" is part of the crucial process of becoming an authentic leader. Cultivating compassion also contributes to other constructive changes in how leaders lead, relate to others, and handle the unavoidable toxicity and stress of the job.

An angry response erodes loyalty and trust and inhibits creativity by jacking up employees' stress levels. An environment where there is fear, anxiety, and a lack of trust makes people stay away. If people are afraid and anxious, we know from neuroscience that their threat response is engaged and their cognitive control is impacted. As a consequence, their productivity and creativity diminish. When we feel safe, our brain's stress response is lower. When the leader responds in a frustrated, furious manner, it is less likely that the people will take risks in the future because they will worry about the negative consequences of making mistakes. In other words, the leader kills the culture of experimentation that is critical to learning and innovation. Compassion promotes a culture of safety, which in turn helps encourage the spirit of experimentation that is critical for creativity.

"Compassion boosts the energy levels of people within an organization and serves as a motivational tool."

When trust, loyalty, and creativity are high and stress is low, employees are happier and more productive, and turnover is lower.

"When the leader responds in a frustrated, furious manner, it is less likely that the people will take risks in the future because they will worry about the negative consequences of making mistakes."

10.3 Humility

The quote "When I talk to a manager, I get the feeling that they are important. When I talk to a leader, I get the feeling that I am important" tells us how important it is to lead with humility. As per the *Cambridge Dictionary*, *humility* is defined as "the feeling or attitude that you have no special importance that makes you better than others; lack of pride."[2] Leaders who are humble and admit mistakes outshine them all. There are several ways to use humility to be a more effective leader.

Humility brings emotional neutrality. It keeps a leader from putting herself above others. At the same time, a humble leader does not put herself below others. Humble people feel just as valuable as every other peer, no more and no less. Humility connects leaders with the purpose and causes them to react in light of the purposes. It teaches leaders to merely disconnect from the competitive reflex in situations where it is not productive. The leader who leads a team that is smaller and focused should feel equal, should treat everyone equal on the team, and should not encourage hierarchies. Humble people maintain better social relationships, avoid deception in their social interactions, and tend to be forgiving, grateful, and cooperative.

The best way to practice humility is through self-introspection. By reflecting on our past interactions with others, we can gauge what went well, what went wrong, and what we could do better next time. Self-introspection can enhance our perspective and lead us to learn from our past actions. Human beings do make mistakes, but by being humble, we can recover from them and earn the trust of others. Humble leaders are very honest and seek input from all directions and all people to ensure that there is no confirmation bias in making decisions. People want to follow leaders who value their opinions.

---

[2] *Cambridge Academic Content Dictionary* (Cambridge: Cambridge University Press, 2009), s.v. "humility," 466.

"Humble leaders are very honest and seek input from all directions and all people to ensure that there is no confirmation bias in making decisions."

Humble leaders care about the environment in which the team is working and ensure that the team members have what they need without needing explicit requests from them. Team performance is typically much higher when team members believe their leaders are genuinely humble.

Humility is the best answer to narcissism, which is rife in a culture of overpraising, entitlement, and privileges. Leaders who do not believe in being humble concentrate their power and remove others with strong abilities, suspecting them to be a threat. They take credit for the good and blame others for the bad. It requires humility to admit that some people on the team are better at specific roles. Micromanaging limits leaders from utilizing their full potential. It also kills morale. Moreover, it is not very humble. Humble leaders find good people, coach them, then let them do their jobs.

"Humility is the best answer to, which is rife in a culture of overpraising, entitlement, and privileges."

When leaders lead with humility, the team will see a difference, which in turn will impact not only the business but also the team members' personal lives.

10.4 Kindness

Kindness is an essential trait of effective leadership that helps to build a healthy organizational culture. Kindness in the work culture enables people to help each other, binding the people together with trust. Kindness serves as a tool for motivation. It includes encouraging others and making them feel good about themselves. Everyone in the organization wants to be successful. Giving constructive feedback in a kind manner, providing a kind word of correction, can often go far in improving employee performance. Kindness reinforces employees' self-esteem and their perception of management. Kind leaders place themselves on the same level as others without losing their authority as leaders. One of the reasons why kindness is not well integrated into organizational processes and leadership building is that it is difficult to evaluate.

"Kind leaders place themselves on the same level as others without losing their authority as leaders."

Kindness mitigates the negative effects of power. Kindness teaches leaders about perspective-taking. Perspective-taking is one of the essential skills that leaders should harness.

In the business world, good perspective-taking helps leaders anticipate what the competitors and collaborators are thinking and as a result make better decisions. Within an organization, perspective-taking helps a leader understand the diverse viewpoints and experiences of all the members of the organization and integrate them into the common vision.

10.5 Generosity

Generosity is one of the essential traits of leadership that strengthens various other traits and mechanisms of leadership. Generous people share information readily, give of their expertise easily, maintain a strong work ethic, and collaborate efficiently. Increased cooperation and collaboration, enjoyment of one's work, sheer goodwill, and helping others to grow are all a result of generosity. Moderate generosity deals with trading evenly, meaning that people give when in need and take back when the others are comfortable. Givers genuinely contribute without expecting anything in return.

Generosity goes beyond financial giving or being involved in charitable work. While true generosity is ultimately an act of giving something without expecting anything in return, we can develop several business models around generosity. Generosity makes a work culture more positive. Hoarding information makes people look power-hungry. Sharing information generously, keeping teams posted on where things stand, helps leaders and teams to make well-informed decisions. Generous leaders guide their people rather than controlling them. Generous leaders offer constructive feedback rather than criticism and empower teams to make decisions with robust frameworks of support.

Generous leaders create a sense of shared success and understand that togetherness is much more powerful than singularity.

The generous leader works hard and invests time and energy in what reinvigorates him or her in mind, body, and spirit. Generosity is a chain reaction, meaning that it inspires others to behave in a generous way. Generosity helps leaders make a difference in transformational projects by generating creative and innovative solutions. Also, generosity strengthens the acceptance of responsibility.

10.6 Mindfulness

The human brain is the most complex and compelling biological object in the world. Greatness comes from the capability to generate higher consciousness. The brain requires frequent sharpening practices to unleash its full potential. As we deal with increasing VUCA (volatility, uncertainty, complexity, and ambiguity), mindfulness can lead us to resilient responses to ignite creativity and innovation. Mindfulness is the ability to be fully aware of what we are doing and not to overreact or underreact to what is going on around us. Mindfulness can be cultivated through mechanisms such as meditation, walking, and listening to music. Meditation can be merged with activities such as yoga. Though mindfulness is widely practiced in Hinduism and Buddhism, it is not specifically a religious practice and does not require anyone to change their beliefs. It is more than just a practice. It brings awareness and cuts down on unnecessary stress. From the neuroscience perspective, mindfulness lowers blood pressure and can affect the area of the brain known as the amygdala, which is linked to fear, anxiety, and stress. Meditation filters out negative emotions, suspends a judgmental mentality, unleashes natural curiosity, and helps one to experience warmth and kindness toward others and toward oneself.

"Mindfulness is the ability to be fully aware of what we are doing and to not overreact or underreact to what is going on around us."

With all the near-term pressures in today's society, especially in business, it is challenging to find the right equilibrium between achieving our long-term goals and meeting our short-term financial metrics. As we take on more significant leadership responsibilities, the key is to stay grounded and authentic, face new challenges with humility, and balance professional success with the more important but less easily quantified measure of personal success. For most business decision-making, we interpret past events and anticipate the future. To bring our attention fully to the present state, we need to interrupt our thinking and quiet our minds. Once we bring quietness to mind, it will make the brain more authentic and curious, leading us to question our observations in an open, honest, and nonjudgmental way.

Through mindfulness, we can shift our attention inward to observe our thoughts and feelings. This practice changes the brain. Mindfulness affects several regions of the brain but most importantly the anterior cingulate cortex and hippocampus. These two parts of the brain have been discussed in earlier chapters.

The anterior cingulate cortex (ACC) is a structure behind the brain's frontal lobe. It is associated with self-regulation and learning from past experience to support optimal decision-making. The anterior cingulate cortex is particularly important in the face of uncertain and fast-changing conditions.

The hippocampus, which is part of the limbic system, is associated with emotion and memory. People with stress-related activities tend to have a smaller hippocampus. Neuroscientists have shown that practicing mindfulness affects brain areas related to perception, body awareness, pain tolerance, emotion regulation, introspection, complex thinking, and sense of self. Mindfulness is a way to keep the brain healthy, to support self-regulation and efficient decision-making capabilities, and to protect ourselves from toxic stress.

10.7 Resilience

Resilience is the ability to recover quickly from difficulties or setbacks. The real test of leadership is not how a leader performs during good times but rather how she performs during periods of turbulence. Leaders should see failures as temporary setbacks and should practice recovering quickly. When dealing with VUCA, leaders should find ways to move forward and avoid getting stuck. Often, leaders will step back from transformational initiatives when they see roadblocks or failures. While it is true that the transformation process is not free of failures, the transformational leader must be able to counter these with resilience. Resilience is a highly sought-after personality trait in the modern workplace. It is a kind of muscle that contracts during good times and expands during bad times. The best way to develop resilience is through hardship.

Difficulties strengthen the mind as labor does the body. Struggles serve as a tool to strengthen leadership abilities. Every failure and obstacle comes with a valuable lesson. Carefully evaluating and learning from these is most important for if a leader is to become more resilient. The struggles make a pathway to tremendous opportunities. Leaders should use struggles as a chance to grow and learn resiliency, which is something that a transformational leader needs. It is not entirely straightforward to prove that leaders have the power of resilience unless they have gone through difficult times. Resilience is a chain of actions. The next level of leaders keep watching how the current leaders act in all situations. Showing resilience will make team members take that lesson forward with them in the hopes of becoming more resilient themselves.

> "Difficulties strengthen the mind as labor does the body. Struggles serve as a tool to strengthen leadership abilities."

In a competitive world, business leaders tend to have a sense of urgency about introducing a new line of products. However, transformation can be a lengthy process. The innovation teams should know that the type of creative ideas that make a difference in business can take time to implement. Creativity has its own schedule, and we may not always see the result immediately; the outcome may be some time later. Having a sense of urgency in the creative process is a barrier to innovation.

Despite the overwhelming consensus and supporting evidence that resilience is vital for success in today's business environment, the truth is that resilience is hard. It requires the courage to confront painful realities, it requires faith that there will be a solution even if one is not immediately evident, and it requires the tenacity to carry on even during hopeless situations. A state of imbalance is manifested in a variety of ways. Some people may experience anger and even rage, projecting blame outward. Others may become depressed and filled with self-doubt.

The condition of imbalance can make a bad situation even worse, eliminating the ability to act with resilience. Anger can turn into the problem by destroying the relationships that are critical for success. Self-doubt can inhibit the proactive behaviors that are necessary for risk-taking. This toxic situation is compounded if the leader is not aware that he or she is out of balance.

> "Resilience requires the courage to confront painful realities, requires faith that there will be a solution even if one is not immediately evident, and requires the tenacity to carry on even during hopeless situations."

Feeling stress can make people stay away from the routines that are so important to healthy living, like exercise, self-reflection, and meditation. Leaders may tend to give up. Investing the time to practice meditation during difficult times makes a leader resilient. It gives the mind greater clarity and can be the source of new, outside-the-box thinking, which is necessary to solve the most complex problems.

Practicing having a positive outlook on adversity is a critical factor for building resiliency as an individual. The leader should set the example for how team members should behave and relate to each other and serve as a role model for a positive outlook on any problems that may arise. If the leader demonstrates a positive attitude at the top, then that will trickle all the way down through the members. Instead of seeing failure or criticism as something personal or negative, the leader should demonstrate that it is an opportunity to improve. Positive relationships are crucial for building resiliency in an organization. Nurturing relationships among the organization's members not only builds their ability to work as a team but also increases performance. The leader should create these relationships by finding time for community activities outside the workplace. The transformational leader must be resilient to create and sustain momentum for the organization and the people he or she serves.

"Every failure and obstacle comes with a valuable lesson, making a pathway to tremendous opportunities."

10.8 Self-Awareness

In 1972, the two psychologists Shelley Duval and Robert Wicklund developed the theory of self-awareness stating that "when we focus our attention on ourselves, we evaluate and compare our current behavior to our internal standards and values. We become self-conscious as objective evaluators of ourselves."[3] Self-awareness strengthens people's nonjudgmental thinking and, according to Daniel Goleman, author of *Emotional Intelligence*, is the key component of emotional intelligence. The ability to monitor our emotions and thoughts from moment to moment is key to understanding ourselves better. Through self-awareness, people tend to act consciously rather than passively. Self-aware people are more likely to be compassionate toward others.

[3] Shelley Duval and Robert Wicklund, *Theory of Objective Self-Awareness* (Cambridge, MA: Academic Press, 1973).

11

Thought Processes for Problem-Solving

11.1 Problem-Solving

Problem-solving is a process of working through the details of a problem to reach a solution. Not limited to mathematics, problems are everywhere. They can be personal problems, organizational problems, business problems, political problems, economic problems, social problems, and virtually anything that involves some decision-making.

According to the World Economic Forum, problem-solving is one of the essential skills needed for the twenty-first century. Leaders of all levels must be proficient in problem-solving because they have to make decisions all the time.

Problem-solving is not a mere ability. Not every problem can be solved by one person alone. Some problems can be solved based on experience, and some problems can be solved with guidance from experts, but most challenging problems can be solved only through collaboration and by applying a right thinking process. Actual problem solvers search for problems proactively and shed light on them. This process requires wholeheartedness, a holistic mind-set, and the courage to welcome problems, challenge the status quo, and provide solutions to the problems. Problem-solving requires strong leadership qualities. When dealing with problems in a VUCA environment, leaders should provide energy to the people involved in problem-solving by inspiring them and making the environment highly collaborative. Famous leaders like Mahatma Gandhi, Martin Luther King Jr., Nelson Mandela, John F. Kennedy, Steve Jobs, and Elon Musk dared to take on problems and provide solutions.

Leaders should broaden observation, embrace curiosity, have a holistic view, perform root cause analysis, and look well beyond the obvious to assess the problem. While this way of thinking can solve many problems, it is also highly necessary to foster collaboration in an organization to tackle problems. While there are several schools of thoughts for solving problems, the right process of thinking must be applied depending on the context of the problem. Also, leaders must possess the right amount of knowledge on emotional intelligence, which is an essential component of problem-solving.

"Leaders should broaden observation, embrace curiosity, have a holistic view, perform root cause analysis, and look well beyond the obvious to assess the problem."

Problems mount very fast, demanding immediate solutions. To fix any problems, leaders sometimes take shortcuts in hopes of finding temporary relief. In the process, they fail to address the root causes. This approach leads to a never-ending cycle that makes it difficult to find any real solutions. Leaders who apply linear vision, contrary to circular vision, end up seeing the problems that lie directly in front of them and ignoring the problems around them. This approach becomes contagious, meaning that a problem that is not addressed will keep creating new problems.

It is not entirely possible to be free from all problems. Indeed, the real problems are opportunity providers. This means that problems are of two types: toxins and opportunity providers. The leaders, as a problem solver, must ensure that toxic problems either do not arise or at least are minimized.

Businesses thrive when problem-solving becomes a seamless process that enables the people and the organization to grow. The time has come to broaden the traditional leadership approach and the usual method of decision-making and to form a new perspective based on complexity science. This framework allows executives to see things from new viewpoints, assimilate complex concepts, and address real-world problems and opportunities. Using this approach, leaders learn to define the framework with examples from their own organization's history and scenarios of its possible future as well as lessons learned from other organizations. This enhances communication and helps executives rapidly understand the context in which they are operating.

Each time, the given problem may be different. Sometimes we may have to combine multiple thinking processes to solve problems. Various thinking processes are as follows:

- Analytical thinking
- Critical thinking
- Strategic thinking
- Entrained thinking
- Fast thinking
- Creative thinking
- Convergent thinking
- Divergent thinking
- Big-picture thinking

"Leaders who apply linear vision, contrary to circular vision, end up seeing the problems that lie directly in front of them and ignoring the problems around them."

11.2 Analytical Thinking

Analytical thinking is a methodical process that involves breaking down complex problems into manageable components and performing step-by-step analysis to derive solutions. Analytical thinking is not just about using computers to perform the analysis. In daily life, we may have to think analytically and draw conclusions. This is done within the mind. Therefore, analytical thinking is a cognitive skill and can be strengthened and developed over time by practice.

Knowingly or unknowingly, we often detect the patterns in specific behaviors and interpret the data to make decisions. One example is driving patterns based on the time, day, and season. Another example is shopping trends. The steps are as follows:

- Gathering relevant information.
- Focusing on facts and evidence.
- Examining chunks of data or information.
- Identifying key issues.
- Using logic and reason to process information.
- Separating more complex information into simpler parts.
- Subdividing information into packets of manageable sizes.
- Finding patterns and recognizing trends.
- Identifying cause and effect.
- Understanding connections and relationships.
- Eliminating extraneous information.
- Organizing information.
- Drawing appropriate conclusions.

Analytical thinking is said to be a left-brain process. We have discussed creative thinking in depth in the chapter “Igniting Creativity.” Let us now examine what will happen on the left side of the brain concerning analytical thinking.

In the left hemisphere of most people’s brains, the logical thinking processes are found. It seems that the mode of operation of the brain’s left hemisphere is linear; it processes information sequentially, one bit after another, in an ordered way. Perhaps the most apparent linear faculty is language.

Speech, being linear, is a left-hemispheric activity. Now, scientists have found that some everyday human tasks activate one side of the brain while leaving the other mainly at rest. For example, a person's learning a mathematical proof might evoke activity in the left hemisphere of his brain.

Some people, for example, lawyers, accountants, and planners, have better-developed left-hemispheric thinking processes, while others like artists, sculptors, and politicians have better-developed right-hemispheric processes.

There is a fundamental difference between formal planning and informal managing, a difference accounted for by the two hemispheres of the human brain. The process of planning and management is sequential and systematic. Planners and management scientists are expected to proceed in their work through a series of logical, ordered steps, each one involving explicit analysis.

Formal planning, then, seems to use processes akin to those identified with the brain's left hemisphere. Furthermore, planners and management scientists seem to revel in a systematic, well-ordered world, and many show little appreciation for the more relational holistic processes.

11.3 Critical Thinking

Critical thinking is about judgment. In a busy life with analytics all around us, the trend is toward more analytical thinking depending deeply on the numbers. While it is true that analytics play a crucial role in decision-making, there are several situations and scenarios where the context comes into the picture for decision-making. Critical thinking improves the quality of thinking by systematically applying intellectual standards. Intellectual standards include the clarity, accuracy, precision, consistency, relevance, soundness, depth, breadth, and fairness of the information gathered from observations, experience, and communication. Critical thinking filters out biases and distortions from a set of information for solving a problem and making a conclusion. Biased thinking is costly for both individuals and an organization. Improving critical-thinking skills is one of the most essential things to improving business outcomes.

"Critical thinking filters out biases and distortions from a set of information for solving a problem and making a conclusion."

Critical thinking has been an integral part of leadership since before anyone started tracking leadership trends. However, given recent changes in academic curriculums, quantitative skills are taking precedence over qualitative skills. Hyperconnectedness and the elements of VUCA are bringing critical thinking to the elite once more.

Critical thinking is a mental process; as such, it varies according to mind-set. Toxic moods such as anger, anxiety, stress, and grief prevent people from thinking critically. On the other hand, positive emotions such as compassion, humility, kindness, generosity, and empathy can help people to think critically and come up with rational conclusions.

While assumptions are used to connect the dots, making decisions based on assumptions without supporting evidence can lead to costly mistakes. Assumption is an enemy of critical thinking. Context-based and intellectual analysis helps to eliminate false assumptions and to draw meaningful conclusions.

Intellectual analysis looks at alternative viewpoints from an emotionally intelligent, nonbiased, analytical perspective to discover truths and solve problems. Critical thinking can be practiced. The concepts that strengthen critical thinking are as follows:

- Apply the why–what–how method to determine how and why the problem arose and what needs to be done to solve the problem.
- Apply big-picture thinking to gather information from 360 degrees.
- Consider alternative viewpoints.
- Use assumptions to increase the breadth and depth of the information but not for the conclusions.
- Use emotional intelligence.
- Avoid favoritism, and suppress biases.

A fundamental difference between analytical thinking and critical thinking is that analytical thinking involves breaking down complex information into smaller parts, whereas critical thinking involves taking outside knowledge into account when evaluating information. Analytical thinking seeks to review and break down the information gathered, whereas critical thinking looks to make a holistic judgment using various sources of information, including a person's existing knowledge.

Analytical thinking is more linear, a step-by-step breaking down of information. On the other hand, critical thinking is a more holistic approach seeking to assess, question, verify, infer, interpret, and formulate.

Analytical thinking can be thought of as a step in the critical-thinking process. When we have a complex problem to solve, we will want to use our analytical skills before applying critical-thinking skills. Critical thinking does involve breaking down information into parts and analyzing the parts in a logical, step-by-step manner, but it also involves taking other information into account to make a judgment or formulate innovative solutions.

Additionally, with analytical thinking, we use facts derived from the information gathered to support our conclusions. Conversely, with critical thinking, we make a judgment based on our opinion formed by evaluating various sources of information, including our own knowledge and experiences.

11.4 Strategic Thinking

Strategic thinking is the ability to look into the future, both short term and long term, and design solutions to fulfill people's needs. The solutions can include products, services, processes, or policies or can take any other form. With strategic thinking, we can focus on the long term while maximizing outcome in the short term. Without strategic thinking, the decisions a leader makes today could have a negative impact on future outcomes regardless of how best they fit into current business conditions.

Strategic thinking is a mental process. It requires deep thinking and much incubation in the brain to come up with decisions. A decision is not something that can be arrived at instantly. Strategic thinking will have the best results when done in a low-stress environment where one can freely think without distraction. That is the main reason why many organizations, whether they are business or public policy, do not expose their strategic thinkers to the general public.

A leader as a strategic thinker should not make any decisions as an individual. Strategic leaders can capture ideas that come from several sources, such as what he or she has written on paper, in a journal, or in a computer but this is insufficient. Leaders must reach out to other leaders and listen to them to understand their thinking. A leader must interact with all kinds of people to know what the impact of the decision will be both within the organization and on the market.

Strategic thinking takes a systemic approach involving multiple revisits of the ideas, forecasting the outcomes of each time frame, and embedding the outcome with the corresponding time frames. It requires taking into consideration the obstacles one expects to meet within each time frame, availability of resources, the costs and benefits of decision-making, and much more.

Strategic thinking aims to create value by challenging the assumptions about an organization's value proposition and uncovering potential opportunities. By understanding the fundamental drivers of a business, strategic thinkers can challenge the conventional thinking by enabling a provocative and creative dialogue among people who can affect the organization's direction. Boards should encourage forward thinking in leaders of all levels by having the foresight to understand what has not yet taken shape.

Strategic leaders should have the ability to imagine in the future by having a reference point in the present. This requires spending much time considering, imagining, and fantasizing about the future by visualizing a more complex future state. It is like living in two parallel dimensions. Strategic thinking is done in four stages involving various leadership traits in the fourth stage. The four stages are as follows:

- ➢ Understand the past.
- ➢ Understand the current business model.
- ➢ Forecast the destiny.
- ➢ Inject unconventional decision-making.

As such it requires a blend of analytical thinking, creative thinking, and critical thinking.

The detailed steps involved in strategic thinking process are these:

- Anticipate
  Leaders must be constantly vigilant to anticipate what is ahead by scanning the environment looking for signals of threats and opportunities.

- Challenge
  Leaders should question the status quo by challenging their own and others' assumptions and encouraging divergent points of view.

- Interpret
  Leaders should be able to recognize patterns, push through ambiguity, and seek new insights.

- Align
  The insights gathered through the analysis must be aligned with the broader interests of the organization, the customers, and the society.

- Decide
  Leaders should evaluate multiple options by following a disciplined process that considers the trade-offs involved and takes both short- and long-term goals into account.

- Reflect
  Reflecting on interactions with various customers, partners, and market segments to better predict industry shifts and also to learn from the successes and failures is critical to improving strategic thinking.

"Leaders should have the ability to imagine the future by having a reference point in the present."

11.5 Creative Thinking

Creative thinking is a mechanism that unleashes the potential of the mind to conceive new ideas. These ideas have the potential to change people's lives all over the world. Creativity is the driving force behind innovation and transformation. Many current world problems can be solved using creativity. Indeed, many problems were solved using creativity for millenniums. Human creativity drove advancements in the arts and sciences, technology, residential planning, transportation, entertainment, and economic prosperity—almost every significant advance achieved by any society.

Creativity has been discussed in detail in chapter 3: Igniting Creativity.

The secret behind creativity is to bombard the mind with new experiences and ideas entirely outside one's field, filtering out the noise and connecting the dots among the remaining ideas.

Unleashing creative potential within an individual is possible by training the brain. Some methods that will help a person to train the brain to unleash his or her creative potential are as follows:

- Empathy
- Curiosity
- Observations
- Listening
- Questioning
- Experimentation
- Metaphoric thinking
- Divergent thinking
- Courage
- Intuition

When we think of any solution to a problem, we usually impose specific constraints. This is called "inside-the-box thinking." By relaxing these self-imposed constraints, we can make the brain move into divergent thinking. The goal of divergent thinking is to generate many different ideas about a topic in a short period. This breaks down the topic into smaller parts so that we may gain insight into various aspects of the topic. Divergent thinking typically occurs in a spontaneous, free-flowing manner such that the ideas are generated in a random, unorganized fashion. Following divergent thinking, ideas and information will be organized using convergent thinking to put those various ideas back together in some structured way. Convergent thinking is mostly analytical. It excludes some of the ideas gathered from divergent thinking. This means that while finding a solution to the problem, the brain functions steadily alternate between divergent thinking and convergent thinking.

12

Leadership Lessons from Wildlife

Leadership skills are not limited to human beings. Other species such as animals, birds, fish, and insects do possess excellent leadership skills. The most exciting things that we can learn from their leadership styles is the way they communicate, guide, collaborate, influence, and help each other. Indeed, several designs and processes that are used to solve problems in society and invent new things use the concept called biomimicry. Birds helped us to design airplanes; fish helped us to design a better swimsuit. Similarly, leadership lessons from wildlife can help us to solve the problems in the business world. The way that other creatures communicate can teaches us how nonverbal unspoken signals can be adapted to design business models.

A few examples of other species that show core leadership principles are as follows:

- Eagles
- Ants
- Elephants
- Horses
- Migratory birds
- Hummingbirds

12.1 Lessons from Eagles

In Hinduism, the *garuda* is a divine eagle-like bird and the king of birds. One airline's name in Indonesia is Garuda. The American bald eagle is the national bird of the United States of America.

While there are several lessons that modern leaders can learn from eagles, the main traits are as follows:

- Mentoring
- Vision
- Transformation
- Fearlessness

The way that adult eagles teach eaglets to fly is quite fascinating. The eagle will carry the eaglet on its back, climb to a high altitude, and swoop down, letting the eaglet go. Then the adult catches the eaglet after a few moments. This process is repeated until the eaglet learns how to fly on its own. If the mother eagle thinks that the eaglet is too weak to learn, then she slowly destroys its nest, forcing the eaglet to learn to fly.

Even when the eagle quietly sits, it continuously watches its surroundings, taking in the whole 360 degrees. Even when it is flying it scans the surroundings. Eagles have compelling eyesight with long-distance focus and clarity. They can spot another eagle soaring from fifty miles away. Their vision, clarity, and focus helps them to see the big picture. The eagle's vision reminds leaders to see reality in the present as well as make predictions with clarity and using big-picture thinking.

Eagles go through a process, called a molt, of losing feathers and through it essentially achieve transformation or metamorphosis. With age, the quality of an eagle's feathers will degrade, so the feathers get replaced. Eagles lose their feathers gradually and symmetrically. In other words, an equal number of feathers is lost on each wing to maintain balance in flying. After going through this metamorphosis, the eagle will live like a young bird. This concept implies that leaders should reflect on their leadership capabilities whether or not improvements are needed and transform themselves so as to be able to lead efficiently amid changing conditions.

Eagles are fearless. They take on prey much more massive than they are. When a storm comes, the eagle soars to greater and greater heights. This tells leaders that they should set their sights on big targets and be confident in achieving the goal.

12.2 Lessons from Ants

The lessons we can learn from ants are especially useful for organizational leadership. The three primary leadership qualities that ants exhibit are as follows:

- Self-organized collaboration
- Setting big targets
- Saving for a rainy day

By working as a team, ants do great work by creating synergy. They do not leave their fellow ants behind when carrying huge objects. They help each other. They know how to communicate with one another. When they carry objects, they all move in the same direction. They are self-organized without much supervision. Ants share information without having any central coordinating facility. This is true even when ants are not working. Ants are classified into three types: soldier ants, worker ants, and fertile ants. Worker ants go searching for food. When a worker ant finds food, it returns to the nest to share what it has discovered without keeping the information selfishly to itself. When ants leave their nest to search for food, they leave behind a trail of chemical scents to help them find their way back home. After an ant finds food, it lays down more scent on the trail, reinforcing the trail. When other worker ants come across the pheromone trail, they abandon their search and follow the trail directly to the food source.

Ants are not afraid of the size of the objects they want to carry. They create synergies through the collaboration. Ants working together can carry an object with a weight more than the sum of the weight that each ant can carry individually. Similarly, leaders, by encouraging collaboration teams, can achieve bigger goals than those that can be achieved without collaboration.

Ants do not eat all the food on the spot. They will carry the food to their nest and save some of it for a rainy day.

12.3 Lessons from Elephants

Female elephants are the leaders of the herd. They teach several exciting lessons, especially one showing the benefits that females bring to the leadership role.

The primary leadership qualities that we learn from elephant leadership are as follows:

- Wisdom
- Problem-solving
- Social intelligence
- Patience
- Compassion

Elephants run a matriarchal society with a group called a herd. A herd typically consists of twelve elephants. It is led by the wisest and oldest female, called the matriarch. The herd typically includes the leader, her young kids, siblings, cousins, et cetera. The leader emerges based on the respect she has earned by the other elephants. The herd relies on the leader to make decisions regarding the course of action. The herd follows the matriarch by walking behind her. If the herd contains mothers with kids, the young elephants follow their mothers, holding onto their tails with their trunks.

Even though the matriarch does not have speed, she makes up for it with her leadership skills, enabling elephants to survive in their harsh environment. The matriarch demonstrates leadership through her wisdom, strength, problem-solving skills, social intelligence, confidence, patience, and compassion. Elephants are known to have an exceptional long-term memory. Matriarchs carry crucial information such as where water and food resources are. The knowledge comes through her seniority. Young female elephants stay with their mothers for life, whereas young males may join another herd. The matriarch spends friendly playful time with her immediate family members and members of her extended family. Matriarchs can make wise decisions using years of experience and wisdom to avoid danger. Any members of the herd may offer a suggestion, but they leave the ultimate decision to the matriarch. Matriarchs have the patience to think and respond to all situations calmly and confidently. Baby elephants are born with few instincts. Mothers and relatives or other female elephants teach the newborn elephants. Matriarchs are compassionate toward their immediate family members as well as toward extended family.

12.4 Lessons from Migratory Birds

Birds migrate with a pattern of moving from areas of decreasing resources to areas of increasing resources.

The primary leadership qualities that one can learn from migratory birds are as follows:

- Leaders take responsibility.
- Others share the leader's responsibility.
- They all collaborate for purposes of synergy.

The primary resources that migratory birds seek are lengthy daylight, temperature, food, and nesting locations. Food is not the sole reason why they migrate, because they leave long before food becomes scarce. The length of daylight and the temperature influence birds' hormones. Together these factors motivate them to migrate to places where they can find resources. They fly back to northern regions in the spring, where they find increased resources.

Birds use their natural powers as well as knowledge to find their migratory routes. There are hundreds of types of birds that migrate seasonally. Some of them have the power to find the direction based on the sun's position and time of year. Some of them have built-in magnetism to distinguish between south and north. Some birds use their knowledge of the landscape, such as rivers, mountains, and valleys, to determine their location.

However, the most exciting part is not about how birds find their way but how they lead the flock to the flyways. Some birds stop during nighttime, and some birds make a nonstop flight from the origination to the destination. The critical factor is the V-shaped formation of birds on their flyways.

The V-shaped formation serves two purposes. First, in the V-shaped formation, each bird flies slightly above the bird in front of it, resulting in a reduction of wind resistance. The front-most bird breaks the wind resistance, and the birds following it can fly more efficiently. The front-most bird conserves energy to break the wind resistance and serves as the leader. Second, the V-shaped formation allows each bird in the flock an unobstructed field of vision, allowing all the birds to see each other and communicate while in flight. The V formation gives birds enough energy to make it to the end of their long migration. Every few minutes, one of the birds from the back of the group come to the front and takes over the lead position, giving the previous leader a chance to take a break. The lead bird's primary role is to help reduce air drag so that the group can fly without consuming more energy.

From these observations, we may conclude that regardless of whatever formal title a person might hold in his or her organization, the leadership position can be shared. When birds fly together in the V formation, they can cover more distance than if the birds were to fly alone. This is the type of synergy that collaboration creates. Teams accomplish more working together than by working independently.

12.5 Lessons from Hummingbirds

Small hummingbirds with colorful feathers show their specialty in nature. They can flap their wings very fast, typically eighty times per second, making a humming noise. That is where the name *hummingbird* came from. They can fly right, left, up, down, backward, and upside down.

The leadership lessons that hummingbirds offer to modern leaders are as follows:

- Have agility.
- Scan for threats.
- Thrive in VUCA conditions.

Hummingbirds get the nectar out of an even tiny flower by continually looking out for aggressive species such as crows that sit in or fly around trees. Also, a hummingbird maintains a stable position in space even when its wings are beating eighty times per second. Disruptive effects such as wind gusts can throw them off.

Being agile is one of the strengths of the hummingbird. Agility helps them to escape predators and outcompete rivals. They take breaks from drinking nectar to scan the skies and trees, searching for potential attackers that may interrupt their meal. Hummingbirds can even chase larger birds such as hawks away from their territories. If a predator catches a hummingbird from behind, its loosely attached tail feathers pull out, giving the bird a chance to get away.

This behavior resembles the current business world and the VUCA environment, where leaders have to deal with disruptive, volatile technological changes continually and adapt to complex demographic needs in a very narrow time frame to keep customers happy while dealing with the stress of competition that is mushrooming everywhere. During the transformation process, leaders must maintain a stable position in disruptive markets, just like the hummingbird maintains balance even during the disruptive wind gusts while getting the nectar from flowers.

12.6 Lessons from Horses

Like elephants, horse have a matriarchal society with the herd led by a female horse. There are several other matriarchal societies, such as lions and honeybees.

Horses teach us several leadership qualities, as follows:

- Showing a presence
- Communication
- Being aware of the surroundings
- Spirit

Horses developed a herd life over a few million years for survival purposes by drawing on each other's strengths, moving toward that which is confident, and adapting to environmental changes. Female horses create and govern the order of the herd and impose discipline. The lead horse asserts her authority through her actions and observes the rest of the herd to ensure they understand. She guides the herd and keeps them safe. Horses use a nonaggressive way in all their actions.

Human brains are trained not to pay attention to nonverbal cues and filter them out. Humans could benefit from better understanding each other's nonverbal communication. This would enhance group dynamics. Horses are always aware of their surroundings and circumstances.

13

Human Experience Transformation

Technology has been advancing for the past few decades, and more and more organizations, regardless of the sector, are depending more on technology. Despite the advancements, organizations are failing when it comes to providing a better experience to humans, whether they are customers, patients, students, or internal employees. The benefits of technological advancements are not effectively reaching all corners.

For example, one finds in every hospital room patients, families, and staff feeling stress and anxiety around high-technology equipment that is continuously beeping. There are numerous reasons why hospitals are lagging behind in providing a better human experience. In most parts of the world, a hospital's administrative staff primarily focuses on monetizing the patient's condition. With that purpose in mind, the staff communicates critical information with a sense of urgency. However, that sense of urgency only enhances anxiety in patients. Moreover, the administrative processes hinder the human experience as they are not streamlined from the patient's perspective. There are multiple bills, duplicate forms, duplicate tests, et cetera.

Human experience is how people perceive their interactions with an organization. It is determined by the way an organization is delivering value to people. Delivered value makes people emotionally engage in using the product or service. The human experience is how an organization makes people feel. It is the human experience that feeds the value back to the organization when the organization successfully executes human-centric strategies.

People interact with an organization in several ways, such as going to a physical location, calling into the contact center, navigating through the website, using the apps, and using the products or services.

Once customers decide whether the product or service is easy to deal with, they will make a decision whether they want to continue with it or not. Once customers find that the interaction is enjoyable, useful, and usable, they will emotionally bond with the organization, product, or service, thereby boosting its reputation.

The experience that is focused on cost optimization does not last long. The factors that are most important to the design process are customer thoughts, emotions, and perceptions about their interactions with the organization, product, or service. As discussed in chapter 3: Igniting Creativity, focus group testing will result in a biased customer expectation. The design process requires real-time engagement of customers and employees to devise new interactions and to come up with innovative customer experiences. Using the cocreative design process, design teams should be able to gather a vast amount of customer insights into a multitude of products and touch points, thereby understanding the journey of the customer.

Touch points describe the customer's interaction with the company and include such things as purchase, service calls, and billing. The touch points are merely a set of discrete actions. However, the customer journey spans a variety of touch points, with each touch point interconnecting and contributing to the overall journey. This means that a better design should pay attention to the end-to-end experience that customers will have with a company from their own perspective.

Understanding customer journeys helps an organization to mobilize employees to deliver value to customers consistently, in line with the organization's purpose.

As digital transformation is setting the bar high in every sector, the real challenge to transformational leaders is to collaborate with the cocreators. As an example, digital players such as Amazon and Uber are continuously reinventing themselves using cocreation and delivering better customer experiences.

Customer experience transformation is a complex and multidimensional task. It requires commitment from senior executives, cross-functional teamwork, more digital enablers, and an agile way of delivery along the journey of transformation, including all its phases. The traditional incumbents need to create customer-centric strategies that can sustain new levels of speed, agility, efficiency, and precision by combining digital technologies with existing capabilities. Transforming the customer journey and implementing customer-centric organizational transformation at scale is possible by way of adopting design thinking and following agile approaches.

As discussed under the section "Design Thinking," applying design-thinking methodologies is the best starting point to begin the process of developing a customer journey instead of merely fixing inefficiencies. The customer's needs and preferences are the starting points. They serve as feedback points, meaning that the customer experience is designed by thinking like the customer. Designs are immediately tested and iterated based on customer feedback. This is called a zero-based journey redesign as it designs the customer journey from scratch rather than merely improving the status quo. One example is redesigning the instant account-opening process by eliminating a large number of steps, enabling account opening anytime and anywhere and fostering a mobile journey. By adapting design thinking in an organization, management will be able to form a new vision and understand how the redesigned services will help to redesign other products or services for a broad range of customer journeys.

Journey maps are evolving to facilitate better management of customer experience programs. Customer journey maps are end-to-end customer experience visualizations that empower companies to make value-driven decisions based on a customer experience model of performance.

Customer experience is not a rigid process. As continuous evolution of digital capabilities is changing customer expectations rapidly, any designed customer experience will have a limited time span. Changing customer dynamics requires fast, frictionless, real-time insights into customer journey management and design. Therefore, any customer experience program must have an agile process to generate insights by employing flexible and dynamic research approaches. By conducting an in-depth experience assessment of current customer touch points and combining this with the empathize phase of design thinking, it is possible to generate valuable insights and initiate a zero-based approach to rethink the customer journey.

Customer experience programs should be positioned as strategic. Several factors determine the success of any customer experience program, as follows:

- Customer engagement
- Business goals aligned with the customers' perspectives
- Innovation mind-set
- Clear purpose
- Design thinking
- Agile approach
- Management commitment

Despite the rise of digital channels, there are still places where customers are failing to adopt digital channels. This is because customers must become self-sufficient to the degree desired. Making customers adopt the digital channels is another process that organizations need to establish. Gauging the voice of the customer through the feedback, including satisfaction scores and verbatim opinions from sources like social media, is essential to transforming the customer experience. This involves a dedicated group tasked with gathering internal and external insights on what truly matters to the target customer, within the industry, and for the organization, and aggregating the insights and producing the analytics on customer experience. To encourage customer adoption of digital journeys, it is critical to find a suitable way of using multiple levers to drive adoption. Providing incentives, offering bonus points or other financial rewards, and limiting access to legacy channels allows companies to accelerate customer digital adoption.

The customer experience depends on a clear sense of purpose to serve the customers' real needs. A company must establishing clear purpose statements and a vision statement and share them to inspire authentic and consistent brand value proposition. Shaping customer perceptions can generate significant added value. Understanding behavioral psychology plays a big role in kowing which customer journey experiences drive customer perceptions and satisfaction levels.

14

Business Model Transformation

Linear transformation is not new to the industry. For example, the emergence of the internet and related technologies brought about the concept of e-commerce. However, this merely transferred the physical store to the online platform. These technologies have never transformed any industry on their own. Exponential transformation has the potential to transform the business model linking digital technologies to an emerging market need. Indeed, business model transformation and digital transformation are connected in two ways. To unleash the full potential of digital technology, a company must transform its existing business model and discover a new business model to use digital technologies to their full potential.

For example, Airbnb realized that technology had great potential and designed an entirely new business model challenging the traditional economics of the hotel business. Their business model came up with a platform producing value for both guests and property owners and producing value to itself, eventually creating the shared economy.

Some of the fundamentals that contribute to an excellent business model are the following:

- Products or services that are better tailored to customers' individual and immediate needs.
- The model that allows the sharing of precious assets. Uber and Airbnb are the best examples.
- A fee structure based on the use of the product or service, rather than requiring customers to buy outright.
- An ecosystem that allows seamless collaboration among partners.

A business model is defined as a way of creating and capturing value by business organizations. It is a system where various features interact, often in complex ways, to determine business success.

A business model relies on the three following building blocks:

- Value creation
- Value delivery
- Value capture

All three of these building blocks are centered on the customer and other people involved in the process. Business delivers value to customers by creating value either alone or by cocreation. Cocreation involves the customers or partners or both. The value delivered to the customer provides returns to the business, which are typically reinvested to create more value and compensate employees and business owners.

How an organization delivers value to its customers by way of its business model also depends on its operating model. All three of these building blocks depend on the customer experience.

There are three ways organizations are deploying digital capabilities to transform their business models:

➢ Modifying existing business models
  Organizations are modifying their existing business models by augmenting traditional capabilities with digital technologies.

- Introducing new business models
  Organizations are introducing new business models using digital capabilities.

- Globalizing the organization
  Organizations are generating additional revenue by expanding the traditional business worldwide with the help of digital capabilities.

14.1 Value Creation

Digital capabilities change the way an organization can create value. That is why this value is often referred to as digital value. Digital value creation comes from the ways in which a business connects with partners and customers, offering new business insights.

Digital relationships provide data that reaches farther into a customer's world than one's competitors do. This data makes possible new relationships with customers and a new level of intimacy, allowing firms to personalize offerings. The digital economy is resulting in new types of value chains, partnerships, and ecosystems.

Business, whether it is done independently or with external partners, heavily depends on market interactions, which require information exchange, coordination, safeguarding, et cetera. When there is not enough information out there, the result is information asymmetry. Digitization embraces the connections among several exchanges and produces more information. Individuals and market participants utilize a multitude of exchange networks that easily form and grow. The vast amount of information available reduces information asymmetry between information producers and information consumers—in other words, between market participants.

Value creation is defined by several key features that include the following:

- Value proposition
- Open innovation and cocreation
- Value chain
- Revenue chains

Value Proposition

The first advancements in technology helped business leaders to improve productivity and efficiency. They also helped to expand businesses to new markets. The fruits of technological advancements are increasing customer expectations, which is putting pressure on business leaders to change the way they design strategies. People are using social networks to find the things they need and achieve their goals. This is making businesses place their focus more on their customers than they've done in the past. Business will need to reshape their products and services, realigning with customer preferences and inform customer of every activity involved in the buying and selling chain. In other words, businesses must reshape the value proposition.

What is a value proposition? Customers evaluate products and services to determine if they can provide desired benefits. Customers typically will not spend much time on evaluation. They use the thirty-second rule, meaning that thirty seconds is long enough to find out why the product or service is superior to competing offerings.

Value proposition is defined as a business value showing why the customers think the product or service should be purchased.

Even though businesses should earn revenue from their products or services, the goal of value proposition is to focus on what the customer wants. Value propositions vary based on market segments or groups of customers.

No matter how much is invested, some products or services fail if the organization does not view the business from a customer's perspective. The best value proposition does not come from merely the quantity of features but from both quantity and quality of features. Harnessing insights about the customers to better understand their pain points and embedding those insights into the value proposition process is a critical success factor. That is where digital enablers play a critical role.

Below are some of the critical factors that need to be considered when developing a value strategy:

- Why the product or service has been developed.
- What exactly the products or services do.
- Who the target audience is.
- Why they should buy the product or service.
- What their pain points are.
- How the product or service remedies the pain points.
- How much originality lies in the product or service.
- How the performance has been improved compared to existing products or services.
- How much customization is done for the segmented markets.
- How easy it is for customers to use the product or service.

Ultimately the value proposition boils down to a statement that paints a clear picture of what the product or service is offering. Let us look at a few examples:

- Blue Apron – "Food is better when you start from scratch."
- Netflix – "Watch anywhere. Cancel anytime."
- Spotify – "Music for everyone."

Open Innovation and Cocreation

Open innovation creates an environment where individuals and organizations can collaboratively develop products. The individual includes suppliers, partners, and the broader business community. The use of "knowledge of knowledge" will help to accelerate innovation. Instead of entirely relying on their own research, organizations can acquire inventions or intellectual property from other companies to advance their business model. The competitive advantage comes from discovering and leasing others' innovations. Open innovation is an inclusive, social way of solving complex problems and bringing innovative solutions.

While open innovation enables collaboration between different organizations and involves the sharing of intellectual property, it does not actively involve customers. The digital economy has made customers a new asset class to organizations. The value is measured by way of how much insight customers bring to the organization.

Cocreation, on the other hand, involves the customers in building the products and services. The most common definition of *cocreation* is "an active, creative and social process, based on collaboration between producers and users."[4]

Cocreation is a way of developing new product and service ideas together with the customers. It is a way of turning customer engagement and direct insights into a creative process. During the course of cocreation, an organization provides public or private platforms granting freedom to customers to participate in the production of things they themselves will use and to exchange valuable insights.

The evolution of digital capabilities and social networking is bringing about fundamental shifts to business thinking in the form of cocreation to achieve value creation. The convergence of business and technologies, a rapidly emerging shared economy, the digital economy, increased connectivity, and well-equipped customers has changed many aspects of the business world. Adapting collaboration is the fundamental driver to best utilize the cocreation approach. Cocreation is gaining importance as consumers are actively creating their own value.

In many organizations, value is jointly created by customers who express their requirements, bring their own insights, and even actively participate in the production process. Collaboration requires organizations to relinquish some of their control over the resources that the customer consumes. By opening what is tagged proprietary information to the consumer and by allowing customers to engage in active dialogue, individualized value propositions are created. This new class of privileged customer will foster transparency into products, services, and processes,

[4] C. K. Prahalad and Venkat Ramaswamy, *Co-Opting Customer Confidence* (2000).

and introduce new ways in which the organizations and consumers can achieve mutual benefit. Cocreation gives consumers the opportunity to utilize an organization's expensive and time-consuming processes, from R&D to maintenance. The prevailing customer base will bring synergies into the organization. In other words, the sum of the creative customer energy is higher than what the company can achieve alone.

Value Chain

In any industry, whether it is manufacturing, or product development, or the hospitality industry, the business process may enact certain activities to find solutions from concept to delivery. All these activities when combined represent the value chain. For the service industry, the value chain starts with the subservices required to create the main service and includes steps required to unite these subservices. In the manufacturing industry, the value chain starts with the raw materials used to make products and all subsequent procurements or production to develop the goods. Digitizing every step in the chain by connecting the underlying activities will generate the digital value chain. Digitally enabled technologies such as 3-D printing, and robotics; other enablers connected using the Internet of Things; and analytical tools form a digital chain. The chain is capable of creating value by connecting individuals and machines across the chain, making it possible to generate and draw insights from vast new oceans of data.

Digital capabilities provide opportunities to service brokers, that were once heavily people-focused, to create value in a new way by enabling new and dynamic business models. The purpose of the digital chain is to digitize service activities to improve the customer experience and create value for everyone in the chain.

14.2 Value Capture

In the rapidly changing digital world, business models have to put more emphasis on value creation. In other words, value creation is becoming a core competitive advantage to businesses. However, unless value creation leads to profitability, a business cannot sustain itself to create further value. While traditional models focus more on value capture compared to value creation, digital business sometimes puts less importance on value-capture strategies, assuming that value creation will automatically capture value. This is perhaps a wrong assumption. Both value creation and value capture should be given priority and should have strategies accordingly. Some digital companies could not survive on their own even after amassing a large number of customers who were gaining the benefit because those digital companies did not have well-designed strategies to capture value.

One example during the rise of e-commerce was Napster, which was launched in 1999. It offered peer-to-peer file sharing without having a proper value capture model. Unfortunately, it was unable to convert value creation into revenue.

Value creation and value capture go hand in hand. A well-designed business model should balance the value to customers with the capture of value by the business. This reminds the broader business community to develop a shared understanding of strategy to capture value.

In the rapidly changing business world, business models are unable to last for decades, and they have finite life spans. When there are changes in technology, consumer demand, or the competitive landscape, the business model and its value capture component must be revised. Continuous sensing of the need for change must be cultivated and built into an organization's structure.

The rise of new revenue models is making even incumbents think of new ways to offer their products and services. For example, General Motors is experimenting with a new model of car ownership that allows customers to trade cars a certain number of times to avail themselves of different types of vehicles. In other words, GM is experimenting with subscription-based ownership.

Let us briefly discuss the revenue models that were introduced recently by a few digital businesses. Customer data drive these value capture models, value-based pricing, auctioning, demand-driven pricing, bundling, unbundling, and sharing.

- The Subscription Model: Companies charge the customer periodically to give access to their products or services. Examples include Netflix, Adobe, and Apple Music.

- The Freemium Model: Companies provide a basic product or service for free, hoping that customers will contribute to the data assets, and then set a specific fee to upgrade to the full offer. Examples include LinkedIn and Spotify.

- The Free Model: This model turns customer actions and behaviors into insights and monetizes those insights by correlating them with advertisers. Examples include Google and Facebook.

- The Shared Economy Model: This model creates a community of consumers and providers or buyers and sellers, providing the digital mechanisms to share the resources. Examples include Uber and Airbnb.

- The Hypermarket Model: This model provides a marketplace where consumers gain more profound insights about the products they want to buy and avail themselves of an immersive purchasing experience. Amazon is an example.

- The Experience Model: This model provides a superior experience compared to competitive players and charges a premium. Examples include Tesla and Apple products.

- The Ecosystem Model: Businesses are moving toward an ecosystem that involves several firms working together. Any company in the ecosystem must maintain an acceptable balance between its profits and the profits of the firm's ecosystem partners.

- Demand-Driven Model: The charges are set based on fluctuations in aggregate demand. Industries such as airlines and hotels use forecasting models based on reservation patterns to maximize profitability during both peaks and valleys.

- Value-Based Model: Instead of determining the price based on production cost or based on what competitors are charging, the value-based model sets the price based on offerings that are worthwhile to the customer.

- Auctioning Model: This model is the best fit for the business-to-consumer environment where businesses compete for customer information. Customers benefit when they contribute to the third-party business that is bidding.

- Unbundle Model: The traditional bundle offers a combined price to induce customers to buy more than they may want. This model makes them obligated to buy unnecessary things. Examples include travel packages. Though specific components of the bundle are most valuable and cheap, the unnecessary components add a heavy burden to customers. The unbundle model, on the other hand, is offered on an individual basis. For example, Spirit Airlines and Frontier Airlines detached baggage and seat preferences from the base price so that customers who travel without baggage and who prefer to sit anywhere can benefit from lower prices.

14.3 Value Delivery

The largest hurdle to success is the culture of many businesses themselves. Structured in a world where digital technologies didn't yet exist, many companies struggle to transform in order to deliver and evolve experiences—both digital and physical. Most organizations still struggle to realize value from their digital products. Delivering valuable digital products requires complex coordination and understanding across the entire organization. These businessnes struggle with how to achieve the right mind-set—not just in how they do things but also, more importantly, in how they think.

Customer experience is a mechanism that delivers real benefits to companies that successfully execute customer-centric strategies. With the dynamic of value creation and a durable competitive advantage, delivering digital services and operations has emerged as a prime mover in reshaping customer experience in almost every sector.

Many organizations that are leading the way in digital value delivery exhibit key cultural mind-sets, as follows:

- Value-Driven
  These organizations are structured around the delivery of value to customers by empowering individuals across the organization to make business decisions.

- Innovation
  Successful organizations have a sustainable method of introducing innovation throughout the product life cycle.

- Experience
  Companies must create and re-create user, customer, and organizational experiences that engage and delight individuals from all touch points while maintaining a focused commitment to the organization's mission, vision, and values.

- Lean Agile
  Lean thinking helps organizations develop the tools they need to scale agile beyond individual development teams to the entire enterprise.

- Culturally Responsive
  It is critical to identify, leverage, and respond to internal and external cultural influences to maximize value.

- Data-Driven
  Success comes from planning and evaluating business using appropriate tools to look at carefully curated data to tell stories with direct and actionable insights.

- Continuous Delivery
  Software becomes valuable once it is delivered, so the delivery process must be streamlined in order to release frequently and continuously.

- Operational Excellence
  Success comes from a focus not only on the creation of digital experiences but also on how those experiences are supported, maintained, and scaled to meet the needs of customers.

15

Digital Transformation

15.1 Adapting Digital Capabilities

Advanced Analytics

Business competitive advantage depends on how efficiently the organization can harvest the mountain of data to make faster and more-accurate decisions, engage customers, employees, and partners in a better way, and discover new business opportunities. Data and analytics have become a competitive asset. The organizations that can adapt quickly and predict trends by continuously analyzing data and developing insights have the potential to disrupt market trends in the digital economy. Advanced analytics are entirely different from traditional business intelligence reports. Advanced analytics are deeply involved in interactions, transactions, information flow, and processes, driving the next wave of productivity and growth.

Descriptive analytics, the most conventional form of analytics, provides a depiction of facts and figures in an understandable format. Descriptive analytics evolved into advanced analytics with the emergence of big data technologies and complex algorithms to help analysts examine the vast data sets to find out the trends, correlations, and customer preferences, and to generate meaningful insights. The vast amounts of diverse data generated by humans, machines, and devices are making it easy to understand continuously changing organization ecosystems, something otherwise not possible with traditional analytics. Advanced analytics serve as digital microscopes that enable organizations to detect hidden insights and promptly act on them. Advanced analytics help to complete the feedback loop between business and technology, creating new business models. Advanced analytics has further evolved and led to the emergence of a new spectrum of digital capabilities such as artificial intelligence, machine learning, deep learning, cognitive computing, and quantum computing.

Advanced analytics consists of 5 C's, as follows:

- Cloud, for computing and producing insights on demand
- Context, for drawing the meaning and finding the correlations
- Community, for shared economy
- Connection, for creating the network of sensors
- Cyber, for model and memory

With the help of digital microscopes, organizations can accelerate discovery, testing, and implementation of analytic solutions and integrate them with the business models.

There are four stages, listed below, involved in enabling advanced analytics for business models:

- ➢ Predictive analytics
- ➢ Prescriptive analytics
- ➢ Monetization
- ➢ Metamorphosis

Predictive Analytics

The value of the data depends on the organization's ability to derive rich insights from it. The insights will help the business to take action that will improve the business and will indicate the next step on the path. Insights provide essential wisdom about the users, and the insights cannot be obtained without analytics. When the data and analytics are coupled with an organization's critical business and operational processes, the insights will give meaning from the business context. That is where the effectiveness of predictive analytics resides. Unlike traditional analytics, where the business uses a set of canned reports, the insight generation process should involve key business stakeholders to provide the full business context and details about the decisions that the key business stakeholders make to support business activities. Digital capabilities should have a provision to produce real-time analytics that can flag anomalies and behavioral changes. Digital capabilities should support leveraging the predictive analytics to uncover individuals' consistent behaviors such as tendencies, preferences, patterns, trends, interests, passions, and associations.

Prescriptive Analytics

This is the stage that takes insights to the next level to make recommendations to customers, employees, and partners by converting the predictions into perspectives. The organization's digital capabilities should have the ability to produce prescriptive analytics to deliver actionable recommendations. Prescriptive analytics requires two additional components on top of the predictive models. The two components are actionable data and a feedback system that tracks the outcome produced by the action taken. The prescriptive model will predict the possible consequences based on the different choice of action and will recommend the course of action for any prespecified outcome.

Monetization

The monetization stage leverages prescriptive analytics to generate net new revenue opportunities to discover unmet customer needs and market demands and to help build new products and services that can be shared across multiple business use cases.

Metamorphosis

This is the most advanced stage of analytics, directly integrating analytics into the business model. The metamorphosis stage exploits the organization's cumulative knowledge of the customer, product, service, and operations to transform the organization's business model to embrace the economic value of the organization's data.

Artificial Intelligence

Artificial intelligence (AI) and machine learning (ML) are two terms that often seem to be used interchangeably, but they are not the same things. Artificial intelligence is a branch of computer science of making intelligent machines that work and react like humans. Some of the activities that artificial intelligence can perform are speech recognition and problem-solving. The intelligence is the computational part of the machines. AI is intended to understand human intelligence but does not conform to the biological behavior of humans.

Artificial intelligence can be broadly classified into two groups, applied and general. General is the more advanced level of intelligence that led to the development of machine learning.

Machine learning is an application of artificial intelligence based on the idea that machines can access data, learn themselves, and perform the tasks.

Artificial intelligence is the science of making computers to solve complex problems that require intelligence when done by humans to enable computers. Artificial intelligence enables researchers and data scientists to construct algorithms that can learn from the data and make predictions. Rather than following a specific set of rules or instructions, an algorithm is trained to spot patterns in massive amounts of data.

Artificial intelligence will play a vital role in digital transformation, enabling new innovative business models. During the journey of digital transformation, AI has the potential to transform the most central functions by bringing speed and accuracy. Artificial intelligence is an umbrella of related technologies such as voice recognition and natural language processing. These technologies help to detect the user's identity and make recommendations that have already transformed some organizations and changed the ways they initially operated. Artificial intelligence will serve as oxygen in the hyperconnected system of devices. The constant availability of artificial intelligence–based machines will reduce the load on human beings. A chatbot is an example of artificial intelligence. Chatbots can chat with a real person. They can fulfill service commitments because they are available around the clock.

Artificial intelligence has been developing concurrently with the rise of computing capabilities. Artificial intelligence is becoming more mainstream and is making an impact on automation and the more knowledge-intensive tasks such as prediction. An application of artificial intelligence is building an autonomous vehicle that requires vast amounts of computing power to interpret all the data harvested from a range of sensors and then enacting the correct procedures for continually changing road conditions and traffic situations. This is where deep learning systems can be "trained" to drive and develop decision-making processes like a human.

Deep learning is an advanced stage of artificial intelligence that processes information in layers, where the result/output from one layer becomes the input for the next one. Deep learning is a set of algorithms that model high-level data concepts by using architectures of multiple nonlinear transformations. It attempts to mimic the activity in layers of neurons in the neocortex, which occupies 80 percent of the brain and is the place where most thinking occurs. Deep-learning algorithms learn to recognize patterns in digital representations of sounds, images, and other data in a real sense. Several types of research spanning decades have attempted to simulate the neocortex's vast array of neurons in an artificial neural network. Advances in mathematics and computers are enabling computer scientists to model the networks of virtual neurons.

Machine Learning

Machine learning is a branch of artificial intelligence based on the idea that machines should be able to learn and adapt to experience and build analytical models. In other words, machine learning is a way of automating the building of analytical models. Feedback and iteration are two significant aspects of machine learning. The models are given access to data. These machines generate the new data out of models, learn from previous computations, produce reliable decisions, and repeat the process. Machines can learn to speak, write, and interpret meanings in videos and images. Advancements in big data technologies brought about the ability for machines to automatically apply complex mathematical computations over and over, faster and faster. Machine learning can analyze both structured and unstructured data at a much higher level of complexity.

Machine learning is still in its early stages. With further advancements, machine learning will have the potential to accelerate digital transformation. Machine learning can reduce human intervention by automating repetitive tasks and helping people to focus more on creativity and problem-solving. Machine learning–based automated systems can classify data on their own, detect objects, recognize faces and speech, find correlations, and predict future outcomes.

At present, machine learning can be classified as either supervised machine learning and unsupervised machine learning. Supervised machine learning requires preparation of sets of data and validating the results manually. Supervised machine learning imposes certain limits because the tasks we want to perform are not scalable easily. In unsupervised machine learning, humans feed the massive data set and find the patterns within it, without humans having first to figure out what the model needs to look for.

Unsupervised learning still needs some human involvement, such as grouping the data the ML creates and assigning a value to the clusters or patterns of data it finds. However, the maturity of machine learning over time will be primarily driven by the quality and quantity of data.

Machine learning should be able to identify the relationships or patterns in a data set and create a model incorporating those relationships.

Machine learning will help businesses to mine customer actions, transactions, and social sentiment to observe customer behavior and personalize the customer experience. In several parts of *The Art and Science of Transformational Leadership*, we have discussed empathy. Can machine learning understand the wants and needs of customers without sacrificing the insights that come from empathy? At present, there are some shortcomings of machines in understanding unstructured human expression. Customers get frustrated sometimes and give a signal that they will not return to a certain business and so forth. Machines cannot understand all the ways human emotion is expressed, whereas humans can learn, classify, and act based on those expressions and emotions. That is where human-supervised machine learning plays an important role. Machines can generate the exceptions requiring human involvement to classify and make corrections to the data so that the machine can make the right decision.

Cognitive Computing

Cognitive computing takes artificial intelligence, machine learning, and deep learning and combines them with cognitive science (the science of how the human brain functions) and computer science.

While both cognitive computing and artificial intelligence can simulate human thinking, only cognitive computing combines the power of humans with the power of machines. With cognitive computing, machines can sense, comprehend, and act on their own.

Artificial assistants provide the right amount of information to us when we ask for it. Smartphones, for instance, serve up mapping functions, calendars, and reminders, as well as give us access to technical knowledge, references, and more.

We trust people if we think they are kindhearted and want us to succeed. We trust them if we understand how they think and if they have the integrity to admit their mistakes and accept blame. Similarly, artificial intelligence will become more trustworthy when it is used collaboratively in a human-led team. For AI to become a collaborator, it will have to be seen as trustworthy consistently and needs to have the smarts and the social savvy to interact in a trustworthy way.

Cognitive computing will serve as a brain interface for artificial intelligence. Cognitive computing relies on deep learning and neural networks. The neural network is a complex tree of decisions that a computer can make to arrive at an answer. The more data the cognitive computing–based machine is exposed to, the more it learns, and the more accurate it becomes over time. A cognitive computing–based machine should serve customers using more in-depth insight, context, and learning by understanding speech, gestures, and even customer expressions.

For example, in a financial institution, monitoring risk and compliance with cognitive capabilities enables assurance across business processes. With the help of cognitive computing, a financial institution can build a system that understands its entire global client base individually, with comprehensive knowledge of both existing and proposed banking regulations across continents, countries, and local regions.

With its access to new analytic insights, the cognitive computing system can filter and digest dynamic internal and external data from the financial ecosystem by capturing market data such as information about industry trends, financial performance, strategic intent, merger and acquisition activity, market risks, and benchmarking. Cognitive computing can unify a view of corporate intelligence based on data from diverse sources, peer connections, and real-time comparisons.

Quantum Computing

Quantum computing, a revolution on its way to disrupt computer science, is being developed based on the principles of quantum physics and the laws of nature. In traditional computer science, a bit is either a 1 or a 0. Therefore the computational power of a computer is dependent on the number of binary transistors contained within its microprocessor. In the 1980s the first Intel processor was made up of twenty-three hundred transistors, but now an Intel processor has more than five billion transistors. However, its computational power is still limited by simple binary options.

As per quantum physics, particles can act like waves, meaning a particle can be particle or wave or particle and wave. Based on the same concept, translating a bit to quantum physics terminology, the qubit has been introduced. A qubit can be a 0 or a 1 or 0 and 1. A qubit can perform two equations at the same time, two qubits can perform four equations, and three qubits can perform eight. That means the computational power is based on an exponent of the number of the qubit. A mature state of quantum computing in the future may help in solving the most complex problems in the universe by tightly integrating cognitive computing with the day-to-day activities of human beings, leading to an exponential transformation of human society.

Internet of Things

The Internet of Things or IoT is a system of interconnected devices that are capable of producing data and transferring that data over a network with or without human interaction. The devices can be mechanical or digital as long as they can produce the data and transfer it. The IoT has the potential to impact how we live and how we work.

Two aspects are fueling the Internet of Things: the number of devices in the universe and the increased bandwidth of the internet. Year after year, the broadband internet is becoming more widely available across several regions, and the cost of connection is decreasing. More devices are coming with built-in Wi-Fi capabilities. The sensors or devices are increasing, and the costs of devices are coming down. With the combination of these two things, the data that is being produced is growing exponentially. The spectrum of devices is vast and includes cell phones, headphones, coffee makers, lamps, washing machines, heaters, coolers, wearable devices, water-level sensors, pollution sensors, street cameras, and a lot more.

The IoT brings endless opportunities and connections and will continually evolve year after year. The IoT will make steady progress in making a positive impact on the lives of people. Let us take an example: if the alarm clock is set to go off at 6:00 a.m., then it can notify the coffee maker to start brewing coffee.

While digital technology is changing the way people live and work, there are still few sectors that need to utilize the potential of digital and improve working conditions. So, the next step in IoT is to move from a connectedness perspective to improve business, life, and society using the insights gained and radically transforming the existing methodologies in operations. Manufacturing requires a digital overhaul, and the value chain needs to be redesigned. IoT, along with other digital capabilities, has the potential to redefine the way people work in manufacturing. The sensors and controls and the communication among them can optimize real-time manufacturing production and supply chain networks, which in turn can enable the rapid manufacture of new products and a dynamic response to production demands.

The IoT can help banks to create more engaging and context-aware customers and improve their overall operational efficiency. For example, a sensor that monitors the activity of agricultural businesses can help to improve underwriting processes and reach new markets.

In summary, the Internet of Things not only will generate valuable data but also, when coupled with other digital capabilities, can consume that data, analyze it, and generate actionable insights. This development will give business leaders the potential to develop new business models around these capabilities. Those business models will have the potential to transform business, creating value and eventually leading to revenue generation.

Blockchain

A blockchain is a digitized, decentralized, encrypted ledger of transactions. Each transaction represents one block in the chain. The transactions are made immutable; as such, they cannot be deleted. Blocks are added through cryptography, ensuring that they are secure. Each blockchain is managed by a network of people involved in the business process, whether they are internal or are external partners. Once recorded, the blocks cannot be altered without an agreement from most of these people, requiring changes to all subsequent blocks. Blocks are maintained in chronological order in the chain such that every block contains a hash of the previous block. A blockchain maintains complete information about different user addresses and their balances, allowing market participants to keep track of digital currency transactions without central record keeping.

The IoT will bring a significant benefit to blockchain technology. Digital devices can supply the information that feeds into the blockchain ledger, enabling secure transactions. Digital transformation that involves the adaptation of the IoT into the organization involves several internal or external electronic parties requiring secure communication, collaboration, and transaction with or without human intervention. The inherent security, efficiencies, and data validity in blockchain will enable these digital transformation efforts. The security and networking capabilities of blockchain can circumvent cybersecurity challenges faced in traditional information sharing in hyperconnected businesses. In other words, in an environment where concerns about security risks, privacy, and hacking are growing along with the adoption of this technology, the blockchain can create highly secure venues for information sharing.

Blockchain can be applied to virtually any industry where multiparty trades, warranties, and transactions such as supply chains are involved. Following are the some of the benefits that blockchain can bring to digital transformation:

Blockchain will build trust without having to rely on intermediaries as the distributed ledger enables businesses to trade and track virtually anything of value without requiring a central point of control.

With blockchain, independent people can come together and operate on their own as a group by eliminating the intermediaries, thereby reducing the cost of operations.

Using blockchain technology and an appropriate algorithm for a group that agrees to work together can accelerate transactions.

If we take the stock market as an example, there is a cumbersome process involved as a result of intermediaries, trade clearance, and regulatory processes. The process takes three-plus days to complete a transaction. Blockchain can optimize the clearing and settlement and reduce the processing time by securely automating the post-trade process and reducing the paperwork associated with trading. Blockchain can eliminate the intermediaries and reduce counterparties and operational risk while providing the infrastructure for faster trade settlement by applying smart contracts to post-trade activities. Blockchain can act as a surveillance system for each transaction. A blockchain can facilitate the tracking and blocking of an illegitimate attempt made by anyone on the network.

Since the blockchain ledger is designed in such a way that all participants have a full record of transactions and, therefore, of the holdings of investors, it can bring complete transparency and trust to the market. Blockchain transactions are faster, as trade confirmations are done through smart contracts by peers instead of an intermediary. As the intermediaries in the system are minimized, costs associated with them, like trades record keeping, audits, and trade verifications, will also be eliminated or reduced. Through blockchain technology, the margining system and payment of margin can be done instantly, and the frequency of valuation of securities deposited as capital can be done daily, compared with the weekly process prevalent now, minimizing the risk.

Automation of certain operations with blockchain can reduce inefficiencies, leading to a cost reduction and lower entry barriers to expand market base and ultimately increase liquidity and investment.

A blockchain aids in automating events processing and, in market surveillance and posttrade activities, addresses problems such as loss of data, insider trading, data fragmentation, reconciliation, and ticket matching.

For the blockchain to unleash its full potential value from restricted mutual distributed ledgers and smart contracts, the industry should adopt widespread changes in business processes. And regulators will have to adopt shared data arrangement for regulatory reporting.

In-Memory Computing Platforms

Digital transformation initiatives require a high-performance, cost-effective computing environment to scale and deliver the services with the new business models that are different from traditional businesses. As the most of the digital capabilities bring new insights and create value by creating new business models out of those insights, executing the model can give tise to challenges if the infrastructure does not support the cost-effective scalability. To mitigate the risk of failing in execution, the infrastructure must have computing capabilities. The steady decline of memory costs and next-generation memory-centric platforms will eliminate latency, improve application performance, and offer an exceptional value proposition to strengthen digital transformation initiatives. The ability to support hybrid transactional/analytical processing (HTAP) makes in-memory computing platforms most relevant for the Internet of Things (IoT) applications requiring real-time analysis of sensor and other external data sources.

In-memory computing refers to the concept of storing data in the main memory in a compressed format to enable faster access to the data and parallel processing across a highly available distributed computing cluster. The in-memory computing platforms sit between the application layer and the data layer to cache disk-based data from RDBMS, NoSQL, and Hadoop. While the underlying NoSQL or Apache Hadoop is kept in the RAM of the distributed cluster built with commodity hardware, in-memory computing platforms make it easy to scale by automatically utilizing the RAM of new nodes added to the cluster and rebalancing the data set across the nodes, which also ensures high availability.

Cloud Computing

Cloud computing, or simply "the cloud," is the model of delivering on-demand computing resources such as applications and data storage capabilities over the internet on a pay-for-use basis. The cloud is a significant enabler of digital transformation, offering the scale and speed that is needed for business models resulting from transformation initiatives. The cloud itself is one of the disruptive innovative business models that changed traditional IT models radically by reducing the time it takes to develop and market.

Digital transformation, which brings new business models, requires organizations to have agility and the ability to scale up or scale down efficiency. The fast-changing world of competitive business requires ready-to-deploy environments for creating and delivering innovative products. The cloud model provides flexibility by providing the quick scaling up or scaling down of services, metered service to pay for what is used, and self-service access. Cloud models come in different forms, such as software as a service, platform as a service, public clouds, private clouds, and hybrid clouds. Platform as a service provides an environment with everything required to support the complete life cycle without requiring the purchasing and managing of the underlying hardware, software, and hosting. Infrastructure as a service provides computing resources including servers, storage, networking, and data center space. Public clouds are owned and operated by the providers and offer rapid access over a public network for affordable computing resources. A private cloud is an infrastructure dedicated to and operated by a single organization, whether it is managed internally or externally. A hybrid cloud is a private cloud combined with the strategic integration and use of public cloud services.

Microservices

Microservices, an architectural style, is an application consisting of a collection of loosely coupled services acting as building blocks for modern distributed enterprise systems. Microservices architecture is business-focused in the sense that instead of treating different technological aspects such as user interface, middleware, and database as separate, it groups them based on the business context. This means that the team that is responsible for one business context owns all the technological aspects as a group. Traditional information technology development is monolithic in nature and is not convenient to innovate and deploy the application quickly. Originating from service-oriented architecture (SOA), microservices break all prior barriers, transitioning toward a simpler model that enables more natural replacement and execution. Since microservices are more focused, lightweight, and more comfortable, their development time is faster when compared to traditional applications. Many successful digital companies such as Netflix and Amazon have publicly disclosed the use of microservices architecture within their application infrastructures. Business organizations can accelerate the process of innovation, testing, and deploying solutions on the market.

Microservices help organizations to scale up their applications efficiently and cost-effectively. Since they can be cloud based, they can provide agility for any organization that adopts them. The services can be spread across multiple servers, offering innovation at a lower cost. Microservices work well with containers, which are another component of agile IT.

Robotic Process Automation

Artificial intelligence (AI) can extract data without being told exactly where it is in a document. The effectiveness of a business depends on extracting raw data and turning it into actionable information. The best way to achieve this is to use robotic process automation (RPA).

The Institute for Robotic Process Automation defines RPA as "the application of technology that allows employees in a company to configure computer software or a 'robot' to capture and interpret existing applications for processing a transaction, manipulating data, triggering responses and communicating with other digital systems."[5] Robotic process automation is a transformative technology that improves service quality, reduces costs, and increases operational efficiency and

---

[5] "What Is Robotic Process Automation?" Institute for Robotic Process Automation and Artificial Intelligence, https://irpaai.com/events/rpa/?id=1, accessed September 25, 2018.

effectiveness. RPA mimics human functions through user interfaces and interprets third-party applications that are configured to execute data and process flows. Nontechnical business users can handle RPA without requiring a higher level of programming knowledge. This helps create a more uniform approach to data management. RPA automates transaction processing and performs recurring processes just like humans.

Visualizations

Visualizations are powerful essential tools that help in digital transformation. There is a saying, "A picture is worth a thousand words." When it comes to analytics, the value of picturization is extremely high. Data visualization is the process of transforming text- and tabular-based data into graphical formats. Graphics include wheels, gauges, maps, heat maps, bar graphs, pie charts, and other statistical chart formats. In a fast-paced environment, visualization adds tremendous value to business professionals, helping them to spot trends and make revenue-impacting decisions with clarity. Visualizations serve as agents to integrate technology with business strategy.

In a traditional approach, we think of data as spreadsheets, charts, and graphs. However, data is merely a collection of information that has been compartmentalized into different groups. Data visualization occurs when we filter complex and fragmented information into easily digestible snapshots. This helps to provide clear evidence of the desired outcome. A picture is worth a thousand words.

Even from the neuroscience point of view, pictorial representations make it easy for the brain to interpret and store the information in the permanent memory. Graphics play a vital role in converting the mind-blurring columns and rows into valuable insights. Since it is more efficient for the brain to process information from visualizations, it is also easy to discover insights and make faster decisions with clarity and confidence.

Other Digital Capabilities

Robots are now standard equipment at many industrial sites around the world. Will they take away jobs from human or create jobs? We always hear from the skeptic critics that robots will take jobs away from humans. It is not a new criticism. The same happened with the rise of computers. Critics whispered that computers would make humans jobless. Indeed, the computer industry created millions of jobs directly and several other additional jobs indirectly. The same is true of robots. For example, they increase productivity and make the manufacturing process more manageable and safer, especially in hazardous production facilities such as those dealing with mining, oil and gas extraction, and chemical production.

Drones are an evolutionary version of robots. Drones bring even more opportunities and new efficiencies. As they are battery-powered and can be operated autonomously, drones can be effectively be used in logistics, avoiding road traffic and thereby making deliveries faster and cheaper, especially to places that are not easily accessible by traditional vehicles.

Virtual reality will enable teams to come together as though they were in one meeting room, making collaboration more effective. An enhanced version of virtual reality where live direct or indirect views of real-world physical environments are augmented with superimposed computer-generated images is called augmented reality or AR.

Augmented reality uses the existing natural environment and gives users the experience of a new and improved world where virtual information is used as a tool to assist with everyday activities. Virtual and augmented realities both hold the power to transform the world by using digital elements entirely. They both can change our perspective but depend on the experience.

Social media is one of the unaidable tools used to reach a wider audience. Social media players like Facebook, LinkedIn, WhatsApp, Instagram, and Skype, among many other social media platforms, engage millions of potential and current customers around the world, erasing geographical boundaries.

Three-dimensional printing is a powerfully potential innovative technology. It will help to democratize the playing field for consumers and small businesses by providing access to materials previously unavailable outside large enterprises and institutions.

16

Transformation Framework

Transforming an organization or the lives of people within society is purely a leadership-based mission that requires a creative and innovative mind-set. Every transformation mission must have a purpose that is driven by the organization's vision. The vision must be shared with the people involved in the process. The success of the mission depends on the culture of the organization or the entity involved in the transformation. The organization must first change the mind-set of people who exhibit rigid and silo-based thinking so as to renew the entrepreneurial spirit. The organization must ignite creativity among its people to come up with novel ideas addressing the complex problems of the organization or within society to thrive in an environment filled with VUCA (volatility, uncertainty, complexity, and assumptions). The organization must foster innovation by way of experimentation. Business models must be transformed by building them around the best human experience. Digital capabilities should be adapted and digital transformation should be embraced to rebuild business models centered on the human experience.

People care less about how an organization is doing than they do about why the organization is doing and what it wants to achieve.

Transformational leaders must continuously inspire or motivate people to make them courageous to take a risk and to foster a culture of collaboration. Transformational leaders and everyone involved in the process must commit to the purpose-driven vision. It is imperative to have emotional intelligence to deal with any situation. Transformational leaders must apply the right thought process based on the context. These aspects have been discussed throughout *The Art and Science of Transformational Leaderhip*. For convenience, those aspects, components, and subcomponents are shown in table 16.1.

TABLE 16.1. Summary of aspects

Aspect	Component	Subcomponent/comment
Purpose-driven vision	Having a clear purpose	The why factor
	Setting the vision	The what factor
Culture	Identifying barriers to transformation	
	Collaborating the silos	
	Removing change resistance	
	Redefining culture	
Creativity	Thinking outside the comfort zone	
	Idea generation	Collaboration for idea generation
		Brainstorming sessions Empathy Curiosity Observations Listening Questioning
	Idea incubation	
	Idea illumination	
	Idea verification	
	Cocreation	

Innovation	Innovation for the context	Incremental
		Breakthrough
		Disruptive
		Continuous disruption
	Design thinking	Empathize
		Define the problem
		Idea divergence
		Idea convergence
		Prototype
		Evaluate
	Agile innovation	
Human experience		
Business model	Value creation	
	Value capture	
	Value delivery	
Digital	Digital strategy	
	Adapt digital capabilities	
	Embrace digital transformation	
Inspiration	Inspiration	
	Motivation	
	Communicating the purpose	
	Sharing the vision	
	Encouragement	
	Leading by example	
	Principles	
	Ethics	
Courage	Courageous culture	
	Fearlessness	
	Fail-fast strategy	
	Proactiveness	

Collaboration	Breaking the silos	
	Relationships	
	Trust	
	Influencing	
	Listening	
	Integrity	
	Transparency	
	Delegation vs. nondelegation	
Commitment	Commitment	
	Consistency	
	Persistence	
	Clarity	
	Focus	
	Responsibility	
	Accountability	
	Flexibility	
	Adaptability	
Emotional intelligence	Empathy	
	Humility	
	Kindness	
	Generosity	
	Compassion	
	Mindfulness	
	Self-awareness	
	Resilience	

Thought processes	Problem-solving	
	Creative thinking	Outside-the-box thinking
		Big-picture thinking
		Divergent thinking
		Convergent thinking
	Analytical thinking	
	Critical thinking	
	Strategic thinking	
	Entrained thinking	
	Fast thinking	

17

Transforming Risk Management into Business Strategy

Financial services firms and the overall industry have undergone an unprecedented structural change over the past decade. Most of the changes came in the form of regulatory demands, implementations of lessons learned from the 2008 financial crisis, and technological advancements. The financial services industry is continuing to work hard to make further progress.

However, even after putting forth several efforts, the industry has been only partially effective in delivering change. The main reason is that the changes are mostly incremental. Moreover, the changes in business models were a result of organic growth that has been evident for several decades. Sudden competition from unexpected competitors is making incumbent financial firms look for disruptive innovations and ways to transform themselves.

The need for transformation is not restricted to a particular type of services. Every financial service firm, whether it is a retail bank, a commercial bank, an investment firm, a mortgage servicer, a broker–dealer, a mergers and acquisitions organization, a wealth management firm, an advisory firm, or a trading firm, needs digital transformation virtually for any service.

17.1 The Purpose of Digital Risk Transformation

There are numerous reasons why financial services firms need to undergo radical transformation. Digital risk transformation will enable the transformation of the risk function, which is seen as costly to financial services firms, to a more strategic function by tightly integrating the risk function with the business function. Digitization of risk function will improve risk effectiveness and efficiency, especially process automation, decision automation, monitoring, early warning, and accurate risk forecasting, and serve more needy people. The transformation framework that was outlined in chapter 16 can be applied to transforming the risk function. Let us discuss the transformation framework in the context of risk management in financial institutions, whether related to banking or capital markets. The reasons why the risk function needs to be transformed include the following:

- Strong competition from new entrants
- Evolutionary changes in customer experience
- Digital-savvy millennials
- Regulatory driven changes
- Legacy infrastructures
- Real-time transactions
- Threats to cybersecurity
- Disintermediation
- Need for quick firsthand information
- Increased interconnectedness
- Need for collaboration
- Increased operating costs
- To accurately forecast future trends
- To manage risk more effectively
- To survive disruptions coming from other markets
- To play an increased role in global growth

Strong Competition from New Entrants

While it is true that large financial services firms such as banks and wealth management firms have a vast customer base and infrastructure, making it difficult for new entrants to enter the business, technology-enabled entrants are trying to take part of the revenue away from the incumbents. Technology-enabled entrants in the field of finance are commonly referred to as "fintech firms." Like Netflix, which displaced Blockbuster without the need for physical locations, fintech players are coming up with agile and innovative ways to cut the costs for customers and improve the quality of financial services by eliminating the need for branch banking and fostering collaboration between customers and lenders and among the customers. Fintech is an evolving segment tightly coupling business models and technology, making services technology-driven and inventing alternatives to the products and services currently provided by the traditional financial services industry. Fintech is disrupting the traditional value chain by reshaping the value proposition of existing financial products and services. Fintech requires new ways of lending and therefore requires new ways of risk computing tightly integrated with the credit decision-making.

Evolutionary Changes in Customer Experience

Customer expectations are changing everywhere. Disruption is contagious. In line with this principle, a superior experience offered by providers can lead customers to expect the same level of service from other firms even if they are not related to the one that is offering the superior experience. This has led incumbent financial services to offer emotionally rich customer experiences at all levels. Traditionally, the improvements that financial services firms are making are incremental as a result of organic growth. Start-ups that typically are agile enough to make radical improvements are offering intuitive and emotionally rich interactive customer experiences, linking customers' purchase habits to those of others. Expectations are not just limited to retail banking and payment systems; they are more important even for the clients, which involves a time-consuming process. For example, the client onboarding process requires several steps, which makes customers feel frustrated with the several levels of requests for information. Even obtaining a mortgage is still a time-consuming process despite the advancements in technology.

Digital-Savvy Millennials

Millennials have grown up with technology and the internet. Millennials are expected to become the largest demographic group in the world by the end of the decade. As they are accustomed to ease in everything, their behavior is fundamentally different from that of traditional customers. Millennials are more open to fresh approaches than their predecessors. If someone is offering products and services to improve the way a millenial may play online games, then there's a strong chance those products or services will gain some serious traction. The openness to new ideas that millennials have is making new entrants feel confident that their innovation is no longer a barrier to competing with the incumbents. This behavior is not limited to purchasing habits but also applies to significant investments. Millennials prefer to do their own research and build portfolios on their own. This has led traditional wealth management firms to provide sophisticated research tools and offer custom products, giving more control to the customers.

Regulatory-Driven Changes

For the past decade, the financial services industry has undergone radical changes both from a business point of view and in terms of technological infrastructure. Regulations mostly have driven these changes. However, new regulations are continuing to be put in place. Banks are struggling to comply with regulatory requirements, including new capital and liquidity regimes, OTC derivatives reform, trading rules from the FRTB, data management, transparency requirements, new investor protection provisions, and a lot more. Expectations were heightened by reporting requirements, data aggregation, analytics, and algorithms needed to produce the reports required by regulators. All these regulations increased the costs to firms. The costs were increased mainly because of the incompatibilities in technologies across silos and the use of old technologies. Digital capabilities can facilitate the delivery of regulatory requirements in an agile manner. The cost of compliance is becoming a challenge to financial services firms, making it difficult for them to undertake major new initiatives. Utilizing innovations in technology, such as artificial intelligence, the cloud, analytics, and robotic process automation, shared services can reduce the cost burden.

Disintermediation

Disintermediation is a process that provides an end consumer with direct access to a product, a service, or information that would otherwise require a mediator. Fintech in retail financial services reduced the need for intermediaries, giving the former a competitive advantage. While it is true that intermediaries cannot be eliminated entirely in capital markets, digital transformation can bring some disintermediation opportunities.

Increased Operating Costs

Traditionally financial services firms addressed their structurally large cost-cutting programs and repositionings. The simplification of tangled IT infrastructure is arguably the most difficult cost to address. Indeed, such cost-cutting programs eventually result in reduced productivity. Moreover, such cost-cutting techniques do not result in any significant savings to the firms. Such indigent cost-cutting mechanisms can cause frustration for investors. Collaborating with external digital technology-enabled fintech firms allows firms to save enormous costs. Such a digital collaboration requires firms to have sophisticated digital capabilities.

Legacy Infrastructure

For the past five decades, the mainframe has played a vital role in the financial industry because the mainframe offers several built-in capabilities. The capabilities include speed, capacity, security, and availability. Since these capabilities are fundamental to everyday business in the financial industry, there was not enough focus to consider replacing them. At the same time, mainframe systems are not agile enough to adopt any needed changes quickly. Also, there is a shortage of skills to support these environments as the younger generation seeks out modern technologies that provide a more creative and agile platform. Therefore, mainframes are impeding the ability of many organizations to transform their business models. To take a share in fintech innovations, financial institutions must create an open data ecosystem that enables seamless sharing of data and insights across the organization and also with partners. This is another reason why banks and other financial service incumbents need to embrace digital transformation.

Real-Time Transactions

The most fundamental change that customers are expecting is instant payment. Real-time payment capabilities help banks to develop and launch compelling new products and services for customer use. The concept of instant is not just limited to payments but also extends to decision-making in other parts of the financial services industry. For example, traders in trading divisions want to know the risk involved in proposed trade so they can make informed decisions. If they depend on the risk metrics that are computed the previous night using overnight batch computing, they sometimes may lose the opportunity to trade because of the fear of risk, although in reality the risk could turn out to be less after overnight computing. Knowing the risk up front will give traders the ability to know potential future exposure and limits, giving them the confidence in trading. Embracing digital transformation by adapting relevant digital capabilities will allow real-time risk computation that is well integrated with the trading systems to play a vital role in this kind of scenario.

Enterprise Risk Management

Risk management will continue to gain attention from boards of directors because geopolitical, social, regulatory, compliance, and cybersecurity issues all influence each other. This increased interdependency requires higher levels of sophistication, with proactive risk visibility, to prioritize mitigation at the enterprise level, requiring the integration of silos and promoting greater information transparency and collaboration. Digitizing core processes to reduce manual intervention will play a vital role in enterprise risk management. Visualizations will also play an important role in providing senior management with easy-to-use, intuitive dashboards. Digital transformation in enterprise risk management can play a vital role in the overall risk culture of the firm.

17.2 The Vision for Digital Risk Transformation

The vision for transforming the risk function by enabling digital capabilities is geared toward creating more value from a business environment that is increasingly volatile, uncertain, complex, and ambiguous. Doing so will prepare financial institutions to operate as usual even in turbulent times and help people not be negatively impacted by adverse economic conditions.

17.3 Igniting Creativity

Often people think that creativity and risk management are opposites. This is because, for most people, risk management means avoiding risk altogether, whereas in reality risk management is all about managing the risk wisely to make a careful decision and being prepared to tackle the issue when things go wrong. As we discussed in earlier chapters, creativity requires the courage to take risks and to think outside one's comfort zone. On the other hand, one might think that risk management has something to do with conservative thinking, which is the wrong perception. Risk management is about having a holistic view of the factors involved in decision-making and making decisions wisely. Risk management can help business not forgo their opportunities.

How does creativity help to manage risk wisely? Creativity is required virtually everywhere. From the regulatory point of view, risks are computed using a defined set of rules and guidelines. In most cases, there will not be a need or scope to deviate from the predefined guidelines. However, there is ample scope for creativity in designing and architecting systems risk quantification. By creatively integrating risk management with business strategy, risk groups can develop a road map of the things they can do with a set of guidelines to change the mind-set of people from being fearful to having a positive outlook.

When it comes to risk management overall, and to have a holistic view of factors, the power of creativity helps us to think beyond our usual way, that is, conventional thinking. In other words, the process of risk identification requires thinking outside the box to think the unthinkable without any constraints. Risk groups should encourage other departments to think creatively instead of setting up barriers indicating what they should not do. The core purpose of risk management is to search for uncertainties by considering both threats and opportunities and addressing them proactively. Applying creative techniques such as observing and questioning "what if," brainstorming, unconstrained thinking, root-cause analysis, visualization, and scenario analysis will help to identify the risks adequately. But merely identifying risks does not solve the problem. Coming up with an action plan that was not previously thought of requires a creative way of thinking. In a world where changes are happening rapidly, risk management should actively embrace and welcome change, recognizing the fact that some risks present an opportunity to improve on the original plan by thinking creatively.

17.4 Fostering Innovation

While banks are steadily making progress toward innovating their resources, operations, business models, architectures, and facilities, there is less focus on digitizing risk infrastructures and models. This is partly because much of the effort is going toward meeting the demands arising from regulations. Moreover, risk management activities are seen as costly to banks. It is true that risk management initiatives will continue to be seen as costly efforts unless they start adding value regarding revenue generation. Current risk management practices face several challenges when it comes to playing a vital role in revenue generation and becoming an integral part of the business strategy.

Innovating the current risk architectures and models has the potential to bring previously unexploited business opportunities. A spirit of bold and ambitious long-term vision for risk management can be realized through the digitization of risk management.

Here are the ways that innovating the risk function through digitization can bring the value to an organization:

- Freeing the risk executives from day-to-day risk computation activities will allow them to focus on decision-making with strategic thinking and work closely with business stakeholders to make better-informed strategic decisions faster.
- Digitization can move the risk function risk ex post facto to risk ex ante to detect emerging risks proactively, evaluate them, and set mitigation strategies in motion.
- The risk function can move from manual risk limit settings to smart limit settings based on intelligent, on-demand, live decision-making capabilities.
- Business functions can rely on risk function in areas such as identifying opportunities, reducing unwanted exposure, and managing investment portfolios by harnessing advanced risk analytics.
- Regulators can have access to near-live data with drill-down dashboards and analytical tools that allow them to create the exposure views they need.
- A digitized real-time view of activities can help regulators to flag and help prevent problems such as irresponsible lending or nonfinancial risk excesses.
- Digitization can help the risk function play a strategic role in banks as the decisions become embedded directly into customer journeys, offering insights into trade-offs for critical decisions.
- Robotic process automation will automate repetitive activities such as risk system entry during underwriting, data anomaly detection, and cleanup, which are currently performed manually.
- The frequency and magnitude of operational losses and fines will decline as automation reduces human error.

- Digitization has the potential to lower capital-holding costs as capital is deployed more efficiently and risk weights decline given an improvement in data quality, process issues, and analytics.

17.5 Technology-Enabled Business Models

Data is oxygen to digital business models. Data is the core strength of many of the successful businesses that evolved in the past decade. The real strength of a business comes from the way the organization converts data into insights. The volume of data is meaningless unless it is harnessed for the insights and foresights it holds. Traditional financial institutions (FIs) are sitting on a significant amount of data scattered across various silos. However, this trend is changing with the evolution of the risk and regulation regime. Thanks to regulations, incumbent financial institutions now have an opportunity to converge the regulatory, operational, compliance, risk management, and business realms with technology. This is helping the FIs to make continuous progress in building data hubs and lakes, consolidating the data from all the silos.

This enables the organization to go beyond reports and break down silos either virtually or really to align business, risk management, and regulatory reporting processes and to strengthen these three lines of defense. However, the indirect benefit of such an initiative is incredible. The benefit comes in the form of analytics and insights about the customers, products, and markets, making a path to new revenue models.

In other words, digital risk transformation is strategic rather than tactical, integrated rather than fragmented, and systematic rather than bolted on.

Digital Capabilities

Highly fragmented data architectures are not enough to provide an efficient or effective framework for digital risk. Therefore, a clearly defined data vision, a well-established risk data aggregation, robust data governance, enhanced data quality, and an agile data architecture should be in place to embrace the digitization of the risk function. The building blocks of a digital transformation to construct a successful digital risk program should include the following:

- Data management
- Agile infrastructure
- Advanced analytics
- Artificial intelligence
- Machine learning
- Cognitive computing
- Visualization
- In-memory computing
- Cloud computing
- Microservices
- The Internet of Things
- An external ecosystem

Data Management

Even before the digital transformation era, the value of a company was tied to the amount of relevant data it could manage. The era of digital transformation made data a crucial asset based on which the organization could generate insights and integrate the risk identification into its business model. Data is oxygen to the digital environment. In a world where data is changing rapidly and machines are making decisions, there is an increased emphasis on the way data is managed. Data governance practices need to be transformed to improve the quality of the data, make risk and business decisions more consistent, and ensure rapid response to data needs.

Agile Infrastructure

The legacy data architectures are often linked to a vast number of sources of truth. This is creating challenges for an organization to harness the exponentially growing masses of data. That is why fixing the infrastructure is a crucial objective of financial institutions' transformation efforts. Moreover, the current state of risk infrastructure is intended to provide predefined reports that require a manual effort to develop the code to generate such reports. This is true even after putting several efforts into eliminating end-user computing or EUC. For risk executives to best utilize the risk data and generate insights, the infrastructure should be made smarter. The "no code" solutions will give more control to risk executives and help them generate insights seamlessly. In other words, the infrastructure must be agile, consisting of innovative data storage solutions, new interfaces, easier access to the vendor ecosystem, and so on.

Advanced Analytics

The use of artificial intelligence, machine learning, and cognitive computing is imperative for risk function transformation. In sectors such as social media, many decision-making processes are automated as a result of using advanced statistical techniques combined with artificial intelligence, machine learning, and cognitive computing to make better predictions and wise decisions. In financial services, too, advanced analytics can handle prediction, optimal actions, and the extraction of insights. While it is true that certain automation requires clearance by regulators and supervisors, there is a broad scope that can be applied to advanced analytics to embed the risk function with the business function. Because a machine learning system learns itself, there is a risk that analytical models to assess risk will become a black box with a lack of ability to explain how the decisions were made within the business context. This lack of transparency may not be acceptable to regulators and customers. Machine learning and data analytics have ample potential to increase processing speed and reduce cost, resulting in better customer experiences. The machine learning models can analyze massive amounts of data with more granularity and go more in depth, helping analysts make better-informed decisions at the individual securities level as well as at the portfolio level. Artificial intelligence and machine learning will change the way risk is being monitored, from ex post facto to ex ante, with real-time analytics to stop losses proactively. It is a first step where traders, asset managers, and risk managers can use artificial intelligence (AI) based on common platforms to monitor counterparty credit risk, which they are currently dealing with independently. Combining the pricing and risk management mechanisms using machine learning involving a variety of heterogeneous and high-volume data such as tick-by-tick quotes of bond prices, market data risk factors such as interest rates, FX rates, inflation rates, commodity prices, and unstructured news feeds can reveal hidden structures in the data.

So far, financial institutions are putting more focus on well-defined, structured data aggregated across groups to generate large amounts of data that need to be reported. Therefore, financial institutions have the competitive advantage in the form of a significant amount of structured data. FIs can monetize this competitive advantage by leveraging this significant amount of structured data with large amounts of low-quality, unstructured, high-frequency data. These include, but are not limited to, outputs from consumer apps, digital interactions with clients, metadata from payment systems, and social media feeds. Combining the structured data with the additional unstructured data, FIs can optimize their business models.

The extensive set of machine learning approaches is well situated to integrate the risk function with the business strategy. The traditional credit risk models depend on linear, logit, and probit regressions to model credit risk for capital requirements and internal risk management. Combining the new set of data as described earlier, the unsupervised method of machine learning can be used to explore the data, while regression and classification methods can predict key credit risk variables such as the probability of default or loss given default. The advantage for FIs is that their extensive records of loan-level data serve as inputs.

Robotic Process Automation

Traditionally, financial institutions generate high volumes of documents and manage them through a combination of legacy systems, manual processes, and emerging technologies. Technology-enabled virtual banking means more options for customers demanding the best possible user experience.

Robotic process automation (RPA) offers different opportunities for harnessing efficiencies and reducing human error across the organization. RPA plays a vital role in the front office, middle office, and back office.

The typical functions that RPA can perform include, but are not limited to, the following:

- Data movement
- Multiple entries
- Reconciliation
- Cross-system report generation
- Mortgage approval process
- Alerts and notifications
- Account purge activities
- Client onboarding checks
- "Know your customer" (KYC) and anti–money laundering (AML) authentication process
- Legal and compliance processes like credit checks
- Identification checks
- Data mapping across systems
- Activity tracking and fraud detection

Data Visualization

There is a saying: "A picture is worth a thousand words." When it comes to risk management, the value of picturization is extremely high. Data visualization is the process of transforming text- and tabular-based data into graphical formats. Graphics include wheels, gauges, maps, heat maps, bar charts, pie graphs, and any other statistical chart formats. In a fast-paced environment, visualization adds tremendous value to risk managers, helping them to spot trends and make revenue-impacting decisions with clarity. Visualizations serve as agents for integrating risk function with business strategy. Even from the neuroscience point of view, pictorial representations make it easy for the brain to interpret and store information in the permanent memory. Graphics play a vital role in converting the mind-blurring columns and rows to valuable insights. Since it is more efficient for the brain to process information from visualizations, it is also easy to discover insights and make faster decisions with clarity and confidence.

However, the visualizations that are generated with a traditional architecture are not good enough to show all the variables to stakeholders. Traditional dashboards only allow stakeholders to explore one risk identification method at a time. The best data visualization must be dynamic, allowing stakeholders to explore all risk identification methods at one time. It needs to context based, time-sensitive, interactive, communicable, and variable based on the purpose of the data. Digitalizing the visualization will give users the ability to exploit its deep connection to the sources to automatically create visuals that take into account the full spectrum of risk factors. Different stakeholders want to see the data differently because of the disparity in their roles; data visualization must be easily customizable by nontechnical business users to produce different types of data to execute based on prescribed responsibilities. The users should be able to alter their queries and analyze new visualizations to capture a holistic view of risk. Therefore, the digitalization of data visualization is an increasingly critical capability needed to integrate risk function with business strategy.

In-Memory Computing

Processing massive amounts of data accumulated over time and combining it with the just-in-time data within a fraction of a second to produce real-time risk analytics requires a different kind of processing. Such real-time risk analytics are needed for business stakeholders if they want to make decisions by considering the potential risk that the business is exposed to. In-memory technology that comes with fundamental pillars of RAM storage and parallel distributed processing can enable these massive just-in-time computations. For example, running market risk and credit risk calculations at the enterprise level instead of at the silo, and on-demand instead of overnight, will improve visibility into potential risks and aid decision-making. Enterprise-level analytics for market risk exposures proactively help to uncover hidden risks in the trading portfolio and help people make informed decisions effectively.

Cloud and Data Lakes

The cloud can not only lower maintenance costs but also improve the reliability of the architectures and infrastructure to apply analytics more quickly. Data lakes can process a high volume of structured and unstructured data, allowing for near real-time data ingestion and processing. They add significant processing power to advanced analytics and signal detection. Data lakes solve many data storage issues, making it possible to store highly granular data and its full history with many types of data, such as structured and unstructured, in the same repository. Cloud adoption fosters innovation because it can transcend barriers of geography, industry, and organization. The cloud accelerates innovation by enabling quick prototyping of new ideas for fast experimentation.

17.6 Design Thinking

Traditionally, incumbent financial institutions have grown big organically without embracing any significant disruptive innovation or transformation. The complexities of the architectures and regulatory demands made the incumbent FIs stay away from innovative methodologies such as design thinking and agile transformation. It is evident that the fintech start-ups are coming up with disruptive business models coupled with rich human experience to challenge the established players. The rise of fintech start-ups may have the potential to take a share of the revenues. In this current environment, design thinking is a useful tool for the incumbent FIs to evolve their business models to meet these challenges and opportunities.

Design thinking, which is a human-centered approach, has been discussed in detail in the chapter "Fostering Innovation." The stages in design thinking that I described from my point of view are as follows:

- Empathize
- Define
- Idea divergence
- Idea convergence
- Prototype
- Evaluation

Let us take a case where we want to build a product that manages risk efficiently and integrates the risk function into the business strategy.

Empathize

Empathy is achieved by immersing ourselves in the users' world to understand their end goals. Empathy is applicable not only to the external consumer but also to the bulk of clients and even internal users. Let us take a scenario where a client comes to the bank to establish a relationship and do business. In a recent regulatory regime, there are several compliance-related steps involved in client onboarding that sometimes make the customer feel frustrated. The process can even make the customer feel that the bank does not trust him. Unfortunately, this is a global problem. Thinking from the mind of the customer, one can imagine how the process can be streamlined. Improving the client onboarding experience for new clients is one of the most critical steps not only for acquiring new business but also for retaining the customer. The initial client experience is one of the first impressions that helps in engaging business going forward. First, the client onboarding process must be simple and convenient. This means that firms and their clients must complete the onboarding process quickly and without any headaches. Clients should not have to go through a bunch of convoluted steps and complex processes. The FIs do not want that either. The process can be simplified using digital capabilities and making the clients more interactive during the process. Digital capabilities will help to ensure that future business success is built on full compliance within defined regulatory requirements by bringing structured data and unstructured data together and also by bringing business function and risk/KYC/AML functions together.

Define

During the define stage, we take the information from the previous stage and synthesize it to define an actionable problem statement with a strong point of view. This helps to organize, interpret, discover connections and patterns, and make sense of the insights gathered. The goal of the define stage is to achieve clarity on the context and the point of view and to frame the challenge in such a way that it will open the door for exploring ideas for a solution. Let us take an example where the customers are living in a remote rural place where physical bank branches are not available without traveling an inconvenient distance. One can empathize with the people in this situation. The define stage will frame the challenge with a strong point of view and clarity to inspire the people involved in solving the problem. For example, "How might we provide banking services to rural farmers so that they can use our financial services to gain access to farming goods easily?"

Idea Divergence

This is the phase where people from different groups and even the customers come together collaboratively for brainstorming and think about diverse ideas to solve the problem that was framed during the define phase. Bringing people from only one group will not result in outside-the-box ideas. Bringing together the risk managers, business strategists, IT staff, compliance staff, and the user experience will help to get a large number of ideas.

Idea Convergence

Not every idea is worth implementing. The idea convergence phase will help people to do some research on the ideas based on experience and then short-list the potential ideas to move on to the next phase.

Prototype

Experimentation is critical to disruptive innovation. Without experimentation, it is challenging to know which solution is going to be disruptive, whether it is a product, service, or process. Traditionally financial institutions did not encourage experimentation, as the model adopted to assess the worthiness of a product was based on return on investment. Competition from the fintech start-ups is making the financial services industry rethink doing more experimentation, even at the cost of forgoing the sunk cost. Indeed, experimentation reduces the risks of innovation and transformation as it is better to fail early without spending a significant amount of money than to fail in the end. Design thinking, which is nonlinear, cannot be expected to deliver the optimal solution to be built in one trial. This is the primary reason why we should have a stage dedicated to prototyping in design thinking, so as to encourage experimentation. Experimentation comes in the form of iterations. An iteration is a cycle of building something, testing it, improving it, and resting it. In this cycle, we can embed the second stage, which is ideation, in order to improve the quality of ideas based on the findings from prototyping.

Evaluation

The evaluation stage, the last stage in design thinking, is often referred to as the testing stage in other versions of design thinking, but the testing of a prototype in design thinking requires methods that go beyond traditional testing. This is where the expertise from the risk function and business strategists helps to assess the real value of the prototype. People in the user groups must be trained to think in an unbiased way, adopt the new solution without any resistance, and provide feedback for further improvements.

17.7 Agile Innovation

Certainly, agility is the secret behind innovation. Indeed, many successful companies made innovation their core business strategy. Innovation is an imperative tool for incumbent financial institutions. Agility is not just related to the way software applications are developed, but also to the infrastructure, architectures, designs, operations, culture, et cetera. While the concept of agility was first used in software development, it has now penetrated industries in greater depth. Agility integrates technology with a broader business strategy and processes.

The complexities of an infrastructure accumulated over the decades have made some of the incumbents less agile, which has limited their flexibility in delivering new services. This is partly because the incumbent financial institutions were early successful companies at the beginning of IT evolution and the systems that were cutting edge at that time have now become the legacy. Simplification of infrastructure and operations will not only help incumbents become more lean and agile but also will boost the success rate of their digital transformation initiatives. Agility in infrastructure will help business and operational processes to be aligned with the customer experience journey. In a business environment where external vendor systems are playing a vital role, an infrastructure should be agile enough to facilitate seamless integration.

Shared economy is gaining in popularity, and therefore the incumbent financial institutions should participate both as a consumer and provider of financial services. The innovation of open banking requires leveraging of existing architectures with APIs and microservices based on functional and nonfunctional requirements. By doing this, FIs will be able to externalize their core products and service offerings while exposing their customers to services from external marketplaces.

Agile methodologies go hand in hand with innovation. An agile way of delivering software is the key to reducing the risk associated with any uncertainties in the process. As regulations continue to evolve, FIs need to fundamentally change the way software is developed and delivered. The perception until recently has been that using the agile approach to multiyear regulatory compliance projects is both risky and impractical. Moreover, the assumption was that there was no need for intermediate deliveries. However, the challenge is that while there are several regulations and some of them are tightly related, developing one rigid solution for each regulation is not economical and also requires repeated efforts. Agile architectures and the agile way of development make it possible to make changes before even finalizing a solution.

Amid a continually changing regulatory regime, the agile methodology is an extremely useful tool to help banks navigate the unexpected changes as requirements may be unclear at the beginning or require further interpretation.

By looking at bulk requirements, we might get the impression that the waterfall method is most suitable for regulatory projects. Agile methodology is a flexible methodology to achieve flexibility in products, services, systems, and architectures, but at the same time it requires special attention and focus from everyone on the team. Especially in regulatory projects, the smaller the team, the greater the productivity. Given the fact that each regulation touches many applications, systems, and groups, agile methodology is the best approach to foster collaboration, transparency, and accountability. Because mistakes on regulatory projects can have severe consequences for organizations as a whole, agile is the way to build a culture of trust and transparency. Senior management must understand why and how agile is used in regulatory projects and support the approach. It also requires a change in employees, who may be accustomed to managing a discrete portion of a project without having a holistic view of the purpose for working collaboratively to remove roadblocks and taking responsibility for the entire project.

The products, services, systems, architectures, infrastructure, and culture that are agile will help with the tighter integration of regulatory needs and internal risk management, and again with business strategy to reuse the investments made on risk and regulatory projects and also to develop products and services with full compliance.

17.8 Leadership Capabilities

Financial institutions are continuously strengthening their capital positions amid heightened regulatory agency expectations. However, the risk management function is still seen as a group of analysts and managers. Transforming the risk management function into a strategic business function will require stong leadership capabilities at all levels. The board must move toward a more anticipatory approach by working closely with risk leaders in helping to identify and mitigate organizational risk. The board of directors should not be afraid to challenge management and should be involved in facilitating transformation throughout the organization.

Strong leaders must be placed in critical roles that involve risk functions. Business leaders cannot solely rely on the auditing functions to identify the risks in their units. It is imperative that business leaders be held accountable for the self-identification and ownership of the risks in their individual units. This is possible with tighter integration of the business function and the risk function. For a financial institution to play a more significant role in innovation, the chief risk officer should be given a clear, highly regarded role within the organization and should be encouraged to challenge business executives as well as the executive management team to foster a strong risk management culture.

In addition to performing regular risk management activities, risk leaders must embrace the following aspects in order to make the organization stronger:

- Risk culture
- Courage to take risks
- Collaboration
- Commitment
- Resilience

An organization's culture is its collective mind-set. The patterns of widely shared assumptions, whether conscious or unconscious, beliefs, and values form the basis of organizational culture. The organizational culture teaches, by way of spoken or unspoken language, the correct norms of behavior to newcomers to the culture. The factors that constitute the culture include the following:

- Inherited culture from the industry
- The mind-set of top management
- People's behavior at the department level

In the context of the financial industry, the culture, in an unspoken way, is driven by money—in other words, greed. However, the misconception is that some people interpret that greed and risk-taking are the same. A culture that measures performance based on the numbers encourages its members to take reckless risks without applying cognitive skills. This can promote self-interest. The success achieved this year can lead to failure in coming years. In other words, people can become victims of their own success. Organizational culture is driven by how the risk is defined and prioritized. In the case of banking industry revenues, these are related to size and leverage. The incentive is structured based on how much profit the deal makes this year rather than how much loss the deal will lead to in coming years. In other words, short-term benefit is weighed instead of a long-term loss.

On the other hand, risk management functions as ex post facto, meaning that risk is assessed after the transactions are performed and the reports are generated. There is not enough seamless integration between business teams and risk teams.

The culture of the financial industry is dominated by the fact that greed is good in a booming economy and the risk function is unnecessary. And in a bad economy, greed is the root of all evil, and risk function must be strengthened. Such a culture needs to be transformed. The risk culture should become more cognitive and should take all aspects of social needs into consideration.

The type of industry culture that is developed based on incentives and penalties can be changed by adopting a new style of leadership and new leadership capabilities. An effective leader can harness employee behavior and lead them to become more productive and competitive by partially detaching them from incentive and penalty-based productivity.

Transforming systems from the way they are currently functioning can boost confidence in taking risks diligently. For example, let us consider, how fintech credit differs from the current way of lending.

18

Quotations from this Book

"Transformation requires courageous leaders who have the ability to imagine and visualize far beyond their current comfort zones to discover unmet needs with a clear purpose and who have the ability to drive the mission to reach such a destination by taking bold actions."

"Knowing the purpose will make a person dig deep to identify his or her true passion."

"Knowing our life's purpose helps us to find our real passion and drives us to achieve something extraordinary."

"Having a purpose serves as the basis for the courage to act, inspires courage to step outside the comfort zone, and fuels the passion for persevering in the face of volatility in a world of uncertainty."

"Sharing the vision at all levels of the organization creates a strong field that brings positive energy into form."

"Through the vision, leaders embrace positive change by turning dreams into reality by way of strong leadership skills, creativity, innovation, and transformation."

"Mission drives us to the desired destination (vision) to serve the purpose."

"When the purpose, vision, and mission are aligned, then the transformational leader thrives and brings disruptive changes to the world."

"Creativity is the driving force behind innovation."

"Creativity is the foundation for turning vision into action."

"The secret of creativity is to bombard the mind with new experiences and ideas entirely outside the realm of one's field, filtering out the noise and connecting the dots among the remaining ideas."

"The environment we live in, the behaviors around us, our thinking, and our emotions cause the brain to reorganize itself, both physically and functionally, throughout our lives."

"Unlocking the mind to think of extremes, to find the problems, and to find the solutions requires an extraordinary amount of energy, relentless dedication, commitment, and cognitive skills."

"While it is very important to find the right solution to a problem, it is even more important to find the right problems and the solutions to those problems."

"Thinking outside the comfort zone is crucial to embracing creativity."

"Most successful entrepreneurs, both past and present, are highly empathetic."

"Curiosity ignites creativity by enabling us to lean into uncertainty with a positive attitude, searching for the clues."

"Observing the problem closer to the context will suppress the biased thinking that was formed based on repetitive experiences in life."

"The purpose of listening is to gain comprehension. Therefore, we should avoid engaging judgment, prejudice, and assumptions at the time of listening."

"During the interview process, we should not influence the outcome for people."

"Mindfulness meditation reduces the reactiveness of the brain, increases resilience, and improves emotional intelligence, resulting in a flow of ideas and igniting creativity."

"People with positive emotions and good moods are more creative in solving problems compared to those with negative emotions and toxic moods such as anger, frustration, and anxiety."

"Diversity helps a leader to consider perspectives and possibilities that he or she otherwise would have ignored."

"Fostering a healthy creative process requires bringing all the people together and getting a comprehensive set of ideas, whether they are analytical, intuitive, conceptual, experiential, social, or values-driven."

"By way of positive change, innovation fulfills people's unmet needs, improves their lives, makes their jobs easier, and makes them happier and more productive."

"Failure is not a hurdle to the innovation process. Failures provide an opportunity to learn new things and strengthen the innovation process."

"The use of 'knowledge of knowledge' will help to accelerate innovation."

"Have the courage to disrupt yourself by having the courage to compete with yourself."

"Do not ignore the founder's mentality even if he or she is no longer with the organization."

"Do not plan the strategy around small goals; plan it by having big-picture thinking."

"Do not fall in love with a creative invention forever. Creative things can quickly become outdated in a rapidly changing world."

"Develop the product strategy that meets the changing behaviors of customers."

"Innovation requires the courage to dream big and pitch completely different ideas."

"Turn your own difficulties into opportunities by building products and helping other organizations overcome similar difficulties by offering those products as a service."

"Give employees the opportunity to use their passion and come up with creative ideas."

"Think extreme and bring extremes to the mainstream."

"Business opportunities come from the risk of uncertainty and unknown factors that are accumulated by rapid changes in customer behavior, disruptive technologies, hyperconnectedness among systems, shifting economic winds, and increased social connectedness."

"Solving problems in the transformation process requires a different approach that involves a better understanding of the context, the purpose, collaboration, empathy, ideation, and experimentation."

"In traditional problem-solving where we use analytical thinking to solve people's problems, we ignore the reasons why people do what they do. On the other hand, empathy allows us to set aside our assumptions about the world and gain insight into users and their needs."

"Empathic concern will lead to game-changing ideas and proactively invent the future on behalf of customers."

"The point of view serves as the spirit for problem-solving and provides a focus, inspires teams, and guides the innovation effort."

"Culture is the collective mind-set of expectations, experiences, philosophy, values, underlying beliefs, and assumptions that spark inspiration in people."

"Leadership that recognizes only short-term benefits cannot create an environment where creativity and innovation thrive and cannot embrace transformation."

"By empowering teams to work across functional units with the autonomy to make real-time decisions, organizations can move forward amid the ever-changing business landscape."

"Collaborative leadership is about breaking down silos and building trust-based cross-functional relationships."

"Inspiration sparks passion in the leader. The passion fuels the purpose, the purpose drives the vision, and the vision makes the leader think creatively and innovatively to embrace the desired transformation."

"The difference between motivation and inspiration is the same as the difference between push and pull. Motivation pushes us to work through stressful situations to accomplish the result. Inspiration pulls us toward something that stirs our hearts, minds, or spirits."

"Inspiration awakens a person to think beyond his or her experiences and limitations and seek out new possibilities."

"Inspiration fuels people, transforming a concern into a possibility and transforming the way we think about our capabilities."

"Organizations will see a real breakthrough in creativity and innovation when employees are inspired instead merely engaged."

"Human biology demands a sense of purpose and meaning for the work we do beyond the monetary reward either in professional life or personal life."

"When people know that they are valued and that their work is valuable, they will approach a challenge with greater tenacity than they otherwise would."

"The best way to lead people into the future is to connect them to the present through a shared vision."

"If a leader shares the responsibility and the vision with his or her people, the people walk with the leader along the path to reach the destination."

"People feel accomplished when they are encouraged to be part of challenging activities."

"When leaders make people feel more valuable, capable, and motivated, they reach their potential, and their lives change for the better."

"To transform an organization, leaders should transform themselves first by leading by example."

"True transformational leaders inspire society by serving as moral agents and extending the freedom to work toward a noble cause and ethical consequences."

"Courage leads a person toward unconventional thinking and outside-the-box thinking."

"The ability to picture the positive results that will come from the mission increases the ability to act."

"Fear keeps millions of individuals from reaching their potential."

"To be a successful entrepreneur, you must have the willingness to go outside your comfort zone for something you believe in and come up with disruptive ideas."

"By cultivating a culture of courage in which people feel secure enough to move outside their comfort zones and take risks, an organization achieves an extraordinary result."

"Not every risk is worth taking. Failing fast and cheap will encourage people to let go of the unwanted risk quickly."

"To be successful transfromational leader, one should step outside the box by leaving all past experiences, mind-sets, and attitudes behind and start to see things from an entirely different perspective."

"Outside-the-box, unfiltered, unbiased thinking, openness to suggestion, and willingness to empathize with others' feelings will open the gates to a flood of ideas."

"The transformational leader should create a safe environment where employees are allowed to fail in order to protect new ideas."

"In a culture where trust is embodied all over the place, people are more productive and willing to collaborate."

"Having influence means more than just having power; it is about taking charge and understanding people's emotions and nonverbal signals."

"Transparency leads to effective collaboration, greater creativity, faster problem-solving, and improved performance."

"Commitment is the most powerful tool that helps leaders stay on the path to the vision."

"To transform an organization, leaders should take bold actions to break and remake the pseudo commitments if they are seen to be roadblocks."

"Trust is the foundation of leadership, and consistency is one of the ways of establishing trust."

"Obstacles are more common on the mission of transformation to realize the vision. Therefore, while on the path to the goal, leaders need to remain agile enough to make corrections but must be persistent to achieve the final goal."

"The real failure is in giving up. Therefore, instead of giving up on the mission, leaders should consider reinventing themselves to achieve the final goals."

"Clarity adds incredible value to the mission to turn a purpose-driven vision into reality."

"Accountable leaders should behave like fixers instead of merely blaming others."

"Responsibility is the stepping-stone for leaders to grow."

"Being flexible allows leaders to respond to unexpected events in an adverse situation."

"Adaptability helps a leader to get adjusted to the changing business environment and to think outside his or her comfort zone."

"Emotional intelligence is the art of accurately identifying emotions as they occur and relating to the context without jumping to conclusions."

"Empathy makes conflict resolution friendlier by promoting constructive and connective relationships."

"Using empathy to understand critical constituents' concerns, frustrations, and feelings will make a leader think of the big picture and broaden the vision."

"Humble leaders are very honest and seek input from all directions and from all others to ensure that there is no confirmation bias in making decisions."

"Humility is the best answer for narcissism, which is the culture of overpraising, entitlement, and privileges."

"Compassion boosts the energy levels of people within the organization and serves as a motivational tool."

“When the leader responds in a frustrated, furious manner, it is less likely that his or her people will take risks in the future because they will worry about the negative consequences of making mistakes.”

“Kind leaders place themselves on the same level as others without losing their authority as leaders.”

“Mindfulness is the ability to be fully aware of what we are doing and not overreacting or underreacting to what is going on around us.”

“Difficulties strengthen the mind as labor does the body. Struggles serve as a tool to strengthen leadership abilities.”

“Resilience requires courage to confront painful realities, requires faith that there will be a solution even if one is not immediately evident, and requires tenacity to carry on even during hopeless situations.”

“Every failure and obstacle comes with a valuable lesson, making a path to tremendous opportunities.”

“Leaders should broaden their observations, embrace curiosity, have a holistic view, perform root-cause analysis, and look well beyond the obvious to assess any problems.”

“Leaders who apply linear vision, as opposed to circular vision, end up seeing the problems that lie directly in front of them and ignoring the problems around them.”

“Critical thinking filters out biases and distortions from a set of information for solving a problem and making a conclusion.”

“Leaders should have the ability to imagine the future by having a reference point in the present.”

CPSIA information can be obtained
at www.ICGtesting.com
Printed in the USA
LVHW091544051220
673432LV00002B/204

9 781532 061899